W9-BPK-013

Acclaim for Paul Cartledge's

The SPARTANS

"The value of this book is as an introduction to, and overview of, a fascinating society in ancient Greece. It is well written and interesting and there is no question about its scholarship."

—*The Journal of Military History*

"[Cartledge] engagingly speculates on events, people and gods of thousands of years ago. . . . Ancient history springs to life."

—*The Wall Street Journal*

"A remarkable chronicle of Sparta's rise and fall. . . . Cartledge's crystalline prose, his vivacious storytelling and his lucid historical insights combine here to provide a first-rate history of the Spartans, their significance to ancient Greece and their influence on our culture."

—*Publishers Weekly* (starred)

"A lucid, literate history of a model society. . . . Chocked with learning lightly worn, and a pleasure for anyone interested in the ancient world."

—*Kirkus Reviews*

"[An] engaging narrative. . . . In his panorama of the real Sparta, Cartledge cloaks his erudition with an ease and enthusiasm that will excite readers from page one."

—*Booklist*

"Commendable and fascinating. . . . A good overview of the people and the issues."

—*Library Journal*

Paul Cartledge

The SPARTANS

Paul Cartledge's authority in the world of classics and ancient history has long been underpinned by his special interest in Sparta and the Spartans. He is Professor of Greek History and former Chairman of the Classics Faculty at Cambridge University. Over the past thirty years he has written and edited twenty books, including *Spartan Reflections, Sparta and Lakonia, Hellenistic and Roman Sparta,* and *The Greeks: A Portrait of Self and Others.* He is academic consultant to the BBC and PBS for the series *The Greeks: Crucible of Civilization* and to Channel 4 and PBS for *The Spartans.*

ALSO BY PAUL CARTLEDGE

*Crux: Essays in Greek History presented to G.E.M.
de Ste. Croix on his 75th Birthday* (co-editor)

Agesilaos and the Crisis of Sparta

Nomos: Essays in Athenian Law, Politics and Society
(co-editor)

Hellenistic Constructs (co-editor)

Xenophon: Hiero the Tyrant and Other Treatises
(co-editor)

Democritus and Atomistic Politics

The Cambridge Illustrated History of Ancient Greece
(editor)

*Kosmos: Essays in Athenian Order, Conflict and
Community* (co-editor)

Aristophanes and His Theatre of the Absurd

*Sparta and Lakonia: A Regional History
1300–362 B.C.*

Hellenistic and Roman Sparta (with Anthony
Spawforth)

The Greeks: Crucible of Civilization

Spartan Reflections

The Greeks: A Portrait of Self and Others

Alexander the Great: The Search for a New Past

The
SPARTANS

The
SPARTANS

*The World of the Warrior-Heroes of Ancient
Greece, from Utopia to Crisis and Collapse*

Paul Cartledge

VINTAGE BOOKS

A DIVISION OF RANDOM HOUSE, INC.

NEW YORK

FIRST VINTAGE BOOKS EDITION, SEPTEMBER 2004

Copyright © 2002, 2003 by Paul Cartledge

All rights reserved under International and Pan-American Copyright Conventions.
Published in the United States by Vintage Books, a division
of Random House, Inc., New York, and simultaneously in Canada
by Random House of Canada Limited, Toronto. Originally published
by The Overlook Press, Peter Mayer Publishers, Inc.,
New York and Woodstock, in 2003.

Vintage and colophon are registered trademarks of Random House, Inc.

Library of Congress Cataloging-in-Publication Data
Cartledge, Paul.
The Spartans : the world of the warrior-heroes in ancient Greece, from utopia to
crisis and collapse / Paul Cartledge.
p.   cm.
Includes bibliographical references and index.
ISBN 1-4000-7885-7
1. Sparta (Extinct city)—History.   I. Title.
DF261.S8C379 2004
938'.9—dc22
2004049331

Author photograph © Nigel Cassidy

www.vintagebooks.com

Printed in the United States of America
15

To Barry Strauss

CONTENTS

PREFACE AND ACKNOWLEDGEMENTS

Who were the ancient Spartans, and why should we care? The events of 11 September 2001 jolted many of us into rethinking what was distinctive and distinctively admirable – or at least defensible – about Western civilization, values and culture. Some of us were provoked into wondering aloud whether any definition of that civilization and its cultural values would justify our dying for them, or even maybe killing for them. Those of us who are historians of ancient Greece wondered this with especial intensity, since the world of ancient Greece is one of the principal tap roots of Western civilization. As J. S. Mill put it, the battle of Marathon, fought in 490 BC between the Athenians, with support from the Plataeans and the invading Persians, was much more important than the Battle of Hastings, even as an event in English history.

So too, arguably, as we shall see, was the battle of Thermopylae of ten years later. This was a defeat for the small, Spartan-led Greek force at the hands of the overwhelmingly larger force of Persian and other invaders, yet it gave hope of better times to come, and its cultural significance is inestimable. Indeed, some would say that Thermopylae was Sparta's finest hour.

Thus, one not insignificant reason why we today should care who the ancient Spartans were, is that they played a key role – some might say *the* key role – in defending Greece and so preserving from foreign and alien conquest a form of culture or civilization that constitutes one of the chief roots of our own Western civilization.

As I write, there is a remarkable concentration of academic and popular interest on the society and civilization of the ancient Spartans. Two television series – besides PBS's, there was a four-parter aired in over fifty countries simultaneously on the History Channel; a Hollywood movie, to be based on the recent historical novel *Gates of Fire* by Steven Pressfield; and no fewer than three international academic colloquia, one to be held in Scotland, the other two actually taking place in modern Sparta itself: one organized by Greek scholars, and including members of the Greek Archaeological Service working there (whose help over the years has been invaluable), the other by the British School at Athens (which has been involved with research in and on Sparta one way or another since 1906, and is currently seeking the funding to establish a research centre in the city). What can there possibly still be to talk about that merits focusing all this media and other attention on ancient Sparta?

This book attempts an answer to that complex question. It is the first properly general book that I have written on the Spartans (for my others, see the Further Reading section at the end of this book); and for the opportunity to do so I must thank, in the first place, my collaborator and kindred spirit Bettany Hughes. I happened to read an article of hers in a weekly newspaper magazine, and learned that Sparta was a current interest of hers. I have since discovered that it is not only Spartan history in particular but the mediating of history in general to a wide public, that we share a passionate interest in.

I should also like to thank my expert and sympathetic agent, Julian Alexander, and the editors of two publications which are an absolutely vital conduit of the type of public or popular history that I am trying here to practise: Greg Neale and his deputy, Paul Lay, of the *BBC History Magazine,* and Peter Furtado, of *History Today.* For publishing pieces by me (and Bettany Hughes) that relate to the current project, I am extremely grateful to them. I have also to thank Edmund Keeley for permission to quote from his and the late Philip Sherrard's translation of Cavafy's 'Thermopylae'.

The original edition of this book was dedicated to my friend and colleague, Dr Anton Powell. I take the opportunity of this new edition to dedicate it to another friend and colleague, Professor Barry Strauss of Cornell University. He finds it hard to share my enthusiasm for Spartan history, let alone to evince sympathy for the ancient Spartans' way of life, but he too has been motivated over many years by a concern to communicate with a broad public, both as a writer of books and articles for the intelligent general reader and as a co-author of a widely read historical coursebook aimed at North American undergraduates. He is not, of course, to be discredited with any remaining errors or infelicities, but I hope he will not be too disappointed to find this book dedicated to him.

TIMELINE

(All dates BC; all down to 525, and some after, are approximate)

2000–1600	Middle Bronze Age
1600–1100	Late Bronze Age (or Mycenaean Age)
1200	Downfall of Bronze Age kingdom of Lacedaemon
1000	Dorians settle Sparta and Laconia
800	Town of Sparta expands to include Amyclae
776	Olympic Games founded (trad.)
735	Spartans invade Messenia: First Messenian War
720	Accession of Theopompus
706	Sparta founds Tarentum (Greek Taras, modern Taranto)
700	First temple of Orthia, Menelaion sanctuary laid out, accession of Polydorus
680	Accession of King Pheidon of Argos
676	Carneia founded (trad.)
675	Death of Theopompus
670	Messenian Helots revolt: Second Messenian War begins, *floruit* of Tyrtaeus

669	Battle of Hysiae (trad.)
665	Death of Polydorus
650	The reforms attributed to Lycurgus
560	Accession of King Croesus of Lydia
556	Chilon Ephor (trad.)
550	Sparta allies with Tegea, Gitiadas adorns Brazen House of Athena, throne of Apollo-Hyacinthus at Amyclae by Bathycles
550	Cyrus II the Great founds Persian Empire
546	Fall of Sardis and kingdom of Croesus to Persia
545	Battle of the Champions (in Thyreatis)
525	Sparta ousts Polycrates tyrant of Samos
520	Accession of Cleomenes I
519	Cleomenes in Boeotia
515	Accession of Demaratus, embassy of Maeandrius of Samos
512	Failed expedition of Anchimol(i)us to Athens
510	Cleomenes ousts Hippias tyrant of Athens
508	Second intervention of Cleomenes in Athens
507	Reforms of Cleisthenes found Athenian democracy
506	Sparta and Peloponnesian League allies invade Attica
499	Embassy of Aristagoras of Miletus, beginning of Ionian Revolt
494	Battle of Sepeia, end of Ionian Revolt
491	Demaratus deposed, accession of Leotychidas II
490	Battle of Marathon

490	Death of Cleomenes, accession of Leonidas I
480	Battle of Thermopylae
479	Battle of Plataea
EARLY 470S	Persian Stoa at Sparta
478	Sparta recalls Pausanias the Regent, withdraws from anti-Persian alliance, Athens founds anti-Persian Delian League
478	Exile of Leotychidas II
469	Deaths of Pausanias the regent and Leotychidas II, accession of Archidamus II
464	Great Earthquake at Sparta
464–460?	Helot Revolt (Third Messenian War)
461	Pericles comes to prominence at Athens
457	Battle of Tanagra
445	Thirty Years' Peace with Athenian alliance
431	Peloponnesian War begins
427	Death of Archidamus II, accession of Agis II
425	Surrender at Sphacteria
421	Peace of Nicias
418	Battle of (First) Mantinea
413	Occupation of Decelea
412	Alliance with Persia
409	Accession of Pausanias
404	Sparta wins Peloponnesian War
401	Raising of 'Ten Thousand' force of Greek mercenaries to support Cyrus the Younger, the Persian pretender

400	Accession of Agesilaus II
399	Remnant of 'Ten Thousand' absorbed into Sparta's anti-Persian forces in Asia
395	Deposition and exile of Pausanias, accession of Agesipolis I, Corinthian War begins
386	King's Peace/Peace of Antalcidas ends Corinthian War
382	Spartan occupation of Thebes
380	Death of Agesipolis I, accession of Cleombrotus I
379/8	Liberation of Thebes
378	Foundation of Second Athenian League, foundation of (second) Boiotian confederacy, creation of Theban Sacred Band
371	Battle of Leuctra, death of Cleombrotus I
370/69	Invasion of Laconia by Epaminondas, liberation of Messenian Helots, foundation of Messene
368	Foundation of Megalopolis
366	Defection of most of Peloponnesian League allies
362	Battle of (Second) Mantinea, death of Epaminondas
360	Death of Agesilaus II, accession of Archidamus III
338	Death of Archidamus III
331	'Battle of Mice', death of Agis III
309	Death of Cleomenes II; accession of Areus I
294	Archidamus IV defeated at Mantinea by Demetrius Poliorcetes
254	Accession of Leonidas II
244	Accession of Agis IV; attempted social and economic reforms

241	Death of Agis IV
236	Accession of Cleomenes III
227	Cleomenes carries out political, social, economic and military reforms
227	Accession of Agiad Euclidas, brother of Cleomenes III, to Eurypontid throne ends traditional dual kingship
222	Battle of Sellasia; Sparta occupied for the first time ever, by Antigonus III Doson of Macedon
219	Death of Cleomenes III at Alexandria
207	Defeat at Mantinea, 4000 Spartans killed; Nabis assumes power
195	Imposition of settlement by Rome; Sparta deprived of remaining Laconian Perioeci
192	Death of Nabis; Sparta under Achaean League domination
188	Philopoemen again intervenes at Sparta
146	Romans defeat Achaean League and establish protectorate in Greece; destruction of Corinth
79–7	Cicero visits Sparta
42	Deaths of 2000 Spartans at battle of Philippi
40	Livia (future wife of Augustus) given asylum at Sparta
32	Sparta sides with Octavian (later Augustus) against Antony
27	Augustus becomes de facto first Roman Emperor
21	Augustus visits Sparta, hosted by local dynast C. Julius Eurycles
2	Formation by now of ex-Perioeci into Eleutherolaconian League
AD 14	Death of Augustus

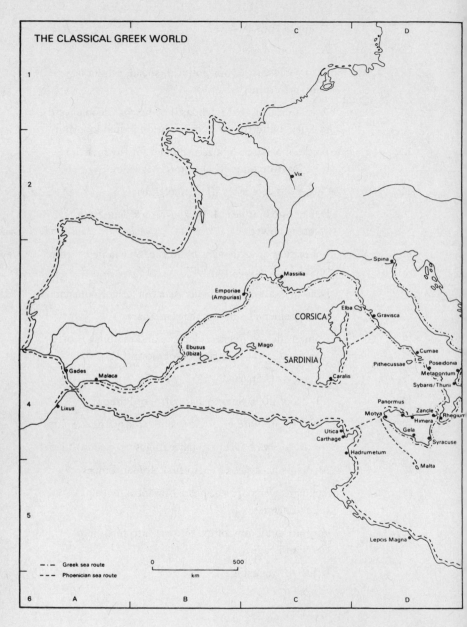

THE CLASSICAL GREEK WORLD

- Vix
- Spina
- Massilia
- Emporiae (Ampurias)
- CORSICA
- Elba
- Gravisca
- Ebusus (Ibiza)
- Mago
- SARDINIA
- Cumae
- Pithecussae
- Poseidonia
- Metapontum
- Gades
- Malaca
- Caralis
- Sybaris / Thurii
- Lixus
- Panormus
- Motya
- Zancle
- Rhegium
- Himera
- Utica
- Gela
- Carthage
- Syracuse
- Hadrumetum
- Malta
- Lepcis Magna

—·—· Greek sea route
— — — Phoenician sea route

0   500
km

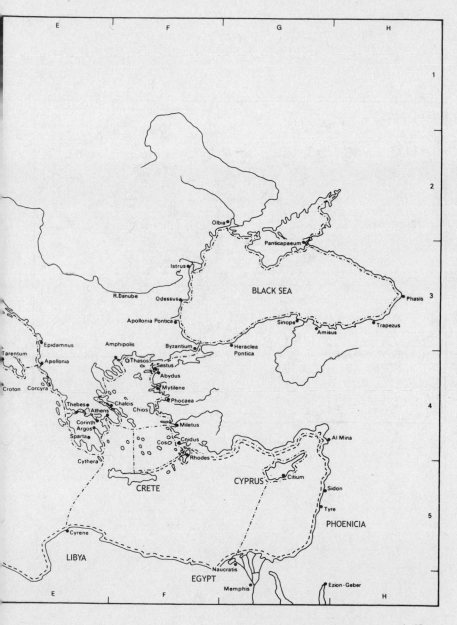

E   F   G   H

1

2

Olbia

Panticapaeum

Istrus

R.Danube   Odessus   BLACK SEA   Phasis 3

Apollonia Pontica   Sinope   Trapezus

Amphipolis   Byzantium   Heraclea   Amisus
Epidamnus   Pontica
Tarentum   Thasos Sestus
Apollonia   Abydus
Croton Corcyra   Mytilene
Thebes   Phocaea
Chalcis
Athens   Chios   4
Corinth   Miletus
Argos
Sparta   Coso Cnidus   Al Mina
Cythera   Rhodes

CRETE   CYPRUS   Citium

Sidon

Tyre   5
Cyrene   PHOENICIA

LIBYA

Naucratis
EGYPT   Ezion-Geber
Memphis

E   F   H

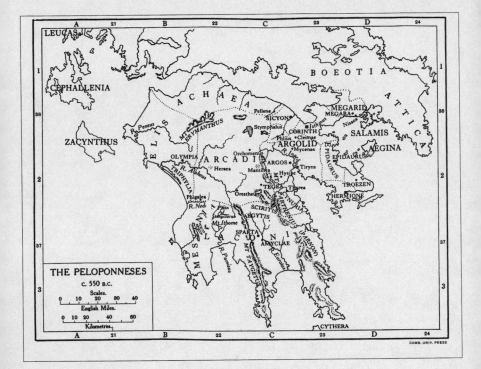

THE PELOPONNESES

c. 550 B.C.

Scales.

English Miles.

Kilometres.

CAMB. UNIV. PRESS

The
SPARTANS

INTRODUCTION

THE MAIN CHRONOLOGICAL PERIOD of focus in *The Spartans* will be from 480 to 360 BC, that is, within the Classical era of Greek history, from the time when Sparta, as head of the new Peloponnesian League, led the loyalist Greeks in their defence of their homeland against a massive Persian invasion, down to the time of Sparta's crisis as a society and collapse as a great Greek power three or four generations later. Within that period we shall follow the story of Sparta's developing difficulties with its Peloponnesian League allies, the major disaster of a massive earthquake followed by a prolonged and potentially deadly revolt of its servile class of Helots, Sparta's increasing differences with and then major military confrontation with Athens and its take-over from Athens as the Great Power of the Aegean Greek world, followed by its severe and ultimately terminal overstretch.

The narrative will be interspersed with snapshot biographies, set off from the main text, that will both bring the story of the past vividly and personally to life, and explore and illustrate underlying historical themes and processes. In order to place the years from 480 to 360 in context, an account will first be given of the formation of the Spartan state in the early historical period of Greece, and especially in the seventh and sixth centuries, together with a backwards glance at the prehistory of the region of Laconia within which all Spartan history must be firmly located. Then, to illustrate the depth of Sparta's plunge from power and grace, the storyline will be continued on as far as the ineffectual resistance led by Sparta to the might of Alexander the Great, and their much happier decision to side with the future Roman emperor Augustus.

Besides the chronological narrative there is another, no less fascinating and important side to our Spartan story, what can be summed up as the Spartan myth. Sparta's enormously protracted period of exceptional success, both as a society and as a great power, naturally attracted unusual attention from outside observers, often admiring, sometimes deeply critical. Despite its ultimate failure, catastrophe and collapse in real-power terms, Sparta's hold over non-Spartan Greek and foreign imaginations grew, and continues today to grow, ever stronger and more complicated. It began with Socrates' pupils Critias and Plato (a relative of Critias) in the late fifth and fourth century BC, and has continued almost without a pause let alone break via the Romans, who liked to think they were genetically related to the Spartans, and such Renaissance and early modern thinkers as More, Machiavelli and Rousseau who admired Sparta's prodigious political stability and order, on through to the Nazis in the twentieth century AD and their contemporary would-be emulators today. Deeply xenophobic, the Spartans were considered in antiquity to be as intriguing, extreme and even alien as they probably should be considered by us today.

Sparta was the original utopia (Thomas More, who coined the word Utopia in 1516, had Sparta very centrally in mind), but it was an authoritarian, hierarchical and repressive utopia, not a utopia of liberal creativity and free expression. The principal focus of the community was on the use of war for self-preservation and the domination of others. Unlike other Greek cities, which satisfied their hunger for land by exporting population to form new 'colonial' cities among non-Greek 'natives', the Spartans attacked, subdued or enslaved their fellow-Greek neighbours in the southern Peloponnese.

The image or mirage of Sparta is therefore at least ambivalent and double-faceted. Against the positive image of the Spartans' uplifting warrior ideal of collective self-sacrifice, emblematized in the Thermopylae story, has to be pitted their lack of high cultural achievement, their refusal for the most part of open government, both at home and abroad, and their brutally efficient suppression for several centuries of a whole enslaved Greek people.

The book will be divided into three Parts. The first, 'Go, tell the Spartans!', which has also been used as the title of a movie based on the Vietnam War, is named after the opening words of the famous contemporary epitaph on the Thermopylae battle-dead attributed to Simonides. It examines the evolution of one of the most intriguing of ancient societies and cultures, one that has left a deep mark on the development of the West. While Athens is justly credited with phenomenal achievements in visual art, architecture, theatre, philosophy and democratic politics, the ideals and traditions of its greatest rival, Sparta, are equally potent and enduring: duty, discipline, the nobility of arms in a cause worth dying for, the sacrifice of the individual for the greater good of the community and the triumph of will over seemingly insuperable obstacles.

This first Part explains how Sparta evolved into the most powerful fighting force in the ancient Greek world without ever completely transcending or obscuring the traces of its origins in a group of villages on the banks of the river Eurotas in the southern Peloponnese. It grew in the first place through subjugating or enslaving its immediate neighbours in Laconia and Messenia, who became known respectively as the Helots ('Captives') and Perioeci ('Outdwellers'), and by controlling easily the largest city-state territory in the entire Greek world, some 8,000 square kilometres, more than twice the territory of the second largest city, Syracuse, and more than three times Athens's territory of Attica (about 2,500 square kilometres).

Consider first Sparta's territorial base in Laconia and Messenia. It is not only the sheer size of the territory that came to be called 'Lacedaemon' that provokes wonder and merits the historian's attention. It is also its agricultural fertility, richness in mineral wealth and secure enclosedness. Above all, we should note the presence of two large riverine plains divided by one of the highest mountain ranges in all Greece, and the occurrence of large natural deposits of iron ore with

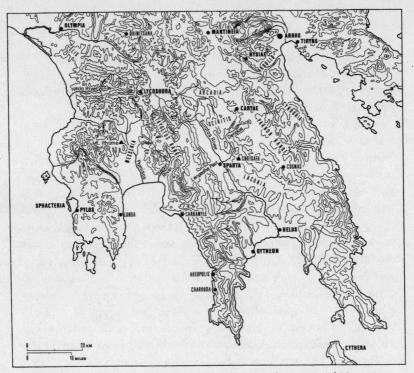

The southern Peloponnese: Sparta's home territory of Laconia and Messenia.

an unusually high iron content. Human settlement is attested in southern Laconia as early as the Neolithic period. The caves at Pirgos Dirou
in the Mani are today a notable tourist attraction for their multihued
stalagmites and stalactites that can be inspected at close hand from a
guided boat. But here a small settlement flourished in the fourth millennium BC, as heaps of bones silently attest. Elsewhere in the southern
Peloponnese, it was not before the third millennium, otherwise known
as the Early Bronze Age, that substantial settlement was established over
a wide area. It was during this millennium and this cultural phase, some
archaeologists and anthropologists believe, that the Mediterreanean
triad of dietary staples – grain, the olive and the grapevine – first put
down unshakeably firm roots. This simple but explosive combination

lay behind the far more impressive developments of the Middle and Late Bronze Ages, dated between about 2000 and 1100 BC.

Well before the latter date, settlements in Laconia numbered in the hundreds, and their size might reach up to several thousands of inhabitants. The main area of concentration was the alluvial valley of the perennial Eurotas river, and in particular its lower or Helos plain, and its upper or Spartan plain. Homer's *Iliad*, a text probably put together in monumental form somewhere around 700 BC but stretching back in its origins at least as far as 1100 BC, the very end of the Bronze Age, contains in its second Book a famous Catalogue of the Ships. This lists the ships that King Agamemnon of Mycenae 'rich in gold' was able to muster in pursuit of his aim of recovering from Troy on the Hellespont the sister-in-law, Helen wife of his brother Menelaus, whom the dastardly Trojan prince Paris had allegedly stolen away. Or so the epic Greek legend had it. It is not possible to authenticate, even in its basic plotline, the story of the *Iliad*, which may be immortal precisely because it is essentially fictional. Anyway, Menelaus's kingdom, as listed in the Catalogue, contained a place called Helos by the sea, and a place – of course – called Sparta. Homeric Helos may have been situated at a place called today Ayios Stephanos (St Stephen), where substantial Late Bronze Age remains have been excavated. But as yet no material remains have been found anywhere in Laconia to match up to the sort of palace that Homer's descriptions (in the *Odyssey* as well as the *Iliad*) would lead one to expect, and it may be that Laconia in the Late Bronze Age was in fact – as opposed to Homeric fantasy – divided up between a number of princedoms none of which could claim overall suzerainty of the region as a whole.

Between 1100 and 700 BC, something quite drastic happened in Laconia, as elsewhere in the Peloponnese and indeed throughout what historians and archaeologists call the Mycenaean world. The palaces of Mycenae and Tiryns in the Argolid, and Pylos in Messenia, and others in other regions of central and southern Greece had been burned and destroyed in about 1200, and the civilization of which they had been the focus melted away, to be succeeded by an era so relatively impoverished culturally that it has often been referred to as a Dark Age. Of course, the darkness was neither total nor uniform over all post-Mycenaean Greece, but in few regions was it as obscure and prolonged as in Laconia. Some of the previous inhabitants remained in place, though scattered and diminished, but they seem to have been eventually dominated by a group or groups of incomers from further to the north and northwest, people who came to call themselves Dorians and spoke a Doric dialect of Greek. These incomers were in the main the ancestors of the historical Spartans. One sign of their novelty is that the site of the main settlement that they built, in Sparta, had not been of any importance during the previous Mycenaean Bronze Age. It therefore carried no direct associations of a more glorious past – such associations clustered rather at Therapne to the south-east and Amyclae a few kilometres more or less due south.

By the middle of the eighth century, the new Spartans felt confident enough to try to spread their influence and control further south in Laconia, incorporating Amyclae along the way as a fifth constituent village to add to the original four (Cynosura, Mesoa, Limnae and Pitana) and transforming Therapne into a major cult-centre devoted to Menelaus and his controversial wife Helen, and to her divine brothers, the Dioscuri, otherwise known as Castor and Pollux. By about 735 the control even of the whole Eurotas valley and its surrounds was not enough, either politically or economically, for the aggressive and expansionist Spartans. They cast their greedy eyes westwards, to Messenia, overlooking – or looking round – the formidable obstacle posed by the intervening Taygetus mountain chain that rises to over 2,400 metres (8,000 feet) at its peak. In what was probably a series of raids and border skirmishes, rather than a concerted invasion as the later sources liked to project it, the Spartans eventually defeated their Messenian neighbours and transformed the inhabitants of the main Pamisus riverine alluvial valley of south-west Peloponnese into serf-like peasants, working what had been their land under compulsion for the benefit of their new and largely unwelcome Spartan masters. As Thucydides was to point out three centuries later, these Messenians were the larger portion of the subject group known collectively as Helots. But probably the idea of Helotage had been developed first or simultaneously in Laconia, in the southernmost part of the Eurotas valley. At any rate, some later sources wrongly derived the name Helots ety-mologically from the town or region called Helos, probably because that is where the major, and original, concentration of Helots was to be found.

These Helots are the single most important human fact about ancient Sparta. Divided into two main groups, the Messenians to the west of Mt Taygetus and the Laconians to its east, the Helots provided the Spartans with the economic basis of their unique lifestyle. They vastly outnumbered the full Spartan citizens, who in self-defence called them-selves Homoioi or 'Similars' (not 'Equals', as it is often wrongly trans-lated; the English word 'Peers' perhaps comes close in meaning, though it, like French 'pair', is derived from Latin *par*, 'equal'.) This was because they were all equal and alike in one respect only, in being members of the dominant military master-caste. The Spartans were exceptionally successful masters, keeping the Helots in subjection for more than three centuries. But they did so at considerable cost. The threat of Helot revolt, especially from the Messenians, was almost constant, and the Spartans responded by turning themselves into a sort of permanently armed camp, Fortress Sparta. Male Spartan citizens were forbidden any other trade, profession or business than war, and they acquired the rep-utation of being the Marines of the entire Greek world, a uniquely pro-fessional and motivated fighting force. Sparta had to be on a constant state of alert and readiness, for enemies within as well as without.

Like other Greeks, the Spartans attributed the foundation of their extraordinary state and society to the reforms of one man. The individual hero credited with this unique achievement was Lycurgus, whose name translates roughly as 'Wolf-Worker'. He was a mixture perhaps of George Washington – and Pol Pot. Quite possibly, too, he was entirely mythical. Winston Churchill once referred to Soviet Russia as a riddle wrapped in a mystery inside an enigma. He could have used the same words of Lycurgus. When faced with the contradictory evidence for this miracle-worker, the

Overleaf: View from ancient Therapnae (sanctuary of Menelaus and Helen) looking west across modern Sparta (founded 1834) towards Mt Taygetus (2404 metres). Byzantine Mistra is visible in the background to the right.

historical and moral biographer Plutarch (writing in about AD 100) was so baffled that he concluded plausibly enough that there must have been more than one Lycurgus. All the same, he chose to compose the life of only one of them, comparing him honorifically with the Roman founding father, King Numa. Aristotle writing in the fourth century BC had been considerably less glowing in his appraisal of the lawgiver's achievements, but Rousseau if anything outdid even Plutarch in his praise.

The legend of Lycurgus postulated a remarkable 'Year Zero' scenario when, at a moment of deep crisis, he was able to persuade his fellow Spartans to introduce the comprehensive and compulsory educational cycle called the Agoge (*agôgê*, literally a 'raising', as of cattle). This system of education, training and socialisation turned boys into fighting men whose reputation for discipline, courage and skill was unsurpassed. He was credited also with utterly reforming the Spartans' political system and introducing perhaps the earliest system of Greek citizen self-government. Lycurgus may have been a myth, in our sense, but it was for the laws that he had supposedly given them that the Spartans who perished at Thermopylae gave their lives so willingly.

Apart from the educational and political systems, Lycurgus was credited with altering decisively the psychological make-up of the citizens. Though the 'Lycurgan' system had many bizarre aspects to an outsider's view, the Spartans' own belief in their ideology was absolute. Throughout Spartan history there were very few defectors – or whingers. At the heart of it all lay paranoia and a preoccupation with secrecy, both in the circumstances wholly rational. While justly famed for their hoplite battle tactics of co-ordinated mass infantry manoeuvres, in which eight-deep shield walls bulldozed the enemy off the field of battle or terrorized them into giving up and running away, the Spartans were also enthralled by espionage and intelligence gathering. They pioneered many methods of secret communication. Sinisterly, the most promising teenage boys on the threshold of adulthood were enrolled in a kind of secret police force known as the Crypteia (roughly 'Special Ops Brigade'), the principal aim of which was to murder selected troublemaking Helots and spread terror among the rest.

This is just one of many aspects of the Spartan system that modern readers will find hard to stomach, or indeed credit. Lycurgus, however, in creating a system in which individuals' first loyalty was to the group and above all the state rather than to family or friends, introduced a novel understanding of what being a *politês* (citizen) meant. It may not have been the intention, but the concept would change the course of Western civilisation. The first Part of the book ends with the Persian Wars of 480–479, the mighty clash between the huge and autocratic Persian Empire and a small grouping of loyalist Greek cities fighting to defend not just their homeland but their way of life. Against all the odds, at Thermopylae, Salamis, Plataea and Mycale, the loyalist Greeks put aside their differences and fought like men possessed, as in a way they were – with an ideal of freedom. They not only repulsed the Persian invasion but laid the groundwork for a remarkable advance of Greek power and culture both east and west, in what we call the Classical period of Greek civilisation and history.

The successful Greek resistance was led overall by the Spartans, and they led from the front. The engagement at Thermopylae, in which King Leonidas commanded a small force of Greek hoplites, including 300 picked Spartan champions, and held up the Persian advance crucially for several days, was technically a defeat. But morally speaking – from the point of view of mores and morale – it was a great victory, and, as Napoleon was to observe, the morale factor in warfare outweighs all other factors in a ratio of three to one. This epic resistance at Thermopylae will provide a suitable climax to the first Part, not least because it is the single most formative element in the composite, complex and enduring Spartan myth.

The second Part of the book is entitled 'The Spartan Myth'. It focuses on the epic confrontation between Sparta and Athens and their respective allies that is usually known for short as the Peloponnesian War but which I shall call the Athenian War (431–404), since I shall be looking at it from the Spartan viewpoint, as the War against the Athenians. The book's exploration of the contradictions and surprises within Spartan society will thus be linked to a strong narrative of the disastrous conflict between

Sparta and Athens and their respective allies, which had its origins almost as soon as their joint repulse of the Persians had ended. Athens and Sparta represented two alternative and increasingly incompatible ways of being. Athens was democratic, individualistic, radical, commercial, sea-based. Sparta was land-based, hierarchical, oligarchically minded, above all conservative, prone to overvalue its version of the past and inclined to dismiss innovations such as coined money and siege warfare. The cold war that broke out between Sparta and Athens in the aftermath of the Persian Wars soon turned uncomfortably hot.

Following the heroic joint efforts of 479, Sparta withdrew from the mainly naval initiative led by Athens to liberate the remaining Aegean Greeks from the Persian empire. Some fifteen years later, the two cities had a major falling-out. Sparta had suffered a violent earthquake in about 464, followed by a large-scale Helot revolt. Other cities sent troops to help put down the revolt, but Athens's contribution – even though masterminded by the pro-Spartan Cimon, who had even called one of his sons Lacedaemonius or 'Spartan' – was soon sent packing. The Spartans simply did not want several thousands of democratically minded citizen-soldiers running loose among their Greek servile underclass in their tightly controlled territory. In 458 or 457, the two fought a pitched battle against each other at Tanagra in Boeotia. A peace of sorts was patched up in 445, but when outright war finally came in 431, no one was surprised.

Greek cities had been fighting each other since time immemorial. The Ephesian philosopher Heraclitus called war 'the father of all, and king of all'. Yet the Athenian War was to prove unprecedentedly and incomparably savage and destructive. Greece, the ancient travel writer Pausanias later wrote, had up until then walked steadily on both feet, but this War toppled it over as if by an earthquake. Nothing could better illustrate its topsy-turvy quality than an episode in the seventh year of the War, in 425. Incredible news reached the outside world of an extraordinary happening on Sphacteria, a small island just off the south-west coast of Messenia and within Sparta's home territory. A 400-strong force of Spartan and Perioecic hoplites, including 120 of the elite Homoioi or Peers, had surrendered there following a twelve-week blockade by Athenian forces aided by descendants of former Messenian Helots. This event shook the Greek world. It simply was not supposed to happen. For it contradicted absolutely the Spartan myth, as laid down and exemplified most famously at Thermopylae, the myth of Never Surrender.

Militarily speaking, the siege of Sphacteria was a side-show in the Athenian War, a war of unprecedented duration, scale and savagery. Psychologically, however, it was devastating. Even the Great Plague (possibly a form of typhus) that struck Athens in 430 and caused the loss of perhaps 30 per cent of the Athenians' fighting forces seemed a relatively normal occurrence by comparison with the Spartans' surrender at Sphacteria. This was, in the words of Thucydides, the Athenian general and the War's principal historian:

> the event that caused more surprise among the Hellenes
> [Greeks] than anything else that happened in the war.[1]

So shocked were the Spartans by what had happened that they sued for peace – even though they had themselves started the war and had by no means yet achieved their stated objective of liberating Athens' Greek subjects. Indeed, adding insult to injury, the Athenians rejected the Spartans' peace overtures outright and hung on to the 120 Spartan prisoners as hostages for the remainder of the first – ten-year – phase of the War.

To the Greeks as a whole, and to the Spartans in particular, it was inconceivable that 120 products of the Agoge education system would surrender after a mere eighty days of privation, thirst and hunger. When questioned about that very fact, one of the prisoners in Athens is said to have given as his reason for surrendering that he hadn't been involved in a fair fight, man to man. He hadn't been fighting against true men in regular warfare using masculine weapons. Instead, he had been brought low by what he called the enemies' 'spindles', which he claimed were incapable of distinguishing a true warrior from a born coward. The reference of 'spindles', Thucydides explains, was to arrows – ignoble, cowardly, long-distance weapons, typically womanish. But what would that Spartan prisoner's wife and the rest of the Spartan women have made of his justification?

The Spartan myth was persuasively labelled a 'mirage' in the 1930s, by the French scholar François Ollier, because the relation between the myth and reality was and is sometimes so hard to perceive without distortion. It remains potent to this day. Perhaps the most interesting and controversial of all its many facets is the position of Spartan women. As ever, Athens provides a useful comparison and counterpoint. An Athenian girl would receive no formal education beyond training for the domestic duties required of a good Athenian wife and mother – weaving, food-preparation, childcare, household management. A daughter was routinely fed smaller rations than her brothers. At puberty she would be sequestered in her father's or other male guardian's house until she was married off to a man who, if he could afford to, would keep her as much as possible out of the public eye and would think it dishonourable even to hear her talked about among unrelated men. She was not allowed to own any significant amount of property in her own right and had no official say in Athens' much vaunted democracy. Significantly, the women of Athens of whom we hear most were not Athenian citizen women at all, but the *hetaerae* or upmarket prostitutes who were powerful but definitely beyond the acceptable social pale.

In sharp and complete contrast, Spartan women were – allegedly – active, prominent, powerful, surprisingly independent-minded, and positively garrulous. Girls had a similar education to that of the boys, though separate. Many could read and write. Young virgins, oiled head to toe, ran races, then danced by night to worship their gods and goddesses. By day, ultimately to attract suitors, they threw the javelin and discus, wrestled – sometimes, again allegedly, with the boys – and performed gymnastics, all completely naked and in full public view, to the consternation of Greek visitors from other cities. They were also keen on the horses. One breeder, Cynisca (sister of King Agesilaus II), was the first woman ever to win a crown at the otherwise relentlessly masculine Olympic Games, in the four-horse chariot-race. 'I won with a team of fast-footed horses' – so read in part her own self-praising inscription. Stormin' Cynisca, indeed, though she should in all fairness have given a mention to the anonymous, and male, charioteer. The reputation of Spartan girls and women for outstanding physical beauty went right back as far as Helen of Troy – or Helen of Sparta, as she of course was originally. But so too did their reputation for being fast and loose. The derogatory epithet 'thigh-flashers' was coined just for them – even though, as we shall see, the Spartan-made bronze figurines depicting typical young female Spartans in athletic (and thigh-revealing) pose tell a story rather of vitality, grace and vigour.

Spartan women could own property, including land, and though they had no official voice in the Spartan warrior Assembly, they clearly found other ways to make their views known and felt. There is even a collection of *Sayings of Spartan Women,* preserved by Plutarch: something unthinkable in the case of Athenian women. Spartan women, moreover, were freed from the everyday drudgery that was their Athenian sisters' normal lot. Helot women and men did the housework for them, cooked, wove, childminded, and so on. The women were left with only the satisfactions of motherhood, which they took very seriously indeed. Sexually, too, they seemed to be independent, although alleged Spartan customs regarding wife-swapping are not entirely easy either to credit or to comprehend. Certainly, with their men often away at war or practising for it, they sought emotional satisfaction with other women. Certainly, strong women acquired such positions of authority that they could be considered a political force or – depending on outlook – menace.

Not that Sparta was any kind of feminist utopia. Much of the physical training, for example, was severely eugenic in aim. But such was the women's apparent emancipation to non-Spartan eyes that Aristotle actually blamed them for Sparta's eventual demise as a great power, on the grounds that they had never submitted themselves satisfactorily to the Lycurgan regimen imposed on and accepted by their men. That was probably a judgment warped by the typically sexist outlook of the average Greek citizen male, but it pays a backhanded compliment to what was surely the most remarkable group of women in all Greece.

Sparta's victory in the Athenian War had been won with great difficulty and at great cost. The War had plumbed new depths of savagery, leading Thucydides to question the Greeks' hold on civilization and humanity. Brutal sieges occurred, massacres of women and children, wholesale rapine and the destruction of entire communities, the selling of thousands of Greeks into slavery, and, not least, ferocious outbreaks of *stasis* or civil war – Thucydides' account of the civil war on Corcyra (modern Corfu) in 427 is a chilling classic of political analysis.

To start with, the conflict was a stalemate of Athenian sea-power versus Spartan land-power, neither side being able decisively to gain the upper hand in the other's preferred sphere. But then, in 415, the Athenians over-reached themselves, inspired by the evil genius of Alcibiades, a kind of false Pericles (who had been his guardian after his own father's death in battle). They despatched a huge armada to Sicily, ostensibly in defence of 'kinsmen' but in reality either to conquer the whole island or at least to secure further resources for a renewal of the war with Sparta that had been temporarily in abeyance since 421. Alcibiades, the prime mover in this high-risk venture, was as much hated by his jealous political rivals as he was loved by the Athenian masses for his flamboyantly extrovert lifestyle. He had entered no fewer than seven four-horse chariot teams at the Olympics of 416 and, after almost inevitably carrying off the crown with one of them, commissioned no lesser a poet than Euripides to write the victory ode for him.

Yet the Sicilian expedition had been launched with the illest of ill omens – a wide-scale mutilation throughout the city of Athens of sacred images of Hermes, the god of travellers. For his alleged implication with this and other sacrileges, Alcibiades was recalled to stand trial on a capital charge, but jumped ship in southern Italy – and went over to the enemy. It was supposedly at his suggestion that Sparta both fortified a garrison post permanently within Athens's own home territory, thereby cutting off the city from its silver resources and prompting thousands of slaves to desert, and sent an effective Spartan general to help with the defence of Sicily, above all Syracuse. Both measures were crucial to Athens's eventual catastrophic defeat.

The Sicilian campaign thus got off to the worst of all possible starts, and was further bedevilled by ineptitude and dithering and difference of opinion within the high command. Moreover, the principal Sicilian enemy city, Syracuse, was exceptionally well equipped both materially and morally to withstand the assault. The Athenian forces, after failing to take Syracuse by siege and suffering a major naval defeat in that city's Great Harbour in 413, found themselves taken prisoner and, if not killed outright, ignominiously consigned to a lingering and painful death by starvation in Syracuse's stone quarries. Out of so many who left Athens in 415, as Thucydides ruefully recorded, so few eventually returned.

In retrospect the Sicilian disaster was the turning point in the Athenian War, though campaigning continued for a further decade, mainly by sea in the eastern Aegean and in and around the Hellespont (Dardanelles). In line with the general paradoxical quality of the struggle, this decade saw Sparta go cap in hand to Persia in order to raise the cash needed to build a fleet capable of defeating the Athenians in their own sphere and on their own element. Inevitably, such a policy of kowtowing to the oriental barbarian met resistance from the conservative Spartan commanders, but one figure, Lysander, proved more than equal to the task, becoming in the process something like a roving King of the High Seas. His personal relationship with one of the sons of the Persian Great King ensured a steady supply of cash to Sparta at the crucial time, and between 407 and 405, Lysander was able to forge the instrument of Athens's doom. In 405 at Aegospotami in the Hellespont, Athens's last fleet was finally overcome. Lysander's treatment of prisoners of war was savage – he had their right hands cut off, and then sent the men back to Athens as a terrible omen of the fate in store for the city. After a siege lasting the winter of 405/4, which left Athenians dying of starvation on the streets, Lysander was free to dictate Sparta's terms of unconditional surrender.

The Athenian empire, with its bold ideas of democracy, free commerce and rational progress, had been eclipsed, never to shine again quite so brightly or in quite the same ways. Sparta, it now seemed, had the chance of building a different sort of empire in its stead. Yet in 400 BC, at the time of the disputed accession of Agesilaus II, the following oracle was unhelpfully in circulation:

> *Boasting Sparta, be careful not to sprout*
> *a crippled kingship...*
> *unexpected troubles will overtake you...*[2]

The Spartans were a notoriously pious, or as we might say superstitious, people, always quick to believe omens, especially inconvenient ones. The third Part of the book, entitled 'A Crippled Kingship', reveals just how that doom-laden prediction came in a way to be fulfilled.

In the space of three decades, a little more than a human generation, Sparta would suffer humiliating military defeat, invasion of its home territory, and, most shocking of all to the system, the revolt and liberation of the greater part of the Helot serfs on whom the Spartans' power and way of life fundamentally depended. The key character in this remarkable peripety was the crippled king of whom the oracle – or so it was of course interpreted in retrospect – had spoken. Agesilaus, the ultimate Spartan, was the embodiment of all the weaknesses as well as the strengths of this extraordinary people, being both literally and metaphorically lame.

Lysander, though an aristocrat, was not a king, and the Spartans were wedded to their curious dual kingship. This went back, traditionally, to the very foundation of the city, and the two kings from two separate royal houses stoutly maintained their lineal descent from the hero-god Heracles. The duality led inevitably to divided counsels – dynastic rivalries, succession anxieties, faction-fighting. But because it was traditional, and because it was divinely ordained, it was deemed good and unalterable. Lysander therefore, unable to gain access to one of the lawful thrones and thwarted in his desire to carve out a kind of alternative kingship for himself, decided to turn kingmaker.

His chosen candidate, in the succession dispute of 400, was his former beloved, the aforementioned cripple Agesilaus, half-brother to the deceased Agis II. Since Agesilaus had not been expected to become king, he had been treated more or less like any other ordinary Spartan, and had, for example, gone through the Agoge, with great success. But against him were his physical deformity, the fact that Agis had recognised a son of his, Latychidas, as his legitimate successor, and – not least – the oracle about a 'crippled kingship'. The powerful Lysander's intervention tipped the balance. The oracle was explained away as referring to a metaphorically crippled kingship, that is, a kingship occupied by an illegitimate person – such as Lysander claimed Latychidas was, because he was the son, not of Agis, but of the Athenian interloper Alcibiades! (The dates would just fit.) Finally, Lysander could point out that Agesilaus's disability had in no way compromised his success in the Agoge and that, in times of huge and disorienting change, Agesilaus would stand for Spartan traditionalism. These arguments prevailed with the Gerousia, Sparta's Senate, and Agesilaus was chosen king.

If Lysander had hoped in effect to rule through Agesilaus, he was quickly disabused and disappointed. Agesilaus had his own agenda, even if that did in large measure coincide with Lysander's vaulting ambition for an Aegean-wide as well as mainland Greek empire. Unfortunately for Sparta, however, Agesilaus proved to be an inflexible, excessively Spartan leader, unable to adapt to a world in a state of flux. He was thus to preside actively as well as passively over Sparta's last victories and spectacular decline during the next three to four decades.

The Athenian War, it soon emerged, had transformed not only the Greek world generally but also Sparta itself. The adage of Lord Acton – absolute power corrupts absolutely – applied vigorously in this case. The cult of frugality and conspicuous non-consumption that had served Sparta well in the past by disguising actual differences of wealth among the self-styled Peers gave way to a more individualistic and self-serving ethic of which Lysander, though himself materially austere, was a talisman. Spartan citizen numbers had already begun to fall steeply, aggravated by greed for accumulations of land and other forms of personal wealth. By 371 there were only about 1,500 adult male Spartan warrior citizens – compared to some 25,000 Athenians, for example. The rapidly increasing disparity of numbers between citizens and Helots became really frightening, and the expedient of freeing supposedly reliable Helots and arming them was a double-edged sword.

Foreign policy too, in Agesilaus's hands, proved massively counterproductive. Within a decade of the Athenian War's end, Sparta found itself fighting not only Persia but also a coalition of the principal mainland Greek states including two of its own former Peloponnesian League allies, Corinth and the Boeotian federation, which were allied with Sparta's oldest Peloponnesian enemy, Argos, and a somewhat revived Athens. Moreover, Sparta's claim to empire was backed by no such ideological manifesto as Athens's support of liberation from Persia and domestic democratic self-governance. All it had to offer was brute force deployed in support of the minority of wealthy citizens in its subject states, against the common people as a whole. Plutarch put it very nicely when he compared the actuality of the Spartans' empire, notwithstanding their claims to having freed the subjects of Athens, to the pouring of vinegar into sweet wine.

Ultimately, the Spartans themselves helped to fashion their own nemesis, in the form of the Thebes-dominated federal state of Boeotia under the inspired leadership of Epaminondas (a philosopher as well as a brilliant general) and Pelopidas. Within just a few years Sparta suffered its first ever major defeat in pitched hoplite battle, at Leuctra in 371, and the first ever invasion by land of its home territory by a hostile force, in the winter of 370/69. After some three centuries of enslavement, the Messenian Helots were at last liberated thanks to Epaminondas and reacquired their own polis or city of Messene, the massive fortifications of which still inspire amazement today.

Sparta as a real-world earthly city never recovered fully from the liberation of the Messenian Helots, though the Spartans clung on to the Helots of Laconia as their severely reduced economic base for another century and a half. Without the Messenians, they were left with a full tradition but less than half a full rationale. Agesilaus, active to the end of his very long life, hired himself out as a mercenary commander to raise funds to refill the city's anyway never very healthy coffers. He died in north Africa, aged 84, and his embalmed body was brought back to Sparta for the extraordinary funeral that was the hereditary right and rite of dead Spartan kings. But by 360 the ritual was an empty one.

Nonetheless, although Sparta never regained its former terrestrial power, the myth and legend of Sparta waxed mightily. The final chapter of the book sketches some of the more interesting and important highways and byways of the Spartan mirage, paying attention specially to the place and roles accorded to Leonidas. The High Priest of Jerusalem, for example, in the early third century BC, found it politically expedient to claim a kinship link with Sparta – going right back to Moses, no less. The Romans, too, were so fascinated by Sparta, seeing in it many of the virtues and values they themselves held dear, that they also invented a spurious link of kinship between their two utterly unrelated peoples.

More tangible benefits were provided by the Spartans themselves for Hellenistic and Roman period tourists, who visited a Sparta that became a kind of theme park or museum of its – significantly imaginary – past. For example, in the third century of our era, the Spartans built a semicircular amphitheatre within the age-old sanctuary of Artemis Orthia, once integral to the Agoge, in order to give sado-tourists a better view of the spuriously antique flogging ritual of *diamastigôsis*, whereby Spartan youths were flogged in front of Artemis's altar, preferably to death, but at least to a state of unbowed bloodiness.

How were the mighty fallen. Perhaps it's not entirely surprising, though, that the philhellenes who wished for the liberation of Greece from the Ottoman empire or the founders of the British public school system in the nineteenth century should have seen in classical Sparta certain virtues worth emulating and instilling. Or that the adjectives 'Spartan' and 'laconic' should have entered mainstream English vocabulary in the ancient Spartans' by then somewhat tarnished honour. At any rate, two great empires, the Roman and the British, do indeed owe a good deal to Sparta: a good deal more, anyhow, than we, the Spartans' cultural heirs in the West, are today always prepared to admit, and at least as much as we owe, directly, to the Athenians. Sparta, to put it laconically, lives.

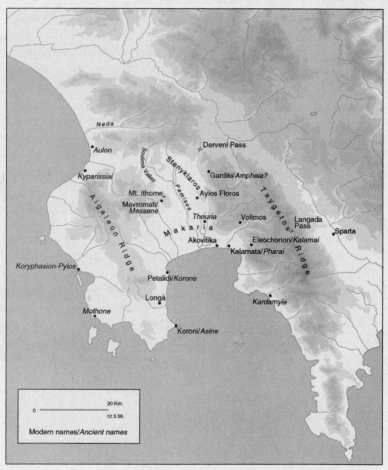

Sparta's western territory: Messenia

PART I

'GO, TELL THE SPARTANS!'

1

UNDER THE SIGN
OF LYCURGUS

THE IMAGE OF SPARTA as a dour, barracks-like camp hardly prepares the first-time visitor for the glorious spectacle that unfolds as one emerges from the uplands abutting Arcadia to the north and enters down the Eurotas valley into the Spartan plain. Stretching before one are two parallel mountain chains, that of Taygetus on the west reaching to 2,404 metres at the peak, and that of Parnon on the east (1,935 metres at its peak). The alluvial plain itself, and its continuation south in the Eurotas valley that runs out into the sea in the Laconian Gulf, constitute one of the most fertile and desirable pieces of land in all southern Greece. Soil, climate and man conspire to yield and garner sometimes two harvests of grain in a single year. Olives and grapevines, the other two staples of the so-called Mediterranean diet, flourish here too – as of course does the forest of citrus trees, but they are a post-Classical import, reminding us that the terrain and vegetation we see today are not necessarily those enjoyed by the inhabitants of two and a half millennia ago.

Hardly surprisingly, this region, known in historical times as Lacedaemon, was believed also to have been the seat of a great king in the ancient Greeks' heroic age – what we scholars more prosaically call the Mycenaean or Late Bronze Age (*c.* 1500–1100 BC). An attempt has been made very recently (*see* biography of Helen p. 48) to relocate the palace of Homer's Menelaus from Sparta to Pellana further north in

Laconia, but that flies in the face not only of ancient legend and religious worship but also of topographical geopolitics. Any real Late Bronze Age Menelaus must have had his palace in or near the site of historical Sparta – perhaps actually where a large settlement, including a building qualifying as a 'mansion', has been scrupulously excavated by the British School at Athens. However, no contemporary palace on the scale of those excavated at Mycenae (seat of Homer's Agamemnon, brother of Menelaus) and Pylos (capital of garrulous old Nestor) has yet come to light in Laconia – and perhaps never will. It is important not to read Homer as a straight history textbook, however archaeologically productive that mistake has undoubtedly been.

HELEN

Helen of Troy – or Helen of Sparta? She was, of course, both. A local girl, daughter of Tyndareus, according to one version of her myth, but yet, according to another version, daughter of great father Zeus and born miraculously from an egg because her mother Leda had been visited by Zeus in the disguise of a swan. Her unsurpassed beauty made her a natural prize for the ambitious Menelaus, son of Atreus of Mycenae, whose older son Agamemnon took Helen's sister Clytemnestra for his bride. However, that beauty also captivated an unwelcome visitor to Sparta: Paris, prince of Troy in Asia, overlooking the straits of the Dardanelles, who – aided crucially by the Cyprus-born love goddess Aphrodite – violated the sacred obligations of guest-friendship and robbed Menelaus of his lawfully wedded wife.

Recently, a Greek archaeologist caused a little stir by claiming that he had located Helen's (and Menelaus') palace, not at Sparta but at Pellana some fifteen kilometres farther north. That claim would have

This unusual pyramid-shaped stele of local limestone is conventionally interpreted as representing Menelaus and Helen: above, the future king of Sparta may be wooing Helen (his brother Agamemnon king of Mycenae had married Helen's sister Clytemnestra); on the right, as wronged husband and king, he perhaps meets her again at the sack of Troy.

astonished the ancient Spartans, who built a new shrine for Helen in Sparta, or more precisely at Therapne to the south-east of the ancient town, where she received worship along with her husband Menelaus and her divine brothers the Dioscuri, Castor and Polydeuces (Pollux in Latin). This was in the later eighth century, a time when the Spartans were, so to speak, rediscovering their roots, seeking to legitimize their recently won domain in south-east Peloponnese by presenting it as the legitimate successor of the kingdom of Menelaus as set out in Homer's *Iliad*. In actual fact, the cult of Helen at Therapne probably reflects a conflation of two Helens: one a goddess of vegetation and fertility associated with trees (also worshipped as such on Rhodes), the other the heroic Helen of Homeric legend. We shall stick with the latter.

More specifically, since Helen served later as an icon of Spartan womanhood and beauty, we must ask, was Helen raped (according to our usage of that term) by Paris or did she go with him consensually, of her own accord? Herodotus, father of history (in the phrase of Cicero), has three very interesting passages regarding Helen. The first comes in his opening aetiology of the Graeco–Persian Wars of the early fifth century, where he traces the history or mythography of Greek–Oriental enmity back through the mists of time and legend. A series of claims and counter-claims is wittily rehearsed, with Herodotus purporting merely to relate the stories he has been told by learned Phoenicians and Persians. Among them features, inevitably, the theft, if that is what it was, by Paris of Helen. Herodotus himself adopts a robust, not to say male chauvinist, view of the matter:

> *it is obvious that no young woman allows*
> *herself to be abducted if she does not wish to be.*[1]

However, an unambiguous tale, not related by Herodotus, of an earlier rape of Helen, effected by Theseus of Athens when she was but a girl rather than an adult wife, tells a different story. Lately, both Elizabeth Cook in her imaginative retelling of Achilles' story and John Barton in his no less powerful *Tantalus* play-cycle have reminded us opportunely of this earlier, darker chapter in Helen's eventful life.

The next reference to Helen in Herodotus is, if anything, even more disturbing, from the historical point of view. For according to him, as he relates it in his account of matters Egyptian in the second book of his *Histories*, she never went to Troy at all, but sat out the ten years of the Trojan War in Egypt:

> *This is the account the Egyptian priests told me*
> *of Helen's story, and I am inclined to accept it, on*
> *the following ground: had Helen really been in*
> *Troy, she would have been handed back to the*
> *Greeks whether Paris consented or not... This, then,*
> *is my own interpretation.*[2]

It was thus, for Herodotus, merely to recover a simulacrum, a phantom double, of Helen's face that Menelaus and Agamemnon and all the other Greeks had launched their thousand ships!

This heterodox version, for obvious reasons unused by Homer, was not original to Herodotus, since we know that it was being peddled as early as the mid-sixth century by the Greek lyric poet Stesichorus, from Himera in western Sicily. And after Herodotus it was again found congenial by the great Athenian dramatist Euripides, who based his surviving melodrama *Helen* upon it; but for most ancients, as for most of us, Helen can safely remain Helen of Troy.

The third mention in Herodotus brings us back from Egypt to Sparta and more precisely to Helen's shrine at Therapne, which was the setting of a classic folktale, beautifully retold by Herodotus for his fifth-century audience. Once upon a time, somewhere in the second half of the sixth century in our terms, a wealthy Spartan couple had a daughter, but, alas, their beloved infant was distressingly plain. So plain that the family's nurse – perhaps a Helot woman – had the following bright idea:

Since she was plain to look at, and her parents,
who were well off, were distressed at her
unsightliness, her nurse had the idea of carrying
her every day to the shrine of Helen at what is
called Therapne, above the shrine of Apollo. She
would take the baby in, lay her in front of Helen's
cult-statue, and pray to the goddess to rid her of
her ugliness.[3]

One day, an apparition – clearly meant to be Helen herself – addressed the nurse and stroked the child's head, whereafter she grew up to be the most beautiful of all the nubile Spartan girls, a suitable match and catch for a leading Spartan. Unfortunately for that Spartan, however, he had a best friend who was childless and who passionately fancied the friend's wife as the bearer of his own future, ideally male, offspring. Even more unfortunately, the best friend just happened to be a king of Sparta, for whom the production of legitimate male offspring was an affair of state and not just of the heart. In his intense desire to procreate this king had already married not just once but twice; now, besotted with his friend's wife, he added insult to injury, obtaining her from him by a low trick.

The product of the union of Ariston – for that was the king's name – with the unnamed female beauty was King Demaratus, whom we shall meet again later in circumstances of alleged illegitimacy and treachery – everyday charges in the fraught world of Spartan royalty. (*See* further his biography, in Chapter 2.) However, before we leave Helen, it is worth mentioning three very different expressions and consequences of her legend. First, as early as the seventh century, the priestess of Apollo at Delphi, the navel of the earth, issued a prophetic utterance on behalf of her lord and master Apollo that was translated by the male priests to include a reference to the women of Sparta, hailing them as the most beautiful in all Greece. That can only have been a bow to Helen of Sparta, whose fame, thanks to Homer, was spreading throughout the expanding Greek world, though it will have surely also put undue pressure, as we have seen, on Spartan girls and their parents to try to live up to Helen's awesome reputation.

Later, in the seventh century, the greatest of the ancient Greek women poets, Sappho from the island of Lesbos, engaged with Helen's reputation more than once. Sappho's verses can be quite conventional, as for example in the small fragment addressed to some beautiful and desired adolescent girl or young woman:

> *whenever I look at you*
> *it seems to me that not even Hermione*
> [daughter of Helen] *is your equal*
> *no, far better to compare you*
> *to Helen, whose hair was golden.*[4]

On the other hand, Sappho could also be deeply and disturbingly unconventional. Flying in the face of normative, male value judgments, she writes, in a poem that happily survived on papyrus for centuries in the dry sands of Oxyrhynchus in Egypt, and was excavated only a century or so ago:

> *Some say a troop of horsemen, some an army on foot*
> *and some a fleet of ships is the most lovely sight*
> *on this dark earth; but I say it is that which*
> *you desire:*

> *... for the woman who far excelled all others*
> *in her beauty, Helen, left her husband –*
> *the best of all men –*
> *behind and sailed far away to Troy; she did not spare*
> *a single thought for her child* [Hermione] *nor for*
> *her dear parents*
> *but* [Aphrodite] *led her astray...*[5]

So Sappho both rejects masculine military values and at the same time excuses Helen's pursuit of the path of Love and Desire as being due to divine *force majeure*. That is not a message that the average Greek husband would have been delighted to hear.

The final expression and consequence I want to mention here is altogether more lighthearted, indeed literally comic. In 411 Aristophanes staged two comedies at the two major annual Athenian play-festivals in honour of Dionysus. One of these was the *Lysistrata*, the first known comedy to have been named after its heroine. Lysistrata, a respectable Athenian married woman, is portrayed respectfully. Seeking to put an end to the war between Athens and Sparta and their allies, which had been raging on and off for some twenty years (twice as long as the Trojan War), she organizes an international conspiracy of Greek women – or rather wives: the big idea is that their withdrawal of conjugal rights, a sex-strike, will force their bellicose but sex-starved husbands to the negotiating table and compel them to make peace (and so be able to make love once again) at last. The Spartan sororal delegate to the convention is one Lampito – she bears a good Spartan name, in fact the real name of the wife of a very recent Spartan king.

Here is how Aristophanes introduces Lampito (played of course by a male actor, in drag):

Welcome, Lampito, my very dear Spartan friend!
[says Lysistrata]
Sweetest, what beauty you display! What a fine colour of skin, and what a robust frame you've got! You could throttle a bull!

To which Lampito replies, in broad local Spartan dialect:

Yes, indeed, I reckon I could, by the Two Gods
[Castor and Pollux];
at any rate, I do gymnastics and heel-to-buttock jumps.

Another Athenian co-conspiratrix joins in the fun:

What a splendid pair of tits you've got!

Lampito affects to be offended by this:

Really, you're feeling me over like a sacrificial victim.[6]

The mainly Athenian audience, in between its guffaws, could hardly miss the allusion to the fact that Spartan women, unlike their own wives and sisters, were given a formal public training in gymnastics and athletics, performed either completely naked or at least partially nude. Perhaps too through these exercises Spartan women, unlike Athenian women, managed to keep their breasts in shape even after suckling babies – unless, of course they regularly resorted to Helot wet-nurses.

The *Lysistrata* ends also on a completely Spartan note, with first a Spartan man individually, and then Spartan couples jointly singing and dancing specifically Spartan songs and figures (the Greek word 'chorus' meant originally dance, before it came to mean collective singing). Notice particularly the final invocation of Helen, 'Leda's daughter':

> *Leave lovely Taygetus again*
> *and come, Laconian Muse, and fittingly*
> *praise the god of Amyclae* [Apollo]
> *and Athena of the Brazen House*
> *and the noble sons of Tyndareus* [Castor and Pollux]
> *who play beside the Eurotas.*
>
> *Ola! Opa!*
> *Prance lightly, that*
> *we may hymn Sparta,*
> *which delights in god-honouring dances*
> *and in the beat of feet,*
> *and where, like fillies, the maidens*
> *prance beside the Eurotas,*
> *raising dustclouds with their feet,*

shaking their hair
like the hair of bacchantes who wield the thyrsus and dance.

And they are led by Leda's daughter,
their pure and beautiful chorus-leader.[7]

In or around 1200 BC, the Mycenaean mansion at Therapne was burnt and destroyed, and the number and quality of the settlements in the region as a whole fell away drastically, so that by 1000 it is possible to speak of Laconia as undergoing a Dark Age. Some shafts of light are dimly visible in Sparta of the tenth and ninth centuries, for example at the shrine of Orthia by the Eurotas that would grow to play a key role in the later Spartan Agoge or Upbringing. However, it is not until the late eighth century, archaeologically, that the light becomes brighter and more evenly diffused. By then, there had been constructed a sanctuary to the city's patron goddess Athena, on what passed for an acropolis in Sparta; this is the Athena who later, in the sixth century, acquires the tag 'of the Brazen House' used by Aristophanes at the end of his *Lysistrata* (above). There was also an important sanctuary of Apollo in Amyclae just a few kilometres to the south of Sparta, also noted in the *Lysistrata*, and it is here rather than in Sparta proper that myth, religion and politics coalesced to produce the first glimmerings of a political history of the origins of the Spartan *polis* or state.

A Greek *polis* was not just a physical space, though it connoted a physical unit combining rural territory with an administrative centre. Nor was it a state in our modern sense – involving the existence of centralized organs of government (executive, legislature, judiciary, armed forces) divorced from and set over and against the people as a whole. Rather, a *polis* was a citizen-state, a state where 'the Spartans' were the city, as it were. Indeed, the Spartans, as we shall see, may have been pioneers in Greece as a whole of a particular kind of participatory citizenship. Spatially and architecturally, on the other hand, they lagged behind most of the rest of Greece, or at any rate the more progressive areas of southern Greece in the relevant eighth, seventh and sixth centuries. Most conspicuously, they never properly urbanized their central place: as Thucydides remarked at the beginning of his *History* of the Spartan-Athenian War, the Spartans conserved an older form of settlement by villages, and the remains of those, he predicted accurately, would be so insubstantial and so unimpressive that future visitors to the site would vastly underestimate the power that Sparta had in fact once been able to wield. Consistently, the Spartans did not erect a substantial city-wall, or indeed any sort of wall, before the second century BC.

One reason for not building a wall was that the Spartans felt relatively secure from possible hostile incursion from outside or from insurrection within. Another was that they affected to regard a city-wall as effeminate; they were proud to rely for self-defence purely on the masculine strength of their own militarily superb bodies. Probably the most important reason of all, to begin with anyhow, was that the city of Sparta comprised, politically speaking, Amyclae as well as the four villages into which Sparta town itself was divided (Pitana, Limnae, Mesoa and Cynosura). So to build a city-wall round Sparta would have been to exclude Amyclae. Just how the amalgamation and incorporation of Amyclae were effected, and precisely why and when, are not known. Suffice it to say that, on the one hand, the incorporation was achieved before – indeed, it was a condition of their being able to do so – the Spartans set out to conquer the rest of Laconia to the south and Messenia to the west across the Taygetus mountain range. On the other hand, the amalgamation never completely submerged or obliterated the distinct identity of the Amyclaeans.

As a token of its special place and status, the cult site of Apollo-Hyacinthus at Amyclae was adorned with an especially splendid visual manifestation in the sixth century, when the Spartans commissioned an Asia Minor Greek, Bathycles from Magnesia on the Meander, to design and construct a multi-imaged 'throne' of stone and precious materials for the cult-image of the god. The cult itself was the object of one of the major annual festivals of the Spartan religious calendar, the three-day Hyacinthia, and Amyclaean soldiers were given a special dispensation to attend, even when abroad on active campaign. Another point of interest here is the combination of Apollo's worship with that of Hyacinthus. In myth Hyacinthus was a beautiful adolescent boy, whom Apollo loved (including sexually) but whom he unfortunately killed by an accidental cast of a discus. Their joint cult therefore symbolized and represented the real-life pederastic relationships between young adult Spartan warriors and the adolescent youths who were undergoing the state-controlled educational cycle. However, the cult was also important for Spartan women and young girls, so it cannot be reduced to a specifically or distinctively masculine, homoerotic affair.

Perhaps one major reason for the Hyacinthia festival's 'national' political importance was rather that it represented in origin the amalgamation of two ethnically distinct peoples, the incoming Dorians and the pre-existing native Achaeans. At any rate, the historical Spartans were Dorians in the fullest sense – speaking a Doric dialect of Greek, exhibiting social and political institutions based on the traditional three Dorian 'tribes' (the Hylleis, Dymanes and Pamphyloi), and worshipping the god who of all the Olympians was most closely associated with the Dorian peoples, namely Apollo. In fact, almost all the major Spartan religious festivals were in honour of one or other Apollo, rather than of the city's patron Athena. The Carneia, sacred to an Apollo represented with the attributes of a ram, was a specifically Dorian festival, celebrated in the month Carneios that was considered sacred by all Dorians (though that did not necessarily prevent the Spartans and their Dorian enemies of Argos from playing fast and loose with their supposedly obligatory and unvarying observance of its sacrosanctity). It was because of their overriding obligation to celebrate the Carneia properly, the Spartans claimed, that they could not send a full levy to Thermopylae in 480.

The other major Apolline festival at Sparta was the Gymnopaediae, and thereby hangs an interesting etymological tale. Traditionally, the name has been translated as the Festival of Naked Youths, deriving the title from *gumnos* and *paides*, but the central action of the festival involved a contest between three age-graded choirs or choruses – Old

The remains of the foundations of the temple of the local goddess Orthia, assimilated to the panhellenic Artemis. The first temple was built in about 700 BC, a small, narrow and generally humble affair of clay and timber on a stone base; this was replaced, after a devastating Eurotas flood, by a rather grander all-limestone version in *c.* 570. What is visible in the photograph belongs to a later, Roman period renovation, by which time the sanctuary of Orthia was the site of an amphitheatre specially constructed to enable Roman sado-tourists to enjoy the spectacle of Spartan youths being flogged within an inch of their life (or beyond) beside Orthia's altar. In better days, the sacred space had been integral to the Agoge or Upbringing, as the site of a number of competitive rituals marking the boys' passage through the prescribed stages of boyhood and adolescence.

Men beyond military age, Warriors of military age, and sub-military Youths – and not just action by the Youths alone. So why call the festival after only one of the three principal groups involved? A more plausible etymology takes *gumnos* to mean not naked but unarmed, and the *paidiai* bit to be derived from the Greek word for dancing (as used for example in the *Lysistrata* passage on p. 55). So in the Gymnopaediae we are probably dealing with a Festival of Unarmed Dancing, organized as such perhaps in the second quarter of the seventh century.

That would in truth have special cultural as well as cultic meaning and relevance, since the Spartans were famed for dancing in general and for one particular military dance, the Pyrrhic (named in honour of Pyrrhos, or Neoptolemus, son of Achilles). Since all the gods of Sparta, moreover, the female ones as well as the male, were represented visually in their cult-statues wearing arms and armour, a festival of unarmed dancing in honour of an armed Apollo would acquire a very particular connotation. This was perhaps the nearest the Spartans got to collectively and communally creating high culture in an Athenian sense. It was to the Gymnopaediae particularly that high-ranking Spartans liked to invite their distinguished foreign friends as guests, treating them to the spectacle of tardy Spartan bachelors being ritually abused for flouting the injunction to marry and procreate. An early non-Spartan poet likened the Spartans to cicadas, because they were always up for a chorus (both choral dancing and choral singing). The Gymnopaediae, celebrated at the hottest time of the year in the hottest place in Greece for its height above sea-level (about 200 metres), gave a characteristically Spartan calisthenic spin to this joyous theme.

In ancient Greece religion and politics were inseparable, and it comes as no surprise therefore to find that the laws of Sparta were ascribed piously to Apollo of Delphi; Xenophon in an essay on the Spartan constitution and way of life composed in the early fourth century calls them 'Delphic-oracle-given'. Invoking divine sanction was of course one way of trying to ensure their observance. Another was to indoctrinate the young through a rigorous educational and social-psychological regime into a condition of habitual law-abiding-ness. The supposedly human figure credited with devising both the laws and the system of educational reinforcement was the wondrously omniprovident Lycurgus.

LYCURGUS

Plutarch, having conceived his great biographical project of writing and comparing the lives of great Greeks and Romans of the more or less distant past, could hardly not write a life of Lycurgus. Indeed, he paid him the huge compliment of pairing him in parallel with Numa, the great lawgiver of the early Romans. However, as he confessed in his prologue to the *Lycurgus*, writing a biography of him was not easy, as everything asserted of him by one source was contradicted by another. Since Plutarch, the indefatigable researcher, cites no fewer than fifty previous writers in this one biography, we can well understand his sense of immense frustration. A modern historian would of course have given up at that point. Therefore we can only be thankful that Plutarch was a moralizing historical biographer and not a historian in the strict sense, for his 'biography' of Lycurgus contains all sorts of details about the Sparta that Lycurgus was supposed to have reformed, that do not appear elsewhere either at all or in the same shape or detail. In a sense, paradoxically, the one thing the work is least helpful for is any attempt to sketch a possible outline life of the man.

If, that is, he was really a man. I have mentioned already the possibility that he was a reified projection of Apollo, under whose divine guarantee 'his' laws were placed. (In strict transliteration his name, Lykourgos, translates as something like 'Wolf-Worker', and 'Wolfish' was one of Apollo's many epithets.) The fact that the Spartans themselves were unclear about his status, although theirs was a society that spent so much effort on remembrance, is surely a significant further pointer to his inauthenticity.

I give just two illustrations of that uncertainty. The first is from the first Book of Herodotus' *Histories*, as he is setting the scene and introducing Sparta and Athens as the two great Greek powers who will play the leading roles in the Graeco–Persian Wars of the early fifth century. He here records a consultation of the Oracle at Delphi by the distinguished Lycurgus himself. No sooner had he entered the shrine than he was hailed as follows:

> *Hither to my rich shrine you have come, Lycurgus,*
> *Dear to Zeus and to all the Olympus-dwelling gods.*
> *I know not whether to declare you human or divine,*
> *But I incline to believe, Lycurgus, that you are a god.*[8]

That Herodotean story conforms to a well-known folktale pattern, and behind it we should see, more prosaically, a consultation by the Spartan state as to how Lycurgus should be worshipped – that is, whether with heroic (semi-divine) or with divine honours. The very fact that the Spartans wished for Delphic clarification and authorization regarding Lycurgus' status, which the Oracle was diffident to provide, indicates that the public memory of him had already grown suspiciously dim.

The Spartans, we know, were very prone to heroize dead Spartans. For example, a stone relief of the sixth century showing a heroic figure carries a single-word inscription 'Chilon'. That is the name of a leading Spartan figure so famous that he acquired a place in some versions of the list of Seven Sages in all Greece, all sixth-century figures, all practical politicians. Chilon was heroized in a one-time, *ad hominem* action, but all Spartan kings were heroized on their death and received heroic honours thereafter *ex officio*. So, we can at least be confident that Lycurgus had not been a king and dismiss Plutarch's belief that he had reigned for eight months. A further clue to his probable inventedness is that, despite the sources' desire to make him a king or at least a member of one of the two royal houses, they cannot decide which one, so that he shifts uneasily between the pedigrees of the Agiads and the Eurypontids.

Plutarch's *Life* contains other interesting supposedly biographical snippets. Lycurgus is supposed to have journeyed to Crete and Asia to collect comparative information on constitutional and social reform. After carrying through his radical land-reform, he is said to have remarked that the whole of Laconia looked like an inherited large estate that had recently been divided up equally and harmoniously among many brothers. He is alleged to have had one eye gouged out in a street brawl. He is supposed to have been especially blessed with the gift of the Spartan gab, and, as such, the source of a rich fund of snappy repartee: for example, when urged (anachronistically!) by a non-Spartan democrat to turn Sparta into a democracy, he supposedly rejoined 'you convert your own household

No genuine portrait of Lycurgus, the wondrously all-foreseeing lawgiver (traditionally dated to the eighth century BC or earlier), exists from antiquity; indeed, it is by no means certain that he ever really existed. This modern statue was erected in the mid-1950s at the expense of Greek-Americans of Spartan origin. The distinctly bookish image of the legislator is perhaps intended as a rebuttal of the ancient canard that all Spartans were totally illiterate as well as generally uncultured.

into a democracy first'. He is held rather delightfully to have dedicated a small statue of Laughter, in order to symbolize the need to sweeten the austerities of a barracks-style life. Finally, once his laws had been adopted and were seen to be working, he is believed to have left Sparta for good, making a last visit to Delphi to consult the Oracle as to the future success of his reforms and then starving himself to death. Alas, all these touching details are at best *ben trovato*. Better for us therefore to apply a little Spartan austerity and suspend belief indefinitely.

Politically speaking, the essence and focus of the comprehensive reform package ascribed to Lycurgus are concentrated in what looks very much like a genuine archaic document known as the Great Rhetra (to distinguish it from a number of smaller *rhêtrai* likewise ascribed to Lycurgus). A *rhêtra* means any kind of saying or pronouncement – from a bargain or contract, through an oracle to a law. Plutarch, who preserves the Great Rhetra, probably believed that it was a Delphic utterance that was enacted, so both an oracle and a law. The fact that it was written in prose, not hexameter verse, did not deter his belief in its authenticity, nor should it deter ours. The occurrence of a number of distinctly poetic turns of phrase, conversely, should confirm his belief that it was an oracle in origin, but when was it delivered, to whom and in what circumstances?

Herodotus dates Lycurgus no more precisely than before the joint reigns of Leon and Agasicles, which fell somewhere in the first half of the sixth century. Aristotle, by connecting him with the swearing of the original Olympic truce, put him as far back as what we call 776 BC. But the mid-seventh-century Spartan martial poet Tyrtaeus does not mention him at all – a very telling silence, especially as he does show clear knowledge of what Plutarch calls the Great Rhetra. In Tyrtaeus too, there is mention of a crucial official consultation of Delphi, though the consultant is not Lycurgus, of course, but the two joint kings Theopompus (who had led Sparta to victory over the Messenians in about 710) and Polydorus, who could have reigned together, in our terms, during the early part of the seventh century BC. Whether or not what Tyrtaeus says is literally true, that is about the right time for any such reform-package attributed to Lycurgus to have been introduced.

Plutarch, acutely, puts his finger on Lycurgus' reform of the Gerousia or Spartan Senate as his first, major political innovation, and it is in connection with this that he quotes the Great Rhetra:

> *Having established a cult of Syllanian Zeus and Athena, having done the 'tribing and obing', and having established a Gerousia of thirty members including the kings* [here called poetically *archagetai* or 'founder-leaders'], *season in, season out they are to hold Apellai* [festivals of Apollo] *between Babyca and Cnaciôn; the Gerousia is both to introduce proposals and to stand aloof; the damos is to have power to 'give a decisive verdict'* [this is Plutarch's gloss on a badly garbled phrase in Doric dialect in the original]; *but if the damos speaks crookedly, the Gerousia and kings are to be removers.*[9]

What is most noticeable, to start with, by comparison and contrast with Tyrtaeus' poem, is the relative status of the kings. In Tyrtaeus they come first and get the star billing, which is what one would expect in a traditional society that had decided to retain a hereditary kingship – or rather a hereditary dual kingship. In the Great Rhetra, however, the kings are, on one hand, downgraded to being mere members of the Gerousia and yet, on the other hand, ensured perpetuity of status and influence by being included in the state's most powerful governing body, the number of which is probably now for the first time being specified as thirty. The other twenty-eight members, who had to be aged at least sixty, included always some relatives of the two kings and was indeed probably restricted to aristocrats, who were chosen in what Aristotle considered a parody of a free and fair election, and held office for life.

As the Theban lyric poet Pindar was to put it in the early fifth century (in a passage quoted by Plutarch),

The councils of old men
Are pre-eminent there...[10]

What this seems to have meant in practice is essentially twofold: first, the Gerousia had the power of *probouleusis* or predeliberation, such that all measures put for decision before the Spartan Assembly, called *damos* or People in the Great Rhetra, were first debated by the Gerousia. Second, it functioned as Sparta's Supreme Court, capable of trying even the kings and serving as ultimate arbiter of what was or was not lawful. So great was the Gerousia's power that, as the final clause of the Great Rhetra seems to be saying, it could even overturn a decision of the *damos*/Assembly if it didn't like the way it was expressed or the way it was reached.

What was this *damos* or Assembly? In Classical times it consisted of all adult male Spartan warrior citizens, those who were of legitimate Spartan birth, who had been through the prescribed state upbringing, who had been selected to join a military-style mess, and who both were economically capable of meeting their minimum contributions of produce to their mess and had not been guilty of some act of cowardice or other disqualifying public crime or misdemeanour. It is unlikely in the extreme that such a warrior Assembly would either have come into being, or been in a position to receive even the limited rights and privileges accorded it under the terms of the Great Rhetra, before Sparta had developed a successful phalanx of heavy-armed infantrymen. This would not have been before about 675 at the earliest, and later still if we put weight on the defeat of Sparta by Argos at Hysiae in the Thyreatis borderland traditionally in 669 BC, which was followed by a major revolt of the recently conquered Messenians. A date in the second quarter of the seventh century seems therefore the most likely for that innovation, and it may be that another passage of foreign poetry cited by Plutarch in the *Lycurgus* refers specifically to the successful completion of the political reform coupled with military success by the hoplite citizens:

> *The spear-points of young men blossom there...*
> *along with the clear-sounding Muse*
> *and Justice in the wide streets.*[11]

The author of those lines, Terpander of Lesbos, flourished at about the right time and may well have visited Sparta, perhaps in connection with the establishment of a competition in poetry and music at the Carneia festival.

Hoplite fighting was a particularly ferocious and demanding kind of face-to-face, hand-to-hand warfare, truly terrifying unless the soldiers had been trained physically and mentally in the rigorous Spartan way. The phalanx would normally line up eight ranks deep, its width determined by the number of files; a large hoplite army of 5,000, such as the Spartans fielded for the Battle of Plataea in 479, would have been over 600 files wide. The hoplite may well have taken his name from the cardinal item of his equipment, the two-handled shield which he wore in an unalterably fixed position on his left arm, depending for coverage of his unshielded side on his neighbour to his right in the phalanx. The Greek word *hopla*, which certainly included the shield, was used to mean arms and armour collectively. A *panoplia* was a full set of hoplite kit, which would consist of a large bronze helmet raised from a single sheet of metal that afforded good protection for the head but rendered the hoplite pretty deaf; a bronze or (later) leather or linen breastplate; a large round basically wooden shield, faced all over in bronze in the Spartans' case; bronze abdominal guard and greaves, and possibly also bronze ankle- and arm-guards; a long thrusting spear of cornel wood tipped at either end with a head and butt-spike of iron; and a back-up iron sword, unusually short, more like a dagger, for the Spartans. Two further items of uniform are peculiarly Spartan: long hair and a

(left) The Spartans' red cloaks were a distinctive feature of the local hoplite uniform. This Laconian-made warrior wears his wrapped around him as if on watch on a chilly night. In fact, as his unusual transverse crest may suggest, he is probably meant to be a general, perhaps even a king. Note the characteristically Spartan long hair, the combing of which before the Battle of Thermopylae astonished the Spartans' Persian enemies.

(right) At the other end of the social spectrum from the illustration above, this dour and rather crude figurine emblematizes the indomitable spirit of the ordinary Spartan hoplite ranker. Note his bell-shaped breastplate and prominent greaves, both signs of the Spartans' attention to detail in matters of war.

bright red cloak (so important that it accompanied a Spartan hoplite in death as well as in life). Effectiveness in action depended not only on sheer weight of numbers but on tight co-ordination, rigid discipline and high morale; these the Spartans ensured by constant drilling, which they were able to undertake as they could afford to maintain the only truly professional army in all Greece.

The quality of bravery required by hoplite warfare was labelled *andreia* in Greek, literally virility or manliness. Women, even Spartan women, were given no place at all in war, even though Spartan girls, unlike girls elsewhere in Greece, were formally educated and socialized, as we shall see (in Chapter 5), in order to make them fit partners for the men and fit mothers of future Spartan warriors. The making of real Spartan men began seriously at birth, when it was not the father, as was normal, but the elders of the male infant's tribal grouping who decided whether or not he should be reared. For his first seven years, a Spartan boy was brought up at home, like any other Greek boy, but after his seventh birthday he was removed from the home environment, for good, to embark on the compulsory and communal educational system known as the Agoge or Raising/Upbringing. Between the ages of seven and eighteen, the boys and youths were organized in 'packs' and 'herds' and placed under the supervision of young adult Spartans. They were encouraged to break the exclusive ties with their own natal families and to consider all Spartans of their father's age to be *in loco parentis*.

One particularly striking instance of this displaced or surrogate fathering was the institution of ritualized pederasty. After the age of twelve, every Spartan teenager was expected to receive a young adult warrior as his lover – the technical Spartan term for the active senior partner was 'inspirer', while the junior partner was known as the 'hearer'. The relationship was probably usually sexual, but sex was by no means the only or even always the major object. The pedagogic dimension is nicely brought out in the tale of a Spartan youth who made the mistake of crying out in pain during one of the regular brutally physical contests that punctuated progress through the Agoge. It was not the youth himself who was punished for this breach of the Spartan code of self-disciplined silence – the punishment fell on the youth's older lover, for having failed to educate his beloved properly. The Agoge lasted until the age of eighteen, when a process of selection was operated to single out those Spartans who were destined for the highest positions of an adult Spartan life – membership of the elite royal bodyguard, holding the top military offices, eventually election to the Gerousia. These elite Spartans formed what was known as the Crypteia or Secret Operations Executive (SOE); their task was to control the Helots as well as prove their readiness for the responsibilities of warrior manhood.

Their selection, like the management of the Agoge as a whole, was presumably in the hands of the Paidonomos, literally the Boy-Herd, who was appointed by the Ephors ('Overseers'). This latter board of five annually elected officials represented the chief executive power in the Spartan state, alongside and indeed sometimes over the two kings. The origins of the office are, however, unclear. One tradition ascribed their creation to the same King Theopompus who conquered Messenia in the late eighth century, but then their absence from the Great Rhetra might be thought surprising – unless it was only after the passage of the Great Rhetra that they acquired the full panoply of powers they wielded in Classical times. By the time of Xenophon, there was a monthly ritual exchange of oaths between the Ephors and the kings, the latter swearing to observe and uphold the laws, the former swearing to support the kings but only on condition that they did indeed observe and uphold the laws. That clearly showed how far the Ephors had come to represent a check on possibly excessively charismatic and powerful kings. So too did the fact that, whenever a king exercised his hereditary prerogative of commanding a Spartan or allied army abroad, he was accompanied by two of the five Ephors who could report back home on the king's conduct, and if necessary initiate legal proceedings against him.

After the Agoge, the required social underpinning of the military style of life was provided by the system of common messes (*pheiditia, sussitia*), also known as common tents (*suskania*). Election to these occurred when the candidates were aged twenty or so, and election was competitive: a single 'no' vote was enough to get a candidate rejected. Some messes were of course more exclusive and desirable than others, none more so than the royal mess, in which both kings dined jointly with their chosen aides when in Sparta. Failure to secure election to any mess at all was tantamount to exclusion from the Spartan citizen body and, perhaps, also army.

The main mess meal of the day was held in the evening. No torches were permitted when passing to or from the mess to dine, allegedly in order to habituate the Spartans to stealthy movement by night (something at which Spartan armies were indeed uniquely proficient). So important was attendance at this daily mess meal that two reasons, and two alone, were permitted excuses for being absent: the requirement to perform a religious sacrifice or absence on a hunting trip. Hunting was of enormous symbolic significance in Sparta, as a manhood ritual pitting man against the fearsome wild boar, but also of considerable practical

This *kylix* or wine-goblet was painted in the mid-sixth century by a Perioecic craftsmen who specialized in such 'porthole' compositions. Hunting was one of only two legitimate excuses for a Spartan's being absent from the main, evening meal in his common mess, and at the very top of the Spartan hunter's menu was the ferocious wild boar – hunted on foot with nets and spears, as is described in gory detail by Xenophon (who had lived some time in Sparta) in the fourth century.

utility, as it not only developed ancillary military skills but also yielded game of various kinds to supplement the typically frugal mess rations. These rations were not, as in the Cretan system of public dining, doled out from a central store, but were provided individually by the members of each mess. Indeed, a man's citizenship depended on his ability to maintain his mess membership, once elected, by contributing fixed minima of natural produce. [*See* Appendix, pages 273–81.]

This produce – mainly grain, olive oil and wine – was produced chiefly by Helots working on the Spartans' allotments known as *klaroi*. The Helots were in fact the foundation not only of the mess system but of the entire Spartan political, military, social and economic edifice. Probably a good number of them existed already in Laconia, especially in the Helos plain of the Eurotas valley, by the middle of the eighth century or soon after. Otherwise, if they did not, it is hard to explain why the Spartans should have sought to satisfy their hunger for new land and unfree labour first by hunting for Helots and *klaroi* across the high Taygetus mountain range to the west. Lycurgus was of course given the credit for the land redistribution in Laconia and Messenia that yielded 9,000 plots and notionally 9,000 Spartan citizens in all, but actually so drastic a measure as land redistribution will have been forced upon the Spartan elite only by the Messenian Helot uprising in the second quarter of the seventh century. It was during this Second Messenian War that Tyrtaeus's martial exhortations in verse were produced and found suitably inspiring. By 650 or so, with the Helot revolt in Messenian adequately quelled, the Spartans found themselves at the very forefront of Greek success and prosperity, owners of the largest city-state territory in the whole Greek world (some 8,000 square kilometres) and a servile labour force to work the most fertile portions of it, the Eurotas and Pamisus valleys.

The name 'Helots' means 'captives', and it was as the equivalent of war-captives that the Helots were subjugated and exploited by the Spartans. On taking office in the autumn each new annual board of Ephors issued a proclamation to all the Spartans to 'shave their moustaches and obey the laws'. Their very next public proclamation was a declaration of war on the Helots. This was designed to place the latter under martial law and to absolve any Spartans in advance from the taint of blood-guilt should they find it necessary or desirable to kill a Helot (as the members of the Crypteia regularly and of set purpose did). However, the Helots were not quite unique in the Greek world as a type of labour force: the Thessalian Penestae, for example, were an equivalent Greek ethnic group enslaved *en masse* to support their free Greek master class. However, the Helots were the most controversial group, not least because they were Greek and shared their masters' culture and language, in sharp contrast to the typical slaves in Greece who were imported foreigners or 'barbarians'. Moreover, the Helots not only managed to revolt more than once, as individually owned chattel slaves never did, but the Messenian Helots eventually in 370/69 revolted into total political as well as personal freedom.

Besides, or rather between, the Spartans and the Helots came a third group of population within the frontiers of the Spartan state. These were known as the Perioeci, the 'dwellers-around' or 'out-dwellers', because they occupied the less fertile hill-land and coastal areas of Laconia and Messenia and so dwelt around the Helots, against whom they served the Spartans as an early warning system and first line of defence. There were said to be one hundred Perioecic communities, each of them dignified with the label of *polis*, but the actuality was closer to eighty towns and villages, and being a Perioecic *polis* gave only local political rights, not a say in the determination of policy in Sparta itself. So Perioeci were formally free subjects of the Spartans, at their disposal for military and economic purposes above all.

Before the catastrophe of 370/69, we hear of Perioeci revolting against Sparta only once, and that was during the so-called Third Messenian War, the mainly Messenian Helot revolt sparked off by a

Overleaf: The Spartans had first conquered the central plain of Messenia in the later eighth century BC, but in the early seventh the Messenians rose in revolt, to be eventually crushed by Spartan hoplite (heavy-armed) infantrymen who might have looked something like those in this modern imaginative reconstruction by Richard Hook. The Spartan poet Tyrtaeus, a contemporary of the Second Messenian War, has left grim testimony of the uniquely fearsome nature of hand-to-hand phalanx fighting.

massively destructive earthquake that hit Sparta in about 464. Otherwise their principal, and increasing, value to Sparta was the provision of a steady supply of hoplites, at first for back-up in their own separate contingents but after 464 to be incorporated within the same regiments as the Spartan hoplites themselves. When fighting in this way, the Perioeci like the Spartans were called 'Lacedaemonians' and presumably therefore wore the letter *lambda* (an inverted V) emblazoned on their shields in the same manner as they.

Since the Spartans at any rate in Classical times were legally banned from engaging in any craft or trade activities, in fact from all economically productive activities of any kind apart from that of warmaking, the Perioeci filled the gap as traders and craftsmen, helped particularly by their situation along the coasts of Laconia and Messenia (their city of Gytheum in Laconia was Sparta's main port and naval dockyard) and their access to some of mainland Greece's richest deposits of iron ore, at Boeae in the Malea peninsula. It was they, or their slaves, presumably who quarried the adequate, blue-ish limestone that was used for building and for statuary in Sparta and the environs. They likewise produced the potters' clay that was turned into the fine painted pottery that, in the sixth century, obtained a surprisingly wide distribution throughout the Mediterranean and up into the Black Sea. And it was they too who both fashioned and exported the series of remarkably high-quality bronze figurines that began with horses in the later eighth century and continued with figurines of hoplites and athletes in the sixth. Of course, it was they too, finally, who served as armourers and weapons-makers, the essential infrastructure of the Spartan military machine.

It is easy to forget the Perioeci when writing a history of the Spartans, especially as they could sometimes be called by the same ethnic-political name, but this history of the Spartans will endeavour to avoid making that serious mistake.

2

SPARTA IN 500 BC

In the previous chapter we tried to set the scene and context within which the critical events and processes of the period 480–360 BC will unfold. That scene and context may be summed up for short as 'Lycurgan Sparta', the Sparta supposedly created *ex nihilo* by the legislative wizardry of one Lycurgus some time well before the sixth century. Actually, any real Lycurgus would have been involved with preserving or reshaping traditions as well as innovating from whole cloth, and that will be the main message of this second chapter too. Here we shall broaden our horizons from the southern Peloponnese to the wider Greek universe. We shall be considering relationships between the two worlds of Sparta and of Hellas more generally, especially in connection with Spartan military expansion and diplomacy. Round about 500, Sparta created the multi-state military alliance we call the Peloponnesian League; this was partly prompted by its then hostile relations with Athens, which had escaped from the fairly benign jaws of a patriarchal tyranny or dictatorship to invent the world's first democratic system of self-government in 508/7. Involved with both of these developments were the beginnings of contact with the Persian Empire that had been formed originally by Cyrus the Great in the mid-sixth century and threatened to engulf the Aegean Greek world by the beginning of the fifth.

Herodotus indeed begins the narrative portion of his *Histories* with the quest of the fabulously wealthy King Croesus of Lydia to discover which was the most powerful state in mainland Greece. He knew a lot about Greeks, since some of them on the coast of Asia Minor were his subjects, and he was by no means entirely hostile to Greek culture, but he feared more the rise of the mighty Persian empire under Great King Cyrus II, which had begun about 560 and by the early 540s was threatening the independence of Croesus' own kingdom. Having decided that Sparta and Athens were then the two most powerful Greek states, and that Delphi was the most powerful oracle in the Greek world, he acted on Delphi's alleged advice that, if he crossed the Halys, he would destroy a great kingdom. Unfortunately the kingdom that he destroyed by crossing the river was his own, and after taking over Lydia, Cyrus sent on his Median general Harpagus to subdue or bring over into his Empire peacefully the Greeks of Asia.

The Greeks typically confused the Persians and their near-relatives the Medes; for example, the epitaph of the tragic playwright Aeschylus, referring to his feats at the battle of Marathon in 490, speaks of 'the long-haired Mede' as being aware of those amazing deeds. Actually, the Medes and the Persians were quite distinct peoples, with very different customs, and the origins of Cyrus' creation of the Achaemenid Persian Empire lay in his reversing the traditional political relationship between them. From now on, the Persians of southern Iran were to be on the conductor's podium, and the Medes of northern Iran were to play second fiddle. The Medes had themselves once been an imperial power, following their victory over the Babylonians at Nineveh in 612. One of their legacies to Cyrus' imperial system was the word that the Greeks transliterated as 'satrap', meaning a viceroy or imperial governor. One of the twenty or more satrapies of the Persian Empire was formed out of what had been Croesus' kingdom of Lydia, with its capital at Sardis. Another was made out of the Greek region of Ionia further to the west, which contained such important cities as Ephesus and Miletus. Nor was that all that the Persians borrowed from the Medes. As we have seen, the highest commander on a particular mission might be a Mede such as Harpagus; he was to be followed during the Marathon campaign of 490 by the Mede Datis, appointed by Cyrus' son-in-law King Darius I.

It was from Ionian Miletus that Herodotus' immediate intellectual predecessor Hecataeus hailed. Herodotus himself came from the Dorian city of Halicarnassus further to the south. Hecataeus was in touch with the latest mode of 'scientific' thinking set in train by Thales, also of Miletus, in the early years of the sixth century. Thales may have referred to his research into the nature of the cosmos as *historia*, meaning 'enquiry'; Hecataeus almost certainly used that word of his own enquiries, but what he researched was not the non-human cosmos but the world of man. He had his frustrations. 'The tales the Greeks tell,' he fulminated, 'are many [that is, contradictory] and ridiculous.' Herodotus, who inevitably followed in the footsteps of Hecataeus to some extent, sometimes literally, and often without direct acknowledgement, would have agreed, but he adopted an apparently more liberal attitude:

> My task is to relate the stories that are told; I don't
> necessarily have to believe them.[1]

The tales that interested him most, and presumably his fifth-century listeners and readers too, concerned the origins of the great conflict between West and East, between Greeks and Barbarians, or what we call the (Graeco–)Persian Wars of the early fifth century. This is how he described his self-appointed task in the Preface to his *Histories*:

> This is the exposition of the enquiry [historiê] of Herodotus
> of Halicarnassus, done so that human achievements may not
> become lost to memory with time, and that the great and
> wondrous deeds both of the Greeks and of the non-Greek
> barbarians may not lack their due glory; and, above all, to
> set out the cause whereby they came to fight each other.[2]

To account for 'why the Greeks and the non-Greek barbarians...
came to fight each other', he began his story as we have seen in about
550 BC, roughly seventy years before his own birth. He would have
been able to talk to probably few if any people who had actually
experienced and could remember events from that far back, but the
sons and especially grandsons of those men would have been around
to tell him tales – all, of course, in their own way, and with their own
particular slant or twist. Such is the state of our evidence in general,
and the quality of Herodotus' *Histories* in particular, that we have
to, and pretty safely can, use Herodotus as our guide to the main
chronological, geographical and political developments in the eastern Mediterranean and the Near and Middle East between about 550
and 479. Everything after 479 he called 'after the Median events',
that is, after the Persian Wars, and that was not his subject. It was
left to others, including his great successor Thucydides, to take up
the thread again in 478.

Herodotus records that the Spartans took an early interest in Cyrus'
advance to the Aegean coast. They reportedly sent an embassy to Cyrus
telling him rather grandly to keep his hands off their eastern Greek
brothers. Cyrus' alleged response was a chilling put-down: 'Who are
these Spartans?' Within two generations his successors would have
good cause to know who they were at first hand, on the battlefields of
Thermopylae and Plataea above all. No less interesting than Cyrus'
apparent ignorance is the Spartans' seeming knowledge of and interest
in the rise of Persia. This is not – yet – the isolationist and ostrich-like
Sparta that appears quite frequently in Herodotus' pages and becomes
an essential part of the Spartan myth, legend or mirage: the Sparta that
went to the lengths of practising ritual expulsions of foreigners, Greek
as well as non-Greek, and refusing, unlike other Greeks, to distinguish
verbally between non-Greek 'barbarians' and foreign Greek 'strangers'
(*xenoi*). Archaeology, happily, confirms this relative outwardness and
openness of Sparta in the second half of the sixth century. This was the
time when, for example, as we saw in the last chapter, Bathycles from

Magnesia, on the Meander in Asia Minor, was commissioned to create a 'throne' for Apollo in Amyclae.

By 500 BC Hellas, as the area of Greek settlement came to be known, stretched from the Straits of Gibraltar in the west to the far eastern end of the Black Sea. This was the result of what modern historians call for short the colonization movement, or age of colonization, though it is important to remember that Syracuse, for example, founded by Corinth in 733 or Taras (Tarentum) founded by Sparta in something like 706 were not colonies in the modern sense of that word, but wholly new and independent foundations from the start. One reason Taras was Sparta's only colony was that Sparta was able to solve the problem of land-hunger that lay behind much of the colonization movement as a whole, by expanding into Laconia and Messenia. In a sense, indeed, the Spartan state of Lacedaemon was not just a conquest-state but more precisely a colonial state. However, a century and a half or so after the foundation of Taras, land-hunger, or perhaps we should say rather renewed imperial ambition, once again gripped the Spartans.

Having expanded first to the south and west, the Spartans in about the second quarter of the sixth century decided to expand their territory to the north, which meant into the inland region of Arcadia in central Peloponnese. The image of Arcadia has come today to stand for idyllic pastoral landscapes of gentle and alluring aspect, but the real ancient Arcadia was a rough, tough, upland zone. It was sufficiently remote for a dialect to survive there that is the closest historical descendant of the predominant dialect of the Mycenaean late Bronze Age Linear B tablets, and sufficiently poor to be a regular source of hungry Arcadians seeking service abroad as mercenaries from at least the beginning of the fifth century. Of course the Spartans were able to manufacture a divine warrant for their incursion into Arcadia, in the form of a Delphic oracle designed to pre-empt the accusation that this was mere naked aggression. Yet Apollo's support took a considerable time to translate into success, and in the end the Spartans had to be satisfied with considerably less than a repeat of their conquest of Messenia.

On one notorious occasion, we learn from Herodotus, the Spartans marched out bearing measuring rods to parcel out the land they thought they would soon be acquiring, and chains to fetter their new Arcadian Helots who would work the land for them, but they suffered a defeat and ended up as prisoners of war wearing their own chains. The battle became known therefore as the Battle of the Fetters, and a century later, Herodotus was shown what were claimed to be the very fetters in the temple of Athena Alea at Tegea; 600 years later, such was the strength of the tradition, the religiously inspired Greek traveller Pausanias was shown allegedly the very same chains. If force would not do the trick for the Spartans, then guileful propaganda and diplomacy would have to be put to work instead.

First, the Spartans discovered and recovered the bones of 'Orestes' from Tegea. Orestes was a Spartan on his mother's side, the son of Agamemnon and the Spartan Clytemnestra, and nephew of the Spartan King Menelaus. The point of the claim that these bones were his was to demonstrate Sparta's 'hereditary' claim over Tegea. (In point of sober scientific fact, the preternaturally large bones uncovered were most likely those of a prehistoric dinosaur.) They were solemnly taken 'back' to Sparta for reburial, where they became the focus of yet another heroic cult. At the same time, probably, the alleged bones of Orestes' son Tisamenus were also brought 'back' to Sparta from the region of Achaea in the far north of the Peloponnese. The point of that gesture was to emphasize the claim of the Spartans to rule the whole of the Peloponnese by hereditary right. In other words, the recovery and reburial of the bones of, respectively, Orestes from Tegea and Tisamenus from Achaea were the mythical, propagandistic face of the utterly down-to-earth, prosaically pragmatic campaign of diplomacy that the Spartans were simultaneously waging, which was designed to bring ideally the whole of the Peloponnese under their diplomatic-military-political sway.

This goal was indeed ultimately achieved, through the establishment of what modern scholars call the Peloponnesian League. In reality, like Voltaire's Holy Roman Empire (neither holy nor Roman nor an empire), the Peloponnesian League was neither wholly Peloponnesian nor what we today would understand by a league. It never embraced all the states of the Peloponnese, Argos being the most conspicuous hold-out. Also, it included from early on some states that were not geographically within the Peloponnese, such as Megara, Aegina and eventually the Boeotians led by Thebes. It was not a league in the modern sense, because the allies were not all allied to each other (though some of them were) but rather all were allied individually to Sparta. Moreover, they were all allied to Sparta on a basis of inequality. In their oaths of alliance, they swore in the name of the relevant gods (for example, Olympian Zeus) to have the same friends and enemies as the Spartans. They swore – some of them, anyway – to come to help the Spartans in the event of a Helot revolt. They swore to follow whithersoever the Spartans might lead them, but the Spartans did not bind themselves to any such reciprocal commitments.

The reasons for that are obvious in the last two cases, but it was not immediately obvious that, or why, the Spartans should not swear to have the same friends and enemies as their several allies. The explanation, in fact, was an imbalance of power. The Spartans were in a position to avoid being committed against their will to adopt a policy that they thought might differentially advantage an ally rather than themselves. Eventually, in circumstances to which we shall return, the allies did acquire the collective right to be consulted before they could be committed to a policy or action desired by the Spartans. There was a let-out clause, too, suitably religious, that enabled them to plead a prior religious commitment in order to gain exemption from an action or policy approved by the alliance as a whole. The balance of power between Sparta, on the one hand, and the allies, on the other, was manifestly clear. Technically, therefore, the Peloponnesian League – in ancient parlance 'the Spartans and their allies' or 'the Peloponnesians' – was a hegemonic symmachy of unequal type. Sparta was the *hêgemôn* or leader, and the allies were *summachoi*, that is committed to both offence and defence on behalf of and at the behest of the *hêgemôn*.

Possibly, the alliance concluded between Sparta and Tegea, at the time of the 'bones' episode, was the first in the series leading to the eventual crystallization of the League. Possibly, it was that concluded by Sparta with Elis, since Elis controlled Olympia, and Sparta's relationship with Olympia was second in closeness only to her relationship with Delphi, the other great panhellenic or all-Greek shrine. Greekness, as we shall see particularly in connection with the events of 480–479, was never a very strong, let alone decisive, factor in inter-state relations; more often than not, Greek cities tended to fight against rather than alongside one another, but the great panhellenic shrines did offer an important component of the mainly cultural unity that a notion of Greekness afforded, and at least for the duration of the four-yearly Olympic Games a truce came into being that was designed to express or enforce panhellenic amity rather than enmity. The officials provided by Elis to oversee the administration of the Games were tellingly called Hellanodikai, something like 'Justices of the Greeks', and it was in the interests of all Greek cities to stay on the right side of them, since victory at the Games by a citizen of, say, Sparta could be parlayed by the city of Sparta into political prestige and influence in other spheres. Influence at Olympia, in other words, was a useful diplomatic commodity, and the Spartans, who were always careful to exploit piety for political ends where feasible, will have taken every precaution to establish permanent and binding diplomatic links with Elis from early on.

The Peloponnesian League alliance may therefore have begun to take shape around the mid-sixth century, but it was to be another half-century before it acquired institutional solidity. An interesting experiment, not subsequently followed up by Sparta, was undertaken in about 525. For the first and only time before 480, Spartans were to be found fighting on a naval expedition on the far, eastern side of the Aegean sea, almost on the land mass of Asia itself. The occasion was a joint expedition with the Corinthians to overthrow Polycrates, tyrant of

Samos, and restore some Samian exiles. Since it will have taken quite some persuasion to convince the landlubbing Spartans to venture so far from home on an unfamiliar element, it must have been either something about the cause or something about its proponents or a combination of the two that made the difference in this unique case.

First, the cause. In later times, the Spartans were to acquire a reputation for overthrowing tyrant regimes of all sorts, that is, illegitimate, extra- or unconstitutional regimes usually exercised by one autocrat. Actually, their record was not quite as consistent, or principled, as the reputation made it seem, so we should look for specific, *ad hoc* or *ad hominem*, reasons in each individual case. In the case of Polycrates of Samos, there were both pull and push factors. For whatever reason, individual Spartans had already established close ties of friendship with individual Samians, links that they renewed or refurbished through mutual visits. For example, in about 550, an otherwise unknown Spartiate called Eumnastus dedicated to Samian Hera a bronze vessel adorned with a rather fetching lion attachment (on which he had his name inscribed). No doubt, some of the exiles expelled by Polycrates were in their turn Spartanophiles. Herodotus records, rather humorously, that the Spartans were unpersuaded by the exiles' rhetoric – which was the reverse of 'laconic' – but were persuaded nevertheless by their cause, though exactly why they were persuaded, he unfortunately leaves unclear.

One factor in their decision will undoubtedly have been the urging of the Corinthians. For, although Herodotus does not spell this out, the Corinthians will certainly have been allies of Sparta already by 525, in fact probably almost as early as Tegea and Elis. This was for powerful geopolitical rather than sentimental reasons, though the two cities were both (unlike either Tegea or Elis) Dorian. The Corinthians controlled the land-passage into and out of the Peloponnese via the Isthmus of Corinth, and they had ports on either side of the Isthmus, meaning that they could launch fleets either eastwards into the Saronic Gulf or westwards into the Corinthian Gulf. Given the unshakeable hostility to Sparta of Argos, just to the south-east of Corinth, it was imperative for Sparta that

Corinth at any rate should always remain 'on side', as a friendly ally. Of course, the relationship worked both ways: the Corinthians needed Sparta as a counterweight to Argos or as a support for their own policy objectives outside as well as within the Peloponnese. However, such was Corinth's position that it alone could afford to, and more than once did, oppose Sparta's will openly and unashamedly on even the most major of issues, such as the declaration of war against a third party or the conduct of an already agreed war. So since the Corinthians were urging a war against Polycrates in 525, that was in itself a powerful argument for the Spartans to consider.

What of Polycrates himself? He was not the first man to seize sole, tyrannical power on the island of Samos, but he was easily the most effective and important person to do so; and Herodotus, who knew Samos well at first hand, dwells on Polycrates' reign ostensibly because of the three great 'wonders' that were constructed under his authority: a one-kilometre tunnel through a mountain to provide Samos' town with an assured and defensible water supply, a large mole, or jetty, to protect Samos' harbour, and a magnificent temple for the city's patron goddess Hera. He was also, as Herodotus very interestingly puts it, the first ruler 'in the so-called generation of mortal men' to exercise a thalassocracy, or naval empire. That is, whereas King Minos of Crete was also reputed to have been a thalassocrat, well before Polycrates, his thalassocracy had been in the dim distant time of myth and legend, not within the verifiably authentic time of human history. Polycrates' naval ambitions led him to intervene, on the one hand, to his west, in the Cyclades, where he established Lygdamis as a puppet tyrant, and, on the other hand, to his east – where he ran into and up against the new oriental great power, the Persian Empire, in the shape of the local satrap of Lydia based at Sardis. It is Polycrates' apparent willingness to get into bed with the Persians that has led some modern scholars to suggest that behind Sparta's decision to overthrow him lay an anti-Persian agenda.

If that suggestion is right, it would not have been the first sign, quite, of the Spartans' willingness to stand up to Persia, but it would have been the first evidence of their willingness to engage in physical and almost direct action against the Persians within or near their own sphere. Unfortunately, the suggestion is not susceptible of anything like proof, so we have to leave it hanging in the air for the moment and return to events closer to home, specifically to relationships between Sparta and Argos. These two states had been set on a collision course from perhaps as early as the second half of the eighth century. There is, at any rate, certain evidence of direct confrontation between them in the extant poetry of Tyrtaeus, which dates to around 670. If the traditional dating of the battle of Hysiae is correct, then the two states fought a pitched battle in 669, which Argos – perhaps (because) led by its dynamic King Pheidon – won convincingly.

The location of Hysiae, in the borderland of Thyreatis to the north-east of Sparta's home territory, tells us by itself that Sparta had been the aggressor. All the more reason therefore for the defeat to have left a lasting and deep wound, a score to be settled. So, as soon as the Spartans felt able to – that is, following the necessary accommodation with Tegea, which lay close to any obvious route for a Spartan army marching to the north-east Peloponnese – they set out to try for a conclusion once and for all. This was in about 545, since the episode is synchronized by Herodotus with Persia's conquest of Croesus and the fall of Sardis, but the manner in which the conflict was conducted was, at least to begin with, strikingly odd.

Rather than committing their full hoplite musters, the Spartans and the Argives agreed to a battle of 300 selected champions on either side, a sort of epic trial of strength. This resulted in an equally striking outcome. After a particularly violent encounter, or series of encounters, just three fighters were left alive on the field: two Argives, one Spartan. The Argives, who were so to speak instinctively egalitarian and democratic, judged that this very superiority of numbers was tantamount to victory – and returned home to Argos to report and celebrate as much. However, the one surviving Spartan, who was clearly neither a democrat nor an egalitarian, refused to concede; on the contrary, he claimed the victory for Sparta, on the grounds that he alone had stayed 'at his post', on the battlefield, as a true hoplite should, and he set up a victory trophy accordingly in the name of Sparta. Of course, the Argives were not going to tolerate that, so they sent out their full force of hoplites to meet the full Spartan levy, and the Spartans then won a truly decisive victory. As a direct consequence, they now controlled Thyreatis and indeed incorporated it within their state territory of Lacedaemon.

Being Spartan, they characteristically celebrated their victory and new possession in a symbolic, religious way: an annual festival known as the Parparonia was instituted at the site of the battle, during which celebrants wore 'Thyreatic' crowns, and bronze figurines, of which good examples survive, were manufactured and dedicated to the gods to illustrate and reinforce the point. Herodotus adds that it was after this victory that the Spartans adopted the distinctive cultural practice whereby the adult Spartan warriors grew their hair proudly and terrifyingly long, but actually that's unlikely to have been tied to any one particular event, no matter how momentous. Conversely, the wound that this defeat inflicted on the Argives was at least as great as that which they had inflicted in 669 on the Spartans at Hysiae. In 420, during a lull in the Athenian War, they asked the Spartans for a re-match – or rather a re-run of the Battle of the 300 Champions... Strangely enough, the Spartans declined the request.

So, by 525, probably, Sparta had in place most of the pieces of the jigsaw that would eventually form the Peloponnesian League proper. It was relationships with Athens that were to provide the context for that organization's definitive emergence. Let us briefly review the history of Athens to that date. Like many Greek cities early historical Athens had been under the control of an aristocracy, who called themselves Eupatridae ('Sons of Good, i.e., Noble, Fathers'). Their monopoly of political and religious power had been modified in the early sixth century by the reforms of Solon, another (like the Spartan Chilon) of the Seven Wise Men of early Greece. However, even those reforms had not been sufficient to stave off tyranny, which came to Athens eventually, a century

Laconian craftsmen in bronze of the late Archaic period specialized in a series of hoplite figurines like this one from a sanctuary of Apollo in southwest Messenia. It was presumably both made and dedicated by Perioeci and so stands for the increasingly vital contribution made by Perioecic hoplites to Sparta's frontline phalanx. The hoplite here is shown wearing particularly elaborate parade armour and accompanied by his faithful hound (of which only part of one leg is preserved).

after it had first emerged in Greece at Corinth and Sicyon. After two previous partial successes, the noble Peisistratus finally established a stable autocracy in about 545, which he was able to hand on to his son Hippias at his death in 528/7. Hence in 525, when Sparta and Corinth were attempting to terminate the tyranny of Polycrates on Samos, Athens was still firmly under the autocratic control of Hippias. Indeed, Hippias had been able to cajole or coerce other members of the Athenian nobility into holding high office – men such as Cleisthenes from the family of the Alcmeonids, who served as eponymous archon in 525/4.

However, by 514 some nobles' patience was wearing thin, and an attempt was made to murder Hippias. This went wrong, in that it was his brother Hipparchus who was assassinated, and Hippias thereafter became considerably less affable and his rule more like what we understand by the term tyrannical. Cleisthenes, despairing of revolution from within, went into exile with a number of his followers and attempted an incursion and coup from outside in about 513, but without success. He therefore turned his attention to Delphi, navel of the earth, and sweetened the disposition of Apollo towards his cause by paying for an extremely expensive refurbishment of his principal temple at the sanctuary. In consequence, whenever the Spartans made one of their traditional consultations of the Oracle, the answer they always got, whatever their actual enquiry, was 'go, liberate Athens from the tyranny of Hippias'. These responses caused them no little embarrassment, since they – or at least the leading men of Sparta, whose opinions were the ones that really mattered – had hitherto been on good, indeed friendly, terms with Hippias and his family. For example, in 519 they had advised the small Boeotian city of Plataea to ally with Hippias' Athens, rather than join the pan-Boeotian league dominated by Thebes. This sowed enmity between Thebes and Athens for many years to come.

Eventually, piety and a shrewd calculation of utility persuaded the Spartans to send an expedition to unseat Hippias in 512 or 511. Rather curiously, they sent this not by land, but by sea, and not under the command of either of the two kings (Cleomenes I and Demaratus) but under that of one Anchimolus, who was no doubt distinguished and from a leading family but is otherwise unknown. Perhaps not altogether surprisingly, this first expedition was a complete fiasco, which necessitated a proper land-based invasion under the command of King Cleomenes in 510. This was a complete success, in that Hippias and his sons were taken prisoner and exiled, and Cleisthenes and his fellow-exiles were able to return to resume normal politics. What had been considered normal politics before the tyranny of Peisistratus no longer worked, however; in particular, it did not satisfy either the middling Athenian citizens who thought they were entitled to a greater share of power or the ordinary poor citizens who thought they were entitled at least to a say. The astute Cleisthenes started to woo this hitherto silent majority of citizens, and in 508/7 he lent his name to a package of reforms that in retrospect can be seen to have ushered in a kind of primitive democracy, Greece's and indeed the world's first example of 'people-power'.

CLEOMENES I
(REIGNED c. 520–490)

Aristotle, in the *Politics* (written in the 330s and 320s) dismissed the Spartan kings as mere hereditary generals and nothing more, since they were so powerless at home that they were condemned humiliatingly to fawn on the Ephors of the day. Cleomenes I, together with Agesilaus II (reigned c. 400–360), is one of the two Spartan kings who most actively challenge that dismissive claim. In fact, being entitled to the supreme military command by birthright was not a small prerogative in a successful and aggressive military society such as Sparta.

We should, I think, do better to follow the lead of Herodotus on the significance of the Spartan kingship. He devotes an entire excursus to its prerogatives at home and abroad, as part of a passage the effect (and surely the intention) of which is to reveal just how strange and different, how 'other', Sparta was in comparison to the general run of Greek cities. It is his narrative, too, that reveals how much power an able and shrewd Spartan king could wield in practice.

This is, however, a little paradoxical in the case of Cleomenes I, since Herodotus seems determined from the word go to cut him down to size. He reigned 'for no long time', he was put on trial by the Ephors, he had to resort to bribery and corruption of Delphi to get a co-king deposed, he failed to get Sparta to act in the decisive way he wanted against Persia, and finally he went stark staring mad and came to a sticky end – deservedly, since Herodotus saw this as divine retribution for his Delphic sacrilege. Happily, though, the explanation for his blatant bias – a combination of Herodotus' own religiosity and his exposure to the carefully contrived posthumous blackening of Cleomenes by his enemies – is pretty apparent, and Herodotus himself supplies much of the counter-evidence we need to write an alternative scenario.

Cleomenes' colourful career began before he was even born, as it were. He was his father Anaxandridas II's first-born son, but he was not born to Anaxandridas' first wife – or indeed his only wife at that time. That first wife had failed thus far to conceive, and it was of course she rather than Anaxandridas who, thanks to the state of the ancient Greeks' knowledge of anatomy and their patriarchalist sexism, was blamed for that failure. Yet Anaxandridas loved her, or at any rate wanted to keep hold of her, and it was only when formally commanded to do so by the Ephors that he finally agreed to take another wife. That second wife came, interestingly, from the family of the sage Chilon and became the mother of the future Cleomenes I, who will have been born some time after about 560 BC. However, Anaxandridas did not abandon his first wife altogether – in fact, he refused to divorce her and so committed bigamy by marrying Cleomenes' mother, 'acting in a totally un-Spartan manner', according to Herodotus. So far was he from abandoning his first wife, in fact, that he proceeded to have three sons with her, and this was to cause the first attested – but probably not the first actual – Spartan royal succession dispute.

When Anaxandridas died, in about 520, the succession to the Agiad throne was contested between Cleomenes and his younger half-brother Dorieus. Herodotus, influenced perhaps by his sources, says that Dorieus' claim rested on his *andragathiê*, his manly prowess, and I take that to be a reference to the qualities he had displayed both during the Agoge and as a young adult warrior, perhaps in the campaign of 525 against Polycrates of Samos among others. Spartan crown princes in each royal house were, uniquely, exempted from the otherwise universal requirement imposed on all Spartans to go through the Agoge, as a condition of achieving citizenship. This exemption was granted perhaps partly for pragmatic reasons, in case a crown prince should prove not to be up to coping with the Agoge's physical and psychological demands, but it was surely mainly for symbolic reasons, to emphasize how extraordinary Spartan kings, as 'seed of the demi-god son of Zeus', Heracles, really were. Dorieus, since he was not heir-apparent, will not have been exempted from the Agoge and seems to have seized his chance to shine.

That is by no means the only interesting thing about young Dorieus. There is also his very name, which means 'Dorian', to conjure with. Of course, all Spartans were Dorians, so why call any one of them that? The explanation seems to be that the naming was programmatic. In mythical terms, the ruling royal families and other Spartan aristocrats claimed to be the descendants of Homer's 'Achaeans', and in particular the royals claimed affiliation with the line of Menelaus. Round about 550, as we have seen, a specially big fuss was made of recovering the supposed bones of the 'Achaean' Orestes from Tegea, and simultaneously the bones of his son Tisamenus from the region of the Peloponnese known as Achaea. This can plausibly be seen as an 'Achaean' policy, to which the naming of Dorieus may perhaps be seen as a riposte, due perhaps to the family of his mother, designed to emphasize that Dorieus was to be more a man of the people, rather than belonging to a snotty, exclusive aristocratic elite.

That, at any rate, seems to have been the sort of line that Dorieus took when making his challenge for the throne on the death of his father Anaxandridas. To which challenge Cleomenes retorted that he

Heracles was one of the very few heroes of Greek myth to achieve elevation to fully divine status, through his famous Labours. He was also considered the ultimate ancestor of the two Spartan royal houses and other Spartan aristocratic families. This powerful sixth-century BC bronze figurine depicts Heracles as a suitable role model for the Spartan hoplite citizenry.

was the first-born son of the dead king, and moreover born after Anaxandridas had become king, as if that made his birth even more royal and legitimating. The Spartans unsurprisingly went with their traditional custom and installed Cleomenes as king, though they could not have suspected quite what they were letting themselves in for. Dorieus, finding that Sparta was not big enough for both him and Cleomenes, took the earliest opportunity to leave home and seek fame and glory abroad by trying unsuccessfully to found a colony in either north Africa or Sicily – which would have been only Sparta's second, after Taras.

Cleomenes next turns up in 519, if we may trust the manuscript reading of the numerals in a passage of Thucydides referring to Cleomenes' arbitration of a dispute between Athens and Thebes. The dispute concerned the status of Plataea, which was Boeotian by geography and ethnicity and whose allegiance was therefore claimed by Thebes, the greatest Boeotian power of that and subsequent times. Cleomenes, however, was concerned about Thebes' power, and Sparta was then on good terms with Athens, which was under the rule of a tyrant called Hippias, son of the tyranny's founder Peisistratus. So he killed two birds with one stone by advising Plataea to ally with Athens and remain outside the Boeotian political fold, thereby endearing himself to Athens and, for no short time, alienating Thebes.

A couple of years or so later, the Samian question came on the Spartans' agenda again, as the Samian leader Maeandrius came to Sparta to appeal in person for aid in ejecting the pro-Persian puppet tyrant. However, not even bribes could persuade Cleomenes, who ordered Maeandrius to leave not just Sparta but 'the Peloponnese', a clear reference to Sparta's claimed hegemony of the Peloponnese as head of a proto-Peloponnesian League alliance. Cleomenes was showing himself to be the big man of panhellenic politics, but he had troubles closer to home, and it was these that in the end unseated and perhaps unhinged him.

Herodotus in his excursus on the Spartan kingship in book VI, which leads into a remarkable riff on the distinctiveness of Spartan laws and customs more generally, pointed out that enmity between the two kings from two different royal houses was part of the traditional fabric of Spartan life. Up to a point that was perhaps true, though one might cite the relationship between Agesilaus II and Agesipolis I as a counter-example. There is no doubting, however, that the enmity between Cleomenes and his Eurypontid co-king Demaratus (reigned *c.* 515–491) was deeply personal as well as institutional. It came to a head in about 506, as part of Cleomenes' efforts to control Athens by installing a puppet regime and getting rid of Athens' nascent democracy once and for all. Both men thereafter looked for reasons to stir up hostility against the other.

Demaratus' own, premature birth was by no means free from controversy, and he may well have met similar resistance to his succession in about 515 to that faced earlier by Cleomenes. How far he opposed Cleomenes on grounds of principle and policy, how far on grounds of personal or family enmity, is unclear. His opposition was at any rate highly effective to begin with. Not only was Cleomenes' expedition against Athens of *c.* 506 turned into a fiasco, thanks largely to Demaratus, but his subsequent efforts to achieve his ends by diplomatic means also failed. It was a credit to his powers of resilience and flexibility that he had regained the position of supreme authority by 499, when another eastern Greek leader, Aristagoras from Miletus, came calling at his door for aid and succour against Persia. Again, however, Cleomenes chose to rebuff his suitor, though this time allegedly it took the sharp wits of his eight- or nine-year-old daughter Gorgo to see through the weakness of Aristagoras' case.

In 494 at Sepeia in the Argolid, Cleomenes carried out a *coup de grâce* against Argos, killing at least 6,000 Argive warrior citizens. Since Argos was to adopt a stance, or pose, of neutrality towards Persia in the coming conflict, it is tempting to infer that Cleomenes' treatment of Argos might have been somehow connected with policy towards Persia, but the first certain evidence that a sea change in his attitude had occurred is not apparent until 491–490. By then Cleomenes, acting on behalf of what Herodotus, graciously for once, calls 'the good of all

Greece', had become firmly and determinedly anti-Persian. In fact, there were no lengths to which he would not go in order to promote his anti-Persian policy.

He bribed Delphi, allegedly, he threatened Sparta with a war from Arcadia, he took hostages from Sparta's ally Aegina, which had given to Persia the tokens of submission it had demanded, and he had Demaratus deposed when he showed signs of supporting Aegina against him, and had him replaced with a distant relative and personal enemy whom he knew would be his unquestioning junior supporter. He also, reportedly, went mad. He started poking his staff of office into the faces of passers-by. Such an embarrassment and liability did he become, that he was put in the stocks under the guard of an apparently reliable Helot, but he had lost none of his powers of persuasion and convinced the Helot to give him his knife, with which he committed suicide by slicing himself into pieces from the feet up, or so informants told Herodotus.

'Look to the end', meaning never judge the success of a man's life until you see how he dies, was a Greek maxim enthusiastically embraced by Herodotus. Cleomenes' end was truly sticky, and Herodotus knew no fewer than four possible explanations of why it had been so gruesome. The one he favoured was the one most commonly held in Greece generally, namely that Apollo punished him in this way for corrupting his oracular priestess at Delphi. The Athenians, however, and the Argives each had their own favoured version of the divine retribution hypothesis, which invoked a sacrilege committed specifically against them and on their territory. Easily the most interesting of the four, though, is the explanation given, supposedly, by the Spartans themselves.

According to this local version, Cleomenes died the way he did because he had become a demented alcoholic through having learned from some Scythian envoys to drink his wine neat, but how plausible is that scenario altogether? The dramatic date for the encounter in question would have been about 512, giving almost twenty years for the demon drink to have its dire effects. If authentic, this would have been the only known meeting of Cleomenes with any barbarians, and the Scythians, who came from the northern shores of the Black Sea, were considered among the most barbaric and barbarous of them all by so seasoned a traveller as Herodotus. How Scythians should have found their way to Sparta is therefore a bit of a mystery, but it is perhaps worth remarking that a century later there was a Spartan called 'Scythian', which presumably implies personal contacts between the two peoples at some stage.

Wine for Greeks was a deeply symbolic and culturally freighted substance, and it was almost never taken neat. The modern Greek word for wine, *krasi*, is derived from the ancient Greek word, *krasis*, which meant mixing, because ancient wine was normally drunk mixed with water, sometimes as many as twenty parts water to one of wine, and served from a mixing-bowl (*kratêr*). Elsewhere in Greece at formal drinking parties called *symposia*, a member of the company was chosen to be 'king' for the evening, and one of his main tasks was to decide upon the strength of the mixture and the number of *kratêres* to be served to the guests. The more *kratêres*, and the less water, the merrier the party.

However, the Spartans were notoriously abstemious and controlled wine-drinkers. They did not celebrate private *symposia* like other Greeks but incorporated the drinking of wine, in severe moderation, into their compulsory communal evening meal. It is very noticeable that the Greek god of wine, Dionysos, was not the recipient of any major festival or cult in Sparta, perhaps because the grapes that went into the making of his divine juice were not produced by free labour, but by Helots. Indeed, the only people in Sparta who were allowed – or rather were compelled – to get disgustingly, incapacitatingly drunk were Helots, and this condition was forced on them as a deliberate demonstration by the adult Spartans to the upcoming generation of how a Spartan should not behave.

So Cleomenes by regularly taking his wine neat, if that is what he did, would certainly have been acting in an unacceptably antinomian way – no better than a Helot, or the most barbarous of barbarians. Would that,

This enormous bronze *kratêr* (wine-mixer) was excavated in the elaborate grave of a Hallstatt-period Celtic princess, at the confluence of the Seine and Rhône rivers. It stands 1.64 metres high and could hold over 300 litres. The style of the figures (which include a draped woman, who served as the handle for the lid) suggests a Laconian origin, as does the subsidiary ornamentation. Presumably custom-made, this vessel is striking testimony both to the Celts' passion for wine and display and to the interaction of Greek and non-Greek cultures, in this instance mediated through the port city of Massalia (Marseilles). It also shows that Laconian craftsmen were by no means isolated from the mainstream commercial currents of the time.

by itself, have been enough to account for his suicide, or the manner of it? I doubt it. Which is one of the reasons why it is worth at least entertaining a fifth, and even more sinister, possible explanation of his death: that Cleomenes was murdered, and on the orders of the man who succeeded him on the Agiad throne, his younger half-brother, Leonidas. The story about his neat wine-drinking might then have been a mere propaganda smokescreen to cover up the fact of the murder of a king, whose person was sacrosanct, and the complicity in that murder of another king. This is the stuff of the detective novel, admittedly, but I would not be the first to be tempted to employ that literary genre when contemplating Sparta's blood-spattered history.

Cleisthenes' appeal to the people of Athens was something that the Spartans definitely did not like and would not stand for. Partly to support a leading pro-Spartan politician called Isagoras, Cleomenes again intervened militarily, perhaps with a view to installing him as a puppet tyrant. At the same time, Cleomenes sent Cleisthenes into exile once again, along with members of some 700 Athenian families, but this proved to be an intervention too far. The moderately wealthy and the poor Athenians united to drive Isagoras out and to insist on retaining the democracy for which they had voted. Cleomenes was forced to reconsider his options. His next plan, implemented in 506, was to invade Athens' territory of Attica with an even larger, all-Peloponnesian army, commanded by not only himself but also his co-king Demaratus. However, in his eagerness, he had failed to observe the diplomatic niceties and treated the allies as though they were his subjects or even servants. The opposition to his high-handedness was led by the Corinthians, aided, crucially, by Demaratus. Although the allied army did cross the Isthmus of Corinth and invade the territory of Athens, when it got to Eleusis it began to disband, and it never managed to link up with the forces of Euboea and Boeotia as planned. Athens was not to be faced with another Spartan invasion for more than seventy years.

KING DEMARATUS
(REIGNED c. 515–491)

Damaratus of Sparta, like Themistocles and Alcibiades of Athens, has gone down in history, or at any any rate historiography, shrouded in ambivalence. These three may all have been patriots – but patriots for whom? Formally, they were all at one time traitors to their native lands. Alcibiades went over, first, to Sparta and then, second, to Persia – at any rate, he conducted discussions with and gave sound advice to a Persian satrap, to the detriment of his own state's best interests. Themistocles's treachery was more blatant. After masterminding the Greeks' naval victory against the Persians at Salamis in 480, which in turn paved the way for the eventual decisive victories at Plataea and, by sea, Mycale in 479, he seems to have decided that Sparta, not Persia, was Athens' principal rival and enemy. How right he was, in a way. This apparent lack of anti-Persian ardour cost him public influence, as Athens founded and successfully developed an anti-Persian naval alliance, and in 470 or thereabouts Themistocles was formally exiled for ten years under the procedure known as ostracism. He now compounded his errors, or sins, by going over to the Persian side, becoming a pensioner of the Persian Great King, and dying within the Persian empire – at Magnesia (home of the sculptor Bathycles).

Demaratus, too, was rejected by his own state, though not of course in a democratic way, since Sparta was not and never would be a democracy of the Athenian type. And he too, like Themistocles, was caught up in a moment of intense Greek–Persian conflict, around the time of the battle of Marathon. Unlike Themistocles, though, he was not formally exiled from Sparta, but chose rather to go into voluntary exile. In a sense, that makes his decision to 'medize', to go over to the Persian side and become a valued member of the entourage of the Persian Great King Xerxes, rather more heinously traitorous. And yet Herodotus, interestingly, despite his own firm commitment to the Greek cause, soft-pedals any criticism of Demaratus. There were a number of reasons for this, and they are mainly the reverse mirror image of the reasons why, as we have see above, his account is on balance hostile to his co-king Cleomenes I. However, that still leaves us asking how Herodotus could, as it were, excuse a traitor to the Greek cause such as Demaratus, whereas he is so bitter towards Themistocles.

Two reasons, I think, explain that preference. First, Herodotus very likely counted among his influential informants the direct descendants of Demaratus living in the Troad (north-west Anatolia, around the straits of the Hellespont or Dardanelles); they were still living there in Xenophon's day, two of them bearing the ringingly royalist Spartan names of Eurysthenes and Procles (the originals were the supposed twin founders of the two Spartan royal houses)! Second, alongside – and sometimes over and above – Herodotus' devotion to the Greek cause as against Persia ran a second political agenda, a panhellenist agenda, the principal plank of which was to reconcile Sparta and Athens in his own day, or at any rate to get them to see that they each needed the other more than they thought, and that they owed each other more than they always wanted to be reminded of. So Herodotus consciously used Demaratus as a character in his panhellenist script, having him point out, poignantly to Great King Xerxes himself, just how much the Spartans would contribute to the Greeks' victory and how far they were exemplars of characteristically good Greek civilization and culture.

Let us return from the big picture to the small, from Greece *versus* Persia to the life of Demaratus. In order to find out about his controversial birth, we have to start in 491 or 490, the year that he was deposed from the Eurypontid throne, on the grounds of illegitimacy, following a confirmatory Delphic oracle to that effect, which had been procured – allegedly by bribery – by his hostile co-king Cleomenes I.

His successor Leotychidas II piled insult upon injury shortly after Demaratus had been deposed by asking him, through a servant, how it felt to be a mere official (he was at the time helping to organize the annual Gymnopaediae festival) after being a king. This had the probably desired effect of convincing Demaratus to exile himself, but before he left Sparta for good, he is said to have sought an interview with his mother. In a remarkable passage in Book VI of Herodotus' *Histories,* Demaratus is presented enquiring of her the truth about his conception and birth.

The ultimate source of Demaratus' woes was the fact that his father Ariston had initially disowned him, on the grounds that he had been born only seven months after Ariston had married and first slept with his mother and so could not possibly be legitimate. The mother in question here is the same beautiful woman who had been plain as an infant but beautified, allegedly, by Helen herself and was then stolen from his best friend by King Ariston (*see* the biography of Helen, in Chapter 1, pp. 51–53). The mother's name is never divulged; this is a quite common feature of ancient Greek reportage of the affairs of women, since it was considered a mark of respect not to use the name of a respectable woman in the presence of unrelated men, but of course royal women might reasonably have been counted as exceptions to that rule, and Spartan women in general were often considered fair game by hostile non-Spartan sources.

Herodotus, however, is far from hostile to Demaratus' mother, and presents her very warmly and positively, writing for her a lengthy interview with Demaratus. Constrained on oath to tell him the truth, and holding a portion of the entrails of a sacrificial victim to remind herself she was under oath, she divulges to Demaratus the secret of his genesis. He was conceived, she told her son, on the third (an auspicious number) night after Ariston brought her to his house as a bride, but yet she could not be absolutely certain that Ariston was the father, since that night she was visited also by a phantom that turned out later to be the local hero Astrabacus (who had a shrine just by the house's courtyard gate). So Demaratus was either the son of Ariston – or of Astrabacus.

That perhaps was not entirely reassuring news to Demaratus. On the other hand, his mother was able to clear up the mystery of his seventh-month birth, to which Ariston had taken such disbelieving exception. Men, his mother said, are simply ignorant of such matters; not every baby in the womb is carried to the full ten-month term (the Greeks used inclusive counting – we would say, nine months). What she does not say, though, is how rare it would be for a baby born so prematurely to survive; even going to term was far from a guarantee of survival for an ancient Greek infant. Nor does she point out that, interestingly, Demaratus was allowed to be reared, even though Ariston had sworn on oath that the child was not his. Presumably the Spartan authorities – the Ephors, perhaps, or the Gerousia – had some say in this matter, as we know they intervened in the near-contemporary case of the Agiad king Anaxandridas' temporary failure to produce a son and heir (*see* the biography of Cleomenes, above, p. 90). The name that Demaratus was given means literally 'cherished by the People (Damos)', so perhaps that was his mother's way of seeking to endear him to his father.

Since Demaratus was allowed to live and, so far as we know, Ariston had no other son, he was, as heir-apparent to the Eurypontid throne, presumably excused, like his Agiad counterpart Cleomenes, from going through the Agoge. The next we know of him is when he had reached the age of marriage, and was probably in his mid-twenties or so. Showing himself a true son of his tricky father, who had stolen a bride from a best friend, Demaratus stole his bride from a distant cousin. The lady in question was called Percalus and she was the daughter of Chilon, so there was probably a good deal of political prestige and influence at stake here on top of the purely personal rivalry. Demaratus, Herodotus reports:

*by a bold stroke anticipated his rival and
married her by carrying her off by force.*[3]

In all Spartan marriages, simulated or symbolic rape was part of the
normal proceedings, but Demaratus seems to have been unusual in carrying out the rape literally. The rival bridegroom was Leotychidas, and
it was he with whom Cleomenes cleverly replaced Demaratus after having had him deposed.

Demaratus next surfaces in the Herodotean narrative as Cleomenes's
co-king, or rather anti-king, in the struggle with Athens. It was
Demaratus, as we have seen, who by taking the side of the Corinthians,
when they objected to the mission against Athens, or at least the manner of it, in about 506, ensured its catastrophic failure. Thereafter
Cleomenes and Demaratus were the deadliest of personal as well as
political enemies, but it was Cleomenes who seems consistently to have
won the struggle between them. At any rate, it is always he, not
Demaratus, who features at moments of important decision. We can
well imagine therefore a Demaratus hell-bent on revenge. In 494 he
probably thought his time had at last come.

Cleomenes had won a massive victory against Argos, but the manner of it was at least questionable, since *prima facie* it had involved two
sacrileges (see above), and the Spartans as a whole were an intransi-
gently pious people. Yet apparently Cleomenes' religious reputation was
still firmly intact, since it was not for his impiety that he was put on trial
at the instigation of his enemies but for failing to capture the city of
Argos (even though he had killed some 6,000 Argive hoplites, provoked
a massive internal social crisis in Argos and put paid to the state as a serious military power for a generation). The prime mover among those enemies was surely Demaratus. Cleomenes, however, defended himself vigorously, cleverly exploiting Spartan ideas of piety and respect for
portents by saying that, when he entered the shrine of Hera outside
Argos, a flame had shot from the breast of the famous cult-statue of the
goddess, which signified that he had already done all that the gods

wished; only if it had shot from her head, he claimed, would that have signified that he was destined to capture the city completely too.

So far as the details of the trial are concerned, Herodotus mentions only the Ephors, but he was never particularly interested in the finer constitutional niceties. So what probably happened was that Cleomenes was accused by his enemies who laid charges before the board of five Ephors and the Ephors decided there was a case to answer. Again, Herodotus gives the impression that it was all the Spartans who somehow tried him. If later evidence for the procedure in other trials of Spartan kings is anything to go by, however, the high court of attainder will have consisted only of the Gerousia, of which Demaratus was a member *ex officio*, and the Ephors. These were the Spartans who by a majority found Cleomenes' defence of his failure to take Argos 'credible and reasonable'.

Three to four years later, Demaratus thought he had another chance to nail his rival. Cleomenes was away in central Greece, on the other side of the Isthmus of Corinth, trying to ensure a united front of resistance to Persia between Athens and the medizing offshore island-state of Aegina. So in his absence Demaratus began, as Herodotus mildly puts it, 'talking against Cleomenes', presumably taking the line that Cleomenes was interfering on the side of Athens, an enemy, against Aegina, an ally of Sparta. It was this that led directly to Demaratus' deposition, on Cleomenes' return from Aegina with his controversial mission accomplished.

After being insulted unbearably by Leotychidas, Demaratus left 'for Persia', as Herodotus elliptically puts it. Perhaps he travelled by way of Lampsacus, as had his fellow-defector Hippias, ex-tyrant of Athens, who had married his daughter Archedice to the son of the pro-Persian tyrant ruler of that Hellespontine city. To judge from the location of his descendants, it was in the Troad that Great King Darius I granted Demaratus his estates, a grant presumably confirmed by his son and successor Xerxes. For the next we hear of Demaratus is that he is in the close entourage of Xerxes during his ill-fated expedition against mainland Greece. Demaratus thus functions for Herodotus, as he perhaps did in real life, as a 'wise adviser'. He points out, for example, to his over-lord and suzerain that the Spartans fear the Law more even than Xerxes' subjects fear him. At Thermopylae in 480, it is he who explains to Xerxes why the Spartans pay particular attention to their coiffure imme-diately before a battle.

Demaratus' last words, in Herodotus, are these:

the gods will take care of the King's army.[4]

They were supposedly spoken just before the battle of Salamis, later on in 480. With their Delphic ambiguity, susceptible of being interpreted retrospectively to mean that Xerxes' army would suffer a defeat, and their explicit piety, they leave the reader with as favourable an impres-sion as it was possible to convey of a man who, formally, was a trai-tor to his country's (Sparta's, Greece's) cause. That surely was just what Herodotus intended, but we, equally surely, must suspend moral judgment on Demaratus and ask rather whether he helped or harmed the Greek cause during the Persian Wars, and whether, before that, his or Cleomenes' policies had been more advantageous to Sparta in the short or medium term. The answer seems clearcut to me.

The immediate consequences for Sparta's relationships with its Peloponnesian allies and for how Sparta handled the high command of armies abroad were serious and extensive. A law was passed by the Spartans that forbade both kings ever again to be in command of the same army outside Laconia and Messenia. When next the Spartans wanted the support of their allies for a further campaign against Athens, in, probably, 504, they had to go through a formal procedure of consultation and voting, by summoning in Sparta a meeting of what we call the Peloponnesian League congress. Here, allied delegates were entitled to speak, as were Spartans, and after the speeches, the allies voted, every ally wielding one vote irrespective of size or geopolitical significance. The very first congress on record resulted in a defeat for the Spartans. Their proposal to reinstate Hippias as tyrant of Athens was rejected by the majority of the allies, led by Corinth, which – at least in the version of its delegate's speech composed by Herodotus – chided the Spartans for reneging on their hitherto (ostensibly) principled opposition to tyrants and tyranny.

However, although a Peloponnesian League congress might thus reject a Spartan proposal, the Spartans could not ever be compelled by the congress to adopt a policy or undertake an action with which they disagreed. For only the Spartans could summon a congress, and that would happen only after they, meeting in assembly, had decided what it was that they wanted to do, irrespective of the wishes of the allies. The allies, after all, had sworn to follow the Spartans whithersoever they might lead them, and not *vice versa*. This new restriction on the Spartans' hitherto unfettered power to command the allies to do their bidding was actually a source of strength rather than weakness. It gave the allies the sense that their wishes might count for something, and the feeling that the organization was based on some degree of mutuality. A quarter of a century later, in 480, it was the Spartans' Peloponnesian League that was to form the indispensable backbone of the loyalist Greeks' resistance to the Persian invasion.

Before we turn to that resistance, in the next chapter, we must first review Sparta's social, economic and cultural development during the period from about 600 to 500 BC. In particular, we want to examine the literary and archaeological record for any signs of the famed Spartan austerity that had become such a distinguishing cultural marker by the time Xenophon came to live in Sparta and wrote his account of Spartan customs and mores in the first half of the fourth century BC.

Tyrtaeus the elegist wrote suitably political and martial poetry, so suitable that it was preserved and regularly sung for many centuries both in the messes at Sparta and round the campfire on campaign. The poetry of Alcman, who flourished in the years around 600 BC, comes as a complete and utter contrast. Indeed, so stark was the contrast that many ancient commentators could not believe that Alcman really was a Spartan born and bred – as he surely was – but instead claimed, solely on the basis of some references in his poems, that he was originally a Lydian from Sardis. Those references are in fact precious testimony, not to Alcman's foreign origin, but rather to the Spartans' openness still to outside influences and artefacts. They always of course needed to import copper and tin to make utilitarian bronze objects, but they were not obviously compelled to import precious, luxury materials such as gold and ivory. Yet these too were made into handsome objects and offered piously to the gods, above all Orthia, by both men and women. Lead and potter's clay, like iron, occurred in abundance locally. The later Spartans' reputation for severe utilitarianism and for disdaining the aesthetic hardly fits with the earlier archaeological evidence. Masses of lead figurines were produced from the mid-seventh century on and catered to needs other than the purely functional. A substantial quantity of fine, painted pottery was not only used for mundane purposes or dedicated to the gods in Sparta but also, from the later seventh century onwards, found its way as far afield as southern Italy, Etruria, southern France, even Spain in the west, to Samos in the east and up into the Black Sea area.

Two further kinds of Spartan artefacts became especially characteristic and especially impressive in the sixth century. First, large numbers of clay masks, of several distinct types, some painted all over, were dedicated at the sanctuary of Orthia, presumably somehow connected with the ritual dancing that took place there, but also betraying artistic influence from the Phoenicians of Carthage in north Africa. Second, there was an impressive series of small bronze figurines, of which those representing adult male hoplites in varying degrees of martial dress and equipment deserve special mention. These too, like the painted pottery, achieved a remarkably wide distribution, both within Laconia and Messenia and as far south indeed as Aden. It has even been suggested with some plausibility that they were made for distribution outside Sparta, as a form of pious propaganda, since most found their way into a religious sanctuary sooner or later.

This gravestone of the fifth century BC shows a Perioecic hoplite warrior. The stone is from modern Areopolis in the Mani, but might originally have come from the site of Perioecic Oetylus. Spartan citizens could be named on their gravestones only if they died 'in war'.

It is true of course that all or most of these artefacts were made by Perioecic craftsmen, with or without the assistance of Helots, rather than by Spartan citizens, and were exported by both Perioecic and foreign traders and merchants. However, they were often made for and commissioned by Spartans, both as individuals and as members of the Spartan community, and by women as well as men. Earlier in this chapter we mentioned the bronze bowl dedicated by Eumnastus on Samos. Likewise we could cite the throne of Apollo in Amyclae, designed by Bathycles, or the later 'Leonidas' marble sculpture of the 480s, and even the 'Persian Portico' of the 470s (*see* next chapter). In 500, in other words, it is still too early to talk of Sparta as the cultural desert or wasteland pictured in the mirage or myth.

3

THE PERSIAN WARS
490–479 BC

S PARTA BEGAN THE 480s under the cloud of a royal death, either by suicide or possibly murder, tainted further by more than a hint of sacrilege. Leonidas, if he was guilty of his older half-brother's murder, however indirectly, will have been conscious of the need to cleanse the pollution. His co-king Leotychidas more certainly owed his position on the Eurypontid throne to a piece of sacrilegious chicanery, and so also had much to prove. This chapter will focus on the major set-piece engagements of the Persian Wars at Thermopylae and Artemisium (480), Plataea and Mycale (479). It will be stressed that, despite Herodotus' judgment in favour of Athens, it was actually the Spartans who of all the loyalist Greeks deserved the lion's share of the credit for the eventual victory, and they who sacrificed so many mighty warriors in the unique circumstances of Thermopylae. It was their unwavering discipline and steely resolution that caused the decisive victory on the battlefield at Plataea.

Leotychidas and Leonidas' successor, the regent Pausanias, played vital commanding roles in the victories of Mycale and Plataea respectively. However, of all the engagements in what the Greeks called 'The Median Events' and we call 'the Persian Wars', pride of place must be given to the heroic if ultimately unsuccessful defence of the pass of Thermopylae led by Leonidas. This episode more than any other has given definite and permanent shape to the Spartan myth or legend (*see* further Part II and Chapter 10), but before Sparta is allowed to emerge from the shadows, its conspicuously unheroic role at Marathon in 490, or rather its non-role, must be dealt with.

The Spartans, through Cleomenes, rejected the overtures of Aristagoras of Miletus in 500, as we saw in the previous chapter. Athens, however, responded to them positively, partly for the sentimental reason of their common Ionian lineage, but mainly because Athens welcomed this opportunity to demonstrate that it was no longer ruled by a pro-Persian tyrant and was a free democracy. Herodotus commented that throwing off the tyrant yoke caused Athens to become a serious military force for the first time, but it was one thing to defeat their Greek neighbours from Boeotia and Euboea by land in 506, quite another to hope to achieve anything more than singeing the Persian Great King's curly beard by sending a smallish force of twenty ships to Asia Minor in 499 to aid the Ionians' revolt.

The revolt lasted six campaigning seasons, but Athens' contribution was relatively minor and confined to attacking and burning – early on – part of Sardis, where the Persian viceroy of Lydia had his capital. Athens had no part in the Ionians' final defeat in 494, at Lade off Miletus, which was followed by the total destruction of Miletus itself. All the same, Athens, along with Eretria on Euboea, were marked down as targets for eventual revenge once the revolt was firmly extinguished. The Persian Empire being as it was, a huge, sprawling, heterogeneous entity, it always took several years to mount a serious campaign beyond the frontiers, so it was not until the late 490s that Great King Darius sent round his peremptory message to the main cities of mainland Greece either to supply him with the traditional tokens of submission, earth and water, or to expect a war of reprisal and revenge. Athens and Sparta, famously, refused, and compounded their refusal by murdering Darius' heralds, a serious breach of religious propriety as well as diplomatic etiquette. Aegina, on the other hand, complied – hence Cleomenes' extreme irritation and high-handed intervention. Argos remained inertly neutral.

When the Persian expedition was finally launched in 490, under the joint command of a Persian royal, Artaphrenes, and a Mede, Datis, its major objectives were first Eretria, then Athens. Eretria was easy meat. The town was burnt, its sanctuaries destroyed, and all the inhabitants carried off as slaves. Later, in a characteristic gesture of a mighty imperial power, Darius had many Eretrians transferred to languish as prisoners and hostages far from their native land, in the deep south of Persia, where the first mention of (petroleum) oil in the historical record was small compensation for cultural estrangement. That left the Athenians – and any Greeks who might care to help them – to face the impending Persian onslaught.

The Spartans said they would help, but unfortunately the force of 2,000 they sent (perhaps a quarter of their full citizen muster) actually arrived after the decisive battle had taken place. The Spartans' announced reason, or excuse, for not getting there on time was that they had been obliged for religious reasons to wait until the moon was full before setting out. As Herodotus puts it elsewhere, twice, the commands of the gods were more important to the Spartans than any commands of mere men, but it is reasonable for us to suspect that sometimes divine commands came to the Spartans at suspiciously opportune moments. At all events, they were keen to see the battlefield, and were generous in their congratulations to the Greek victors, the Athenians, chiefly, and their allies from Plataea (there partly thanks to Cleomenes' earlier diplomacy).

The Battle of Marathon – the battle the Spartans managed to miss – is one of the most famous in all ancient Greek, and indeed not only ancient Greek, history. It was a triumph of David over Goliath, due not least to the strategic genius of one of Athens' generals, Miltiades, but also to the courage of men who were fighting in their own back yard not only for their homes but also for an ideal, for more than just preservation of the status quo. Reportedly, there were some 6,400 casualties on the Persian side – these were the corpses the Spartans were keen to inspect – as against only 192 (exactly) dead Athenians and an uncertain number of Plataeans. The Plataeans were buried under an honorific mound on the plain of Marathon; the Athenians likewise, only their mound was palpably the larger and more impressive.

The Athenian hoplites who had won the day were given as an honorific title a new compound noun, 'the Marathon-fighters', and even in the late fifth century and beyond their courage and valour were still regularly hymned in official Athenian ceremonies marking the burial of war-dead. Those 192 who died were paid the religious honours due to heroes, and one modern view argues that they are commemorated as such visually in the huge marble frieze originally adorning the Parthenon (built on the Athenian acropolis between 447 and 432). Another public Athenian monument that is arguably also a Marathon war memorial is the so-called Treasury of the Athenians erected beside the Sacred Way within the precinct of Apollo at Delphi.

This large terracotta vase with mould-made applied decoration in relief was excavated in the centre of ancient Sparta in the middle of a funerary mound. The grave-plot presumably belonged to a family of Spartan citizens, who will have been flattered and gratified by the scene of successful hunting depicted on the amphora (cf. Ill. p. 71).

The chagrin and jealousy of the Spartans, or at least of those Spartans who shared the views on Persia of Cleomenes, can well be imagined. Conversely, ex-King Demaratus was simultaneously finding himself a cosy niche within the Persian Empire and indeed within the innermost Persian court circle, where he could act as a uniquely well-informed and trusted adviser to the Great King himself. Darius, his first benefactor, died in 486, to be succeeded by his son Xerxes, supposedly with explicit support for his cause from Demaratus. However, if Xerxes was already burning to complete the unfinished Greek business left over at his father's death, he had other, more immediately grave imperial matters to attend to in Egypt and Babylonia. These occupied the first two years or so of his reign, and it was not until 484 that preparations could be got under way singlemindedly for the young Emperor's great project: the conquest of mainland Greece and its incorporation in the Persian empire.

Herodotus liked to imagine that Xerxes was in more than one mind over the advisability of the Greek campaign in general, but that may have been not least because it suited the historian's artistic purposes. If only Xerxes had decided not to go... then he would have spared himself and the Empire the misery of defeat. If only he had listened to the wise advice of his uncle Artabanus. If only. Actually, it is unlikely that he hesitated for very long. Greece must have seemed a pushover. After all, the Greeks were notoriously fickle and politically divided among themselves. Support from the islanders and mainlanders for the Ionians' revolt had been patchy, at best, and Demaratus was not the only leading Greek to consider a berth with Persia the preferable option to a defeated homeland. The Greeks' principal mode of warfare by land, hoplite fighting, would avail them little against his numberless hordes. Had Xerxes had all his wits about him, he might have taken more heed of the major Greek military development of the 480s, Athens' creation, under the inspired leadership of Themistocles, of a first-class, soon to be world-class, fleet of trireme warships. He might have noted also that Sparta, perhaps precisely because of

Demaratus' defection, was more determined than ever to resist him – after a few typically religious wobbles.

On learning of the planned expedition the Spartans as normal consulted Apollo's oracle at Delphi, only to be told in effect to give up and give in. For, the oracle said, either Sparta would lose a king in battle or the Persians would overrun Laconia. Deeply troubled, the Spartans took the unusual step of holding frequent meetings of their Assembly, which otherwise met only once a month, about the time of the full moon. At these extraordinary meetings there was only one, ostensibly religious, item on the agenda: which Spartan(s) would be willing to atone with their life for the murder of Darius' herald that the Spartans had carried out in 492 in the run-up to the Marathon campaign? Eventually, two noble – in more than one sense – Spartans did volunteer, and this remarkable act of self-sacrifice on behalf of the good of Sparta was a fascinating anticipation in miniature of the much grander and larger self-sacrifice that the Spartans collectively were to make at the time of Thermopylae, in 480. Xerxes, however, was not interested in killing these two Spartans, or even in treating with them. So, in autumn 481 the relatively few Greek cities that could agree to offer any sort of collective resistance met to plan their joint response to the prospective Persian military offensive.

The delegates met, symbolically, at the Isthmus of Corinth, near a sanctuary of Poseidon that every two years hosted one of the four major panhellenic religious festivals, the Isthmian Games. The Isthmus was also, then, probably the limit of most Spartans' vision and ambition. Even after it had become unambiguously clear that Spartan forces would have to be committed in central and northern Greece, far from home, there was still evidence of a hankering to draw the line, literally, at the Isthmus, to fortify that six-kilometre neck of land and turn the Peloponnese into a kind of fortress. Fond hope – as Herodotus rightly perceived and stated. For the invasion force under Great King Xerxes was, crucially, to be an amphibious one. That is, the conquest of Greece would necessarily depend on co-operation between his land army and the naval forces.

The Spartans were notoriously men of the land, not the sea, so the warship depicted on this ivory plaque (perhaps originally attached to an item of furniture, excavated in the Orthia sanctuary) could perhaps illustrate a mythical scene, for example the abduction of Helen by Paris, or the retrieval of Helen by Menelaus (*see also* Ill. p. 255). The sailor squatting on the ship's ram on the right appears to be relieving himself, while the sailor above him is snatching the chance to fish. The exotic material of the plaque had to be imported from outside the Greek world, from Syria or further east or south.

Only if Xerxes' fleet were defeated would the strategy of defending the Isthmus line have even the smallest hope of success. There, of course, was the Spartans' Achilles heel. They had no fleet to speak of, and any fleet that they might muster would be rowed by Helots, who might not be totally loyal.

Nevertheless, the few Greek cities and peoples who swore a binding religious oath at the Isthmus of Corinth in autumn 481 jointly to resist the Persians committed themselves unanimously to overall Spartan leadership. Such was the prepotency of Sparta as head of an alliance that provided the bulk of the loyalist Greek resistance that even the fleets of the united Greeks were commanded formally by Spartans, men with little or no military experience of the unpredictable element of the sea.

In 480, at last the Persian horde by land and armada by sea set off west. Attempts were made to ease the passage of the vast Persian forces outside the existing Empire, with mixed success. According to Herodotus, whole rivers were drunk dry *en route*, and, more plausibly, large numbers of ships and men were said to have been lost to storms. The immediate pre-invasion muster of the Persian army took place by land at Drabescus in Thrace. Herodotus reports a total of 1,700,000 land troops backed up by well over 1,000 ships. Sober modern estimates by the best military historians cut down the Persians' land forces to numbers estimated from as low as 80,000 to a quarter of a million, and the navy to roughly 600 ships.

Advance west and south from Drabescus was unproblematic – as far as the pass of Thermopylae. For a start, the Greeks of the mainland were deeply divided, traditionally and systematically, and on the specific issue of how, or even whether or not, to resist Xerxes. When Herodotus at a climactic moment of his narrative invokes a definition of Greekness, the list of unifying factors he cites noticeably does not include political co-operation, let alone union. It was wholly unsurprising that the sworn allies who had met at the Isthmus did not include the Greeks of Thessaly, whose territory contained the first possible line of defence, the vale of Tempe between Mount Ossa and Mount Olympus. So the loyalist Greeks in spring or summer 480 sent a force to hold the Tempe line, under the command of the Spartan Euaenetus ('the well-praised') and the Athenian Themistocles ('famous for his observance of Right'), in an attempt to ensure the loyalty of the Thessalians to the Greek cause.

Unfortunately it was soon discovered that the Tempe line could easily be turned, and Euaenetus and Themistocles had no option but to withdraw southwards. The immediate political consequence was that the Thessalians according to the new jargon word 'medized'; that is they, in effect, if not necessarily always actively and willingly, took the side of the barbarian invader. The second – or rather the first – potentially defensible line for the loyalist Greeks was in practice the pass of Thermopylae. Here occurred the first serious head-on encounter between the Persian invaders and the resisting Greeks.

The 'Hot Gates' – Thermopylae in ancient Greek – are a narrow pass in central mainland Greece. This formed the natural route for an invading army coming by land from the north that had as its principal aim to destroy the armies of Athens and Sparta, and their allies in southern Greece. Here in high summer, roughly August, 480 a small force, representing a wavering grouping of loyalist Greek cities headed by Sparta and Athens, made their heroic stand against the oncoming might of a massive Persian invasionary force. In 1940 a reassuring analogy was aptly drawn between the few loyalist Greeks of 480 BC during the Persian Wars and 'the Few' who were then resisting the might of Nazi Germany in the Second World War.

The topography of the Thermopylae region has, since antiquity, been altered by natural forces almost out of all recognition, so that now the sea is several kilometres away from where the fighting took place. For 480, we must imagine a narrow pass, scarcely wide enough for two chariots or wagons to pass each other comfortably, between mountain and sea, punctuated by a series of three 'gates'. It was at the so-called Middle Gate that the loyalist Greek defence force took up its position; this is where the modern memorial has been erected, to the right of the National Highway as you drive north. On the other side of the Highway there may be visited what has been designated, probably correctly, as the hillock where the Greeks made their last stand.

However, this is to anticipate. Even in this dire crisis, Sparta did not manage to send a full muster of its 8,000 or so adult male citizen warriors but despatched instead only a token 300, commanded by one of its two kings, Leonidas. The other loyalist Greek allies, too, held back from sending their full complements to defend the pass, so that out of a capacity force of perhaps 20–25,000 Peloponnesian loyalists, there were only some 4,000 present. Why so? The reasons they all gave at the time were religious, the Spartans alleging their absolute overriding obligation to celebrate their most important annual national festival, the Carneia in honour of Apollo, and the other Peloponnesians emphasizing likewise their unswerving commitment to celebrate the Olympic

Games in honour of Zeus. Undoubtedly, religion in ancient Greece was always a genuinely powerful historical factor, but we may reasonably suspect that another, more mundane and less creditable but entirely understandable, motive was more potently at work here – namely, panic fear: fear that the Persians were simply too multitudinous to be resisted, either at Thermopylae, or possibly anywhere else. After all, the vast majority of the several hundreds of other mainland Greek cities had already voted with their feet and decided willy-nilly to join or at least not oppose the Persians rather than try to beat them back.

The loyalist Greeks from north of the Peloponnese were also present in only very small numbers at Thermopylae, because this defence force was represented as just an advance guard. So, there were no Athenians or Megarians present, and, more controversially, only a few Boeotians, including a mere 400 from the Boeotians' principal city of Thebes. Later, after Thermopylae, all the Boeotians except Thespiae (an enemy of Thebes) and Plataea (an ally of Athens) 'medized', so that the reputation of the Thebans especially was blackened when the Persians were in fact eventually beaten back in 479. It was therefore alleged that, in 480, the 400 Thebans at Thermopylae had been present only because Leonidas compelled them to be, as hostages in a way for the loyal behaviour of their compatriots back home. Apart from these, there were perhaps a thousand troops each from the two local Greek peoples most directly affected, the men of Phocis and the men of Opuntian Locris. A total of some 7,000 in all, maybe.

At any rate, Sparta did send Leonidas and 300 chosen champions (of whom two were prevented at the last minute from fighting, by serious eye disease; one of these two hanged himself from shame on his return to Sparta, the other redeemed himself in a heroically suicidal death at Plataea the next year). Our main narrative source, Herodotus, tells us the 300 had been selected in part on the grounds that they all had living sons, so that their family lines would not die out when they were, inevitably, massacred. One wonders, however, just what the wives of these men were thinking. Of one wife's conduct only are we given

Immediately dubbed 'Leonidas' by a workman when excavated in the Acropolis area of Sparta in 1925, this finely worked lifesize marble figure in fact must depict either a god or a hero and was possibly part of a group of opposed figures set in the pediment of a temple (*see* pp. 270). Note the suitably macho rams that decorate both the helmet's cheekpieces, and the moustache-free upper lip, a typically Spartan feature. Fragments of an inscribed shield were also found.

any specfic information, in the form of a much later anecdote preserved by Plutarch among his collection entitled *Sayings* [Apophthegmata] *of Spartan Women*. As Gorgo was encouraging her husband Leonidas, when he was on the point of setting off for Thermopylae, to show himself worthy of Sparta, she asked him what she ought to do herself. He replied:

Marry a good man, and bear good children.[1]

In fact, Gorgo had already produced his son and heir, Pleistarchus, and she did not to our knowledge remarry after Leonidas's death.

GORGO

Not the least extraordinary thing about Gorgo is her name. What was her father, King Cleomenes I, thinking when he so named her? That she would petrify anyone who looked her in the eye? Surely not. Yet 'Gorgo' means 'Gorgon', as in the myth of the Gorgon called Medusa, whose head Perseus had had to cut off in order to rescue Andromeda from the sea monster. A truly terrifying name, but perhaps in Sparta it was not felt to be quite as odd as all that. An older male contemporary of hers was called Gorgos, and he was a high-ranking Spartan who served as *proxenos* or official diplomatic representative of the city of Elis at Sparta, a sort of honorary consul. To honour their *proxenos*, the Eleans set up a fine marble seat for him at Olympia, where they controlled the Olympic Games festival, and had his name inscribed upon it. The date of the lettering is around 525 BC.

Gorgo was born fifteen or so years later, since she was about eight or nine when she makes the first of her two appearances in Herodotus' *Histories*. The fact that a particular named Greek woman makes any appearance at all in a history of Greece would have shocked Herodotus' brilliant successor, Thucydides, because he hardly ever refers to women either as individuals or collectively, and certainly never presents a woman as having a decisive impact on the course of the Peloponnesian War. Herodotus, on the other hand, has scores of references to women, both collectively and individually, and indeed makes relationships between women and men, especially sexual relationships, one of the key points of reference of the ethnographic part of his work. Mainly these references concern non-Greek women, since the chief point of Herodotus' ethnography was to illustrate how many and various are human social and sexual customs, and how different – not necessarily worse – other peoples' customs could be from Greek norms.

Sparta, however, was a major exception to the rule that the Greek cities observed pretty much the same customs as each other, in respect of the position and behaviour of their women. Herodotus makes it abundantly clear by a variety of means that women in Sparta were different, even 'other'. For example, we are given his versions of the stories of King Demaratus' quasi-miraculous conception and birth, and of King Anaxandridas' supposedly 'quite un-Spartan' bigamy, but an even more telling illustration than these is the role played by Gorgo in Herodotus, or perhaps we should say the roles attributed to Gorgo by him.

In 500, aged just eight or nine, she was at home when her father returned from doing some public business, followed by a foreign suitor, Aristagoras of Miletus. He had come to Sparta on a matter of the highest diplomatic urgency, to try to persuade Cleomenes to support a planned revolt of Ionian and other Greeks from Darius I Great King of Persia, but Cleomenes had refused to commit Spartan land troops to a campaign against the Persian Empire that might take them as much as three months' march inland from the familiar Mediterranean Sea, and ordered the Milesian to quit Sparta before sundown. Having failed with words, Aristagoras, presumably knowing of the Spartans' baleful reputation for corruptibility, offered him a vast bribe of ten talents (several individual fortunes), when little Gorgo piped up: 'Daddy, you had better go away, or the foreigner will corrupt you.'

Of course, neither Herodotus nor his informants had any idea what exactly Gorgo had said, though her supposed use of 'the foreigner' (*xeinos*) to refer to Aristagoras nicely captures Sparta's characteristic trait of xenophobia (fear of *xeinoi*). The historically interesting point is that Gorgo could plausibly be represented as a power behind the throne, wise well beyond her tender years. Some fifteen or so years later, by which time Cleomenes had died in obscure and troubled circumstances and Gorgo was married to her father's younger half-brother and successor, Leonidas, and the mother of future king Pleistarchus, she makes her second decisive intervention in Spartan and Greek history. A messenger arrived in Sparta bearing an apparently blank wax tablet (two leaves of wood, covered with wax and folded together). 'No one,' Herodotus relates, 'was able to guess the secret' – no one except Gorgo, that is. She calmly told the authorities that if the wax were scraped off, they would find the message written in ink on the wood beneath, and so indeed it proved. This was no ordinary message, either, but one sent by the exiled ex-King Demaratus, warning the Spartans of Xerxes' decision to make war upon Greece.

It is not said in this story whether or not Gorgo was herself literate, though there is reliable evidence that Spartan women could at least read, if not also write, and the implication here is that writing was not something alien to Gorgo's experience. However, the main point is that Gorgo was sharper and smarter than all the other Spartans, especially the men in authority, and that she was able to make an intervention on the public stage and in the public sphere, a sphere that elsewhere in Greece was normally reserved exclusively for men. The same message is conveyed by the six apophthegms, or memorable sayings, attributed to her in the Plutarchan collection of *Sayings of Spartan Women*.

Two of these are variations on the Aristagoras story related above, one of them 'improving' on the words put in her mouth by Herodotus:

> *Daddy, the* miserable *foreigner will corrupt you*
> *if you don't* throw him *out of the house* pretty soon. [2]

The third alludes to her father's alleged drink problem and warns him that, the more wine people imbibe, the more intemperate and depraved they become. Hindsight seems to be at work here. The fourth, Gorgo's exchange with her husband Leonidas as he is about to depart for Thermopylae and his death, we have cited above. The remaining two are in some ways the most interesting of all, since they deal with gender politics, and so I quote them in full:

> *When a male foreigner wearing a finely woven robe*
> *made advances to her, she brushed him off saying*
> *'Get lost – you can't play even a female role.'* [3]

*On being quizzed by an Athenian woman, 'Why is it
that you Spartan women are the only ones who rule
your men?', she replied 'Because we are the only
women too who give birth to (real) men.'*[4]

The first of these is an allusion both to the Spartans' supposed contempt
for theatre and play-acting and to their ruggedly masculine view that a
man in luxurious dress was effeminate. It was the rich men of Sparta,
according to Thucydides, who first of all the Greeks abandoned luxurious dress and adopted clothes that were as plain and simple as those
that ordinary poor people could afford.

The second one, though, is even more revelatory. It is repeated in
slightly different words within one of the apophthegms attributed to
Lycurgus, in a collection of male Spartan utterances also supposedly gath-
ered by Plutarch. This clearly indicates its central relevance to the social
organization of 'Lycurgan' Sparta. For, according to normative Greek
constructions of gender and gender-roles, it was an essential part of the
nature of woman to be inferior, whether mentally or physically, to man,
and therefore it was necessary for all women to be subordinate in practice to all men both in private and, *a fortiori*, in public.

Aristotle, in the first book of his *Politics* and elsewhere, spells out
exactly what it is that in his view causes women's natural and so unalterable inferiority. His shock and horror in the second book of the *Politics*
are therefore palpable when he says that the men of Sparta are
gunaikokratoumenoi, 'ruled by their women'. In the apophthegm under
discussion, Gorgo does not deny that this is indeed the case, but, tactfully
enough, she diverts attention from the Spartan women's role as wives to
their role as mothers: only Spartan women, she says, unlike you pathetic
Athenian and other women, give birth to real men! Gorgo is thus doubly
identified with the gender-identity and – alleged – women-dominated
power-structure of the Spartan state. As we shall see in a later chapter,
some modification at least of the latter view is required.

Before we leave Gorgo, let us return again to her familial and especially her marital situation, concentrating this time on the importance of the inheritance of wealth and property. The cardinal fact about her, apart from her being born the daughter of a reigning king, was that she was an only daughter, an heiress, what the Spartans called technically a *patrouchos*, literally 'holder of the patrimony or paternal inheritance'. Her father Cleomenes was one of four sons of his father Anaxandridas, so that on Anaxandridas' death, had all four been alive then, his estate would have been split at least four ways (more if there were any daughters, since daughters in Sparta also inherited in their own right, if probably a smaller portion than their brothers). The other three sons, born to Anaxandridas' first wife, were in birth order Dorieus, Leonidas and Cleombrotus, but Dorieus had died relatively young, leaving Leonidas as Cleomenes' oldest sibling.

Leonidas ought to have been of marriageable age (in Sparta that was twenty-five or so for men) by about 510, yet he either did not marry then, or his first wife or wives had died by the time he married Cleomenes' heiress daughter Gorgo in the late 490s, when she had reached the marriageable age for Spartan women, that is, her late teens. The reasons why Leonidas should have wanted to marry Gorgo then are blatant: she was Cleomenes' only child, and would therefore inherit all his wealth, and he himself was next in line for the Agiad throne, since in the absence of a son, the royal succession in Sparta devolved to the late king's nearest male kinsman, and Leonidas was Cleomenes' oldest surviving half-brother. Cleomenes, in giving his blessing to the marriage, was following Spartan royal custom, since marriages between close blood kin, especially between an uncle and a niece, were by no means unprecedented – indeed, marriages between uncles and nieces were quite common elsewhere in Greece too, and for the same reason, basically a concern to keep the property intact within the male family line.

Gorgo, in other words, was performing the quite usual function allotted to elite women in the ancient Greek world, of being a marital vehicle for the devolution of property and with it property-power among elite males. It would be wrong, however, to think of her as merely a passive pawn in these transactions. From everything we know about her, Gorgo had a mind, and a voice, of her own.

The Thermopylae defence, effectively, was seen by the Spartans as a suicide mission, a sort of kamikaze exercise undertaken in an entirely rational frame of mind. This is confirmed by the story of Xerxes' scout reporting that the Spartans had been seen oiling themselves as if for an athletic contest and combing their – exceptionally – long tresses. As interpreted for Xerxes by Demaratus, this behaviour symbolized the Spartans' resolution to fight to the death if required – as they knew they would be. By the other Greeks, the Thermopylae operation was no doubt seen very differently. A brave resistance would be followed, for the survivors, by an honourable retreat in order to fight or die another day. Hence the very normal reaction of panic among most of them, as reported by Herodotus, when the Persian horde first approached the pass of Thermopylae. Another factor causing alarm was the locals' knowledge that the pass could be turned by a single path called Anopaea through the mountains to the south of them. Leonidas naturally attempted to seal this potential gap with a force of 1,000 Phocians, men familiar with the terrain and conditions and who had immediately the most to lose.

After the Persian forces had arrived, there was a delay of three or four days before the actual assault commenced. This was perhaps intended to pile psychological pressure on the Greeks until it became intolerable, or, more mundanely, to enable Xerxes to make a link with his storm-tossed fleet that was finally safely in harbour at nearby Cape Sepias. When the assault was at last launched, it was on Day One of what was remembered as an epic three-day encounter. The Greeks had rebuilt an old wall at the Middle Gate, behind which they resisted by fighting in relays. Their spears were longer than those of the enemy, who were also unable to make their sheer superiority of numbers tell in the confined space available. The Spartans added to the Persian forces' discomfiture by deploying the sort of tactics that only the most highly trained and disciplined force would have been capable of even contemplating – a series of feigned retreats followed by a sudden about-turn and murderous onslaught on their over-confident pursuers.

Day Two went pretty much as Day One, though one can well imagine the increasing frustration and irritation of Xerxes, but then he had his lucky break. A Greek traitor, a local Judas who knew all about the Anopaea path, opportunely made his presence known to Xerxes. His name (*see* p. 270) has gone down in infamy, at the time a cauldron of boiling hot condemnation motivated at least in part by a desire to obscure the fact that so many whole cities or peoples of the Greeks had already medized, or soon would. Thanks to him, on the night of Day Two and early morning of Day Three, the Persians outflanked the defenders of Thermopylae and, coming at them from the rear as well as the front, bound them in an unbreakable pincer grip. Xerxes had taken no chances. He confided the special night mission to members of his elite force, his personal bodyguard of 10,000 Immortals (as the Greeks called them: they liked to imagine, falsely, that they took their name from the fact that immediately one of them fell in battle he was replaced by a reserve, thereby maintaining at all times the maximum effective of 10,000).

Perhaps Leonidas is to be blamed for not reinforcing the Anopaea path with a larger or at any rate a more effectively determined defence force. Perhaps on appreciating the desperate situation of encirclement for what it was, he could have asserted his authority more unambiguously (it was said that he dismissed most of his remaining troops, but a more cynical view holds that this was just a cover-up for the fact that most of them simply melted away). What is not in question to even the very tiniest degree is the extraordinary resolution and courage with which he, his Spartans and the few thousands of other Greeks who chose to remain with him to the end fought on Day Three.

A truly laconic quip emblematizes the quality of the Spartans' final stand. When told that there were so many archers on the Persian side that their arrows would blot out the sun, the Spartan Dieneces, one of the 300, promptly replied:

So much the better – we shall fight them in the shade![5]

Since arrows were regarded by the Spartans as the weapons of the womanly and weak, in contrast to the spear and sword of the face-to-face, hand-to-hand hoplite fighter, this was a neat way of evading in words the point – both literal and metaphorical – of the deadly host of arrows that would shortly overwhelm them.

DIENECES

Dieneces appears just once in Herodotus' account of Thermopylae, towards its end, but it is a telling appearance, for in a company of the most extremely brave, he yet was able to give 'the most signal proof of valour'. The Greeks had a special word for the sort of excellence that was displayed conspicuously on the battlefield, *aristeia*, and this was applied most famously to the deeds of the Greek heroes related in Homer's *Iliad* – hence the *aristeia* of Diomedes, of Patroclus, and – above all others – of Achilles. *Aristeia* in this sense was a feminine singular noun, but the Greeks also used precisely the same letters for a neuter plural word meaning, not the valour itself, but the prizes for valour, which they awarded competitively after battles such as those of Thermopylae and Plataea. When Herodotus tells us that Dieneces was adjudged 'the best' of the Spartans who had fought and died at Thermopylae, he is saying that he was the man chosen by the surviving Greeks to be awarded the *aristeia*.

The Greeks were deeply imbued with the competitive spirit; their word for competitiveness, *agônia*, has given us our word 'agony', which tells a lot about the nature of Greek competitiveness. Being adjudged 'the best' therefore meant a very great deal. It would have been nice if we had been given more information on how Dieneces had come to be in a position to reap this supreme reward. The American novelist Steven Pressfield, in his *Gates of Fire*, has made a very good job of imaginatively reconstructing Dieneces' life trajectory, crediting him, for example, with introducing a new and specially rigorous form of training for Spartan warriors. That, though, is pure speculation. All that we can infer for certain is that he had passed through the Agoge with flying colours, been elected to a common mess, and then showed himself to be of such martial calibre, as well as being married and having at least one living son, as to be picked for the elite 300 to accompany Leonidas at Thermopylae.

Of one particular aspect of his quintessentially Spartan prowess, we are specifically informed by Herodotus: his skill in the peculiarly laconic form of apophthegmatic repartee. Hence the truly laconic utterance we have just quoted, about fighting in the shade. This, by implication, would enable the Spartans to fight even more fiercely and effectively, and even longer, than they would have done anyhow.

Herodotus adds that Dieneces was said to have left on record other similarly memorable sayings – if only he had decided to quote them too!

Leonidas also showed himself a true Spartan by the words with which he allegedly ordered his men to take their early morning meal before the final encounter: 'This evening, we shall dine in Hades.' Presumably he was also aware of the oracle from Delphi that was later said to have been issued at the time, to the effect that only the death of a Spartan king would ensure an eventual Greek victory against the Persians. At any rate, he fought and died like a man possessed by a consciousness that he was fighting for something greater than mere maintenance of the political status quo. This morale factor in the Spartans' comportment at Thermopylae, already present among the Athenians at Marathon, is a major part of the explanation of the Greeks' ultimate triumph.

According to Herodotus, the Persian losses at the beginning of Day Three were even heavier than those sustained on the previous two days. Perhaps so, if, as is likely, the Greeks fought with almost reckless abandon. The death of Leonidas himself merely increased the intensity of the Greeks' effort, for now they were fighting, Homerically, to preserve the king's body from appropriation and undoubted ill-treatment by the barbarian enemy. The final scene occurred on the low hillock mentioned above. With their weapons gone or broken, the Greeks fought literally tooth and nail, using their bare hands and their mouths. Yet even at the finish the Persian weapon of choice was the arrow, safely released at a distance. The bestial vengeance that was allegedly wreaked upon the corpse of Leonidas, including decapitation, would certainly have borne witness to the fact that Xerxes' Persians had been tested almost to the limit.

Formally, of course, Thermopylae marked a first, terrible defeat for the Greeks in pitched combat against the invading oriental horde, hardly an encouraging sign that they would win out in the end. Yet the epitaphs that later marked the site, including one of the most famous epitaphs in all history, clearly indicate that the Spartans at least felt more than merely shame at the memory.

Go, tell the Spartans, stranger passing by,
That here, obedient to their laws, we lie.[6]

The same message of pride and defiance was conveyed by the stone lion marker later erected at the site, since the king of the beasts symbolized martial prowess; it was for the same reason that the defeated Greeks set up a stone lion monument, that still survives more or less today, at Chaeronea in Boeotia in 338. However, the Thermopylae monument was also a nice echo of Leonidas' own name, which means 'descendant of Leon', since *leôn* was the Greek for 'lion' (*see* Chapter 10).

The example these men set of patriotic struggle to the death, perishing gloriously in the cause of a free Greece, provided precisely the morale booster that the desperate loyalist Greeks needed at that moment. This famous and heroic defeat at Thermopylae was, looked at from that point of view, a sort of victory. Great King Xerxes, who was present in person at the battle, is reported to have been astonished by the Spartans' conduct throughout. He was labouring under a number of cultural misapprehensions. He had to be told that the Spartans behaved as they did because they were fighting for an ideal dearer than mere life itself: the ideal of freedom. Freedom – the freedom to develop their unique and uniquely influential civilization – is indeed what the Spartans and the other Greek loyalists eventually secured by repulsing the Persians in the following year, 479.

This was the year of the two decisive and, for the Greeks, victorious battles of Plataea by land and Mycale by sea. Xerxes, however, experienced them only at second hand and by report, since after the Greeks' great naval victory at Salamis, masterminded by Themistocles and won essentially by the Athenian fleet, he had returned hotfoot to Susa – to the scene dramatically re-imagined eight years later in Aeschylus' winning tragedy, the *Persians*, of 472 (a text of which has survived). Behind him in Greece, Xerxes left as overall commander Mardonius, son of Gobryas, one of the seven noble Persians who had restored the Achaemenid monarchy from a period of usurpation in the late 520s and placed Xerxes' father Darius I on the throne. Mardonius, in other words, was *crème de la crème*, no mere makeweight or stopgap commander, but even he was no match for the Greeks' overall field commander of 479, the Spartan regent Pausanias.

Pausanias was in that position of command because, as first cousin, he was the closest male relative on his father's side to Leonidas' underage son and heir Pleistarchus and therefore appointed as both the boy's personal guardian and the Agiad regent of Sparta. He grasped this opportunity with both hands, securing the major command by land ahead of King Leotychidas, who instead became the first and practically the last Spartan king to hold a naval command.

REGENT PAUSANIAS

Pausanias bursts from nowhere on to centre stage of Greek and international politics in 479. He cuts a generally attractive figure in the pages of Herodotus, who was even prepared to question the charge of medism against him that arose well after the Persians had been finally defeated. Other sources though, especially Thucydides and, paradoxically, Simonides the praise-singer, tell a different story, of perhaps understandable but nevertheless inexcusable arrogance, even *hubris*, and treason.

Pausanias was born perhaps in about 510, son of Cleombrotus, the youngest full brother of Dorieus and Leonidas.

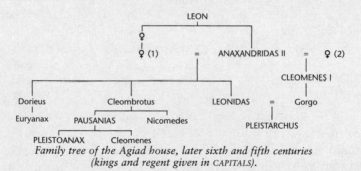

Family tree of the Agiad house, later sixth and fifth centuries (kings and regent given in CAPITALS).

In the absence, followed by the death, of Dorieus, Leonidas had succeeded his older half-brother Cleomenes but had perished at Thermopylae, leaving an underage son Pleistarchus. It was for him that Pausanias served as regent on the Agiad throne for some ten years before he too, like Dorieus, was disgraced. Whereas Dorieus died abroad, Pausanias obeyed the summons of the Ephors to return home from Byzantium in about 470. Accused of treason, he sought sanctuary on the Spartan acropolis, only to be walled up in the temple of Athena of the Brazen House and starved to death.

That lurid end was perfectly in accord with the style of the rest of his attested life. After commanding to victory at Plataea the largest Greek army ever yet assembled, he indulged in a number of grand theatrical gestures while still on the field of battle. Honourably, he refused the invitation of a Greek ally to mutilate the corpse of Mardonius as the Persians had allegedly mutilated that of Leonidas at Thermopylae. Instead, in order to reinforce the contrast between the Persian and the Greek (and more especially the Spartan) ways of doing things, he ordered his Helots to prepare an ordinary plain Spartan mess meal, so that his soldiers could see by how much that differed from the bloated magnificence of the banquet prepared in Mardonius' captured tent. Also, partly because it was not the Spartan custom to dedicate in their sanctuaries spoils taken from defeated enemies, he ordered the Helots to collect up the Persian spoils from the battlefield, including much gold and silver plate, and to dispose of them as they wished. Herodotus relates a vicious as well as false story that the medizing Aeginetans bought it from the Helots at knock-down prices because the unworldly Helots had no idea of its true value and as a result became rich. Vicious because it exposes the Aeginetans for being mercenary and deceitful as well as traitorous, but Pausanias' grand gesture of abnegation rings true enough.

After the defeat of the Persian invasion, the original Greek allies, enlarged now by the addition of Greek former subjects of Persia in the islands and the Asiatic mainland, decided to continue the war, and it was natural that Pausanias should continue to be in overall command, with his GHQ in Byzantium, but his arrogance soon alienated the allies. He was recalled to Sparta in 478, only to return to Byzantium the following year, apparently without official authorization. The sort of arrogance that led to his recall was perfectly displayed in an inscription he caused to be added to a large bronze mixing-bowl dedicated at the entrance to the Black Sea:

This memorial of his valour Pausanias dedicated to lord Poseidon commander of Greece of the spacious dance,

at the Black Sea, by birth a Spartan, son
of Cleombrotus, of the ancient lineage of Heracles.[7]

The two elegiac couplets were ascribed to Simonides, plausibly enough, as Pausanias was surely the prime mover in commissioning Simonides to write an epic-style encomium to commemorate the Spartans', but more especially his own, deeds of valour at Plataea. Large portions of this remarkable text, written on papyrus and preserved in the dry sands of upper Egypt, have recently been published. Here is a short extract (with suggested restorations in square brackets):

[From the Eu]*rotas and from* [Sparta's] *town they* [marched],
accompanied by Zeus' horsemaster sons,
[the Tyndarid] *heroes, and by Menelaus' strength,*
[those doughty] *captains of* [their fath]*ers' folk,*
led forth by [great Cleo]*mbrotus' most noble* [son],
... *Pausanias.*[8]

The poem casts light on the sort of heroic and personalized commemoration of his feats that Pausanias considered appropriate. Even his paid composer Simonides is said to have warned Pausanias to remember that he was but a mortal, not a god, or even a hero.

The Black Sea couplets were bad enough for his reputation, but Pausanias exceeded even this by his gross behaviour at Delphi. The united loyalist Greek cities, all thirty-one of them, commissioned as their victory-monument what is known for short as the Serpent Column. This consisted of a stone base bearing a bronze column in the shape of three intertwined snakes, with at the top – resting on the snakes' heads – a bronze cauldron reminiscent of the cauldrons given as prizes at the Funeral Games of Patroclus described in the *Iliad* and at other heroic contests. The names of the victorious cities, beginning with the Lacedaemonians (Spartans), were inscribed on the bodies of the snakes. They can still be made out, just, where the rather sad remains of the monument now reside, in the centre of the ancient Hippodrome in Constantinople (originally Byzantium, now modern Istanbul). However, Pausanias wanted his personal piece of the commemorative action too, so he caused to be added to the base a further inscription of his own, another elegiac couplet by the ever fertile Simonides:

> As leader of the Greeks, when he had destroyed the
>   army of the Medes,
> Pausanias set up this memorial to Phoebus [Apollo].⁹

As if Pausanias had destroyed the Persian army at Plataea all by himself... Small wonder that, as Thucydides adds, the Spartans had the inscription erased at once.

Pausanias was deprived therefore of the overall command of the Greek forces, and shortly thereafter the Spartans withdrew altogether from the active anti-Persian military campaigning, led now by Athens and its new Delian League naval alliance. Pausanias found Byzantium congenial and remained there for getting on for a decade, during which allegedly – this was the story accepted by Thucydides but queried by Herodotus – he sought and was promised the hand in marriage of a daughter of Xerxes with a view to making himself grand satrap of all Greece in the Persian interest.

Whatever the truth of that, in about 469 he was again recalled to Sparta, accused this time not of medism but of what was in a way a far more heinous crime in Spartan eyes, intriguing with Helots. The informant was hardly a usually reliable source, since he was Pausanias' boyfriend, a Greek slave from Argilus. (He has been transformed imaginatively into a Hellenized Syrian in Valerio Massimo Manfredi's novel *Il Scudo di Talos*, translated into English as *Spartan*.) However, his testimony was good enough for the Spartan authorities, who were prepared to believe that he had offered Helots not merely their freedom but also Spartan citizenship.

This alleged offer is capable of a very different, far less sinister interpretation, if what Pausanias was in fact doing was anticipating the official Spartan practice that became common in the Athenian War of offering Helots a conditional form of freedom in return for their military services. Such liberated Helots were called *Neodamôdeis*, which means something like New Citizen-type people, though in practice they enjoyed nothing like the privileges of full Spartan citizens of the right birth and education. Be that as it may, the charges were enough to make Pausanias take fright and sanctuary, in religious space on the Spartan acropolis. Starved near to death, he was removed just in time to prevent his polluting sacred space by dying within it.

Only later, after recourse to the Delphic Oracle, was Pausanias posthumously rehabilitated and given an unprecedented token of honour in the form of two bronze commemorative statues. Much later still, his name was linked with that of Leonidas as recipient of annual games held in their joint honour.

Mardonius, leader of the Persian land forces following Xerxes' return to Asia, overwintered during 480/479 in Thessaly. In the summer of 479 he moved south to reoccupy and re-destroy the city of Athens, as he had in 480. The Athenians, in effect city-less, made desperate appeals to the Spartans to come out of the Peloponnese across the Isthmus to help them where their help was needed, in central Greece. Eventually, the Spartans responded, in their own time and at their own pace, and joined forces with the Athenians and other loyalists in Boeotia, where Mardonius had withdrawn. Boeotia too was now a Persian subject-ally, except for Athens' ever-loyal ally Plataea, and it was in the territory of Plataea that conclusions were finally tried.

Pausanias may have commanded some 40,000 allied hoplite troops. Of these his own Spartans numbered 5,000, probably amounting to two thirds of the full potential levy. They were accompanied by the same number of Perioecic hoplites and, according at least to Herodotus' figures, no fewer than 35,000 Helots, who not only served as batmen and

The scene on this vase, made in southern Italy, depicts what appears to be a Spartan hoplite (long hair, shaven moustache) confronting a mounted spearman. Note the new type of helmet, less constricting than the earlier all-encompassing model. The style of the painting would place it in the context of the first phase of the Athenian War. Taras (modern Taranto) in Apulia was Sparta's only genuine overseas colonial foundation (founded *c.* 700 BC).

auxiliary personnel but also fought as light troops. Apart from the Spartans, the other key hoplite contingent on Pausanias' side was provided by Arcadian Tegea. The Persians, who probably still considerably outnumbered even the inflated Greek forces, took up their position along the River Asopus, initially on the south bank. Mardonius began the battle with a cavalry attack, playing to his main strength. The Greeks responded with archers, one of whom struck the Persian cavalry commander's horse, and the Persians were repulsed. First blood to the Greeks.

The issue of the main battle, however, lay not with archers or cavalry but with the Greek infantry, the Spartans positioned on the honorific right flank, the Athenians and Tegeans on the left of the line, the Megarians, Corinthians and others in between. Yet it was only after an inordinate delay of eight days that decisive battle at last was joined. One modern explanation of the delay is that Mardonius really did not want to fight a set-piece, pitched encounter but hoped to achieve a psychological victory by forcing the loyalist Greek army to disband.

Certainly the delay caused Pausanias very difficult and delicate problems of maintaining control and morale, and perhaps led even to his seriously contemplating swapping round the positions of his Spartans and the Athenians.

At all events, he did decide to withdraw, during the night. He may in fact have intended to withdraw only his centre rather than his entire force, but the idea that a retreat to Plataea had been ordered somehow got around, and chaos and confusion ensued. On learning at least a part of the true situation in the morning, Mardonius sent his cavalry to attack the Spartans, Perioeci and Tegeans. These now found themselves cornered and subject to a barrage of arrows. Pausanias somehow found the time to ascertain the will of the gods through sacrificial divination before ordering his hoplites to charge the much less well-equipped Persian infantry.

This was Pausanias' finest hour, or at any rate minutes. The Greeks, especially the Spartans, maintained their ranks and cohesion unbroken, rendering the Persian cavalry impotent to attack them. After breaking into the Persians' stockade north of the Asopus, the Greeks carried out a massacre. Plataea, though a damned near-run thing, had in the end been a complete and decisive victory for the loyalist Greeks. Never again would a Persian army invade the Greek mainland – rather, under Alexander the Great, it would be a Macedonian and Greek army that would invade and overrun Asia, a century and a half later. Not that the Persian empire ceased for a moment to be a major factor in Greek diplomacy and politics, but the result of Plataea confirmed the verdicts of Marathon and Salamis.

In retrospect, the battles of 480 and 479, above all that of Thermopylae, can be seen to have been a turning point not only in the history of Classical Greece, but in all history, Eastern as well as Western. Counter-factual 'What if...?' history may of course sometimes be just a pleasing distraction for historians, but it can also be a highly useful way of exploring cause and effect. What if, for example, the resistance at Thermopylae either had not happened at all, or had been much less frighteningly determined and effective than, under the leadership of Leonidas and his Spartans, it actually was? What if the loyalist Greeks had lost in 480–479, and the Persians had absorbed the Greeks of the mainland as well as of the islands and the western Asiatic seaboard into their far-flung Empire?

As it was, thanks to the Spartans' remarkably successful transformation of their society into a well-oiled military machine, and their diplomatic development of a rudimentary multi-state Greek alliance well before the Persians came to Greece, there was a core of leadership for the Greek resistance to coalesce around. The Spartans' suicidally doomed but utterly heroic stand at Thermopylae showed that the Persians could be at least resisted, giving the small, wavering and uncohesive force of loyalist Greeks the nerve to imagine that they might actually one day win. With charismatic Spartan commanders of the character and calibre of King Leonidas and Regent Pausanias to unite behind, the Greek land forces were able not only to stand up to but to defeat their many times more numerous but ill-assorted and easily demoralized foes.

PART II

THE
SPARTAN
MYTH

4

THE '50-YEAR PERIOD'
478–432 BC

In the immediate aftermath of the Persians' defeat and retreat, Athens set up a new anti-Persian naval alliance, what we call the Delian League (because the oaths were sworn, and the league's treasury was kept, on the sacred Aegean island of Delos). Sparta, unsurprisingly, was no part of this, not least because membership would have involved conceding the political initiative and hegemonic status to Athens, as Sparta's own allies did to Sparta in the Peloponnesian League. The Delian League was a wholly new organization, brought into being by the new oaths of allegiance and alliance. On the other hand, the Hellenic League, as modern historians call it, which had been created at Corinth in the autumn of 481, was not entirely superseded by the Delian League. As we shall see, as late as 464 or so, the Spartans could still attempt to conduct their diplomatic relations with Athens within the framework of that earlier anti-Persian alliance.

What was a little more surprising was that Sparta did not immediately give up direct involvement in hostilities against Persia after the Greeks' victory at Mycale, even though that inevitably meant conducting naval operations at a great distance from home. In 479 Leotychidas had won the Battle of Mycale, commanding jointly with Xanthippus, father of Pericles, but in 478, leading an expedition of revenge and reprisal overland against the formerly medizing Thessalians, he was allegedly caught with his hands in the till, as it were, or rather with a sleeve – a distinctively Persian garment – full of silver inside his tent; and on account of this blatant bribery and corruption he was recalled to Sparta and deprived of any further command. Pausanias the Regent, however, was sent out to continue the united loyalist Greeks' naval campaign directly against Persia from a base at Byzantium.

Unfortunately, his arrogance, alleged pro-Persian leanings (apart from rumoured marriage negotiations involving a high-ranking Persian woman, he was supposed to favour wearing Persian dress – anticipating Alexander the Great by a century and a half), and possible incompetence in the naval sphere soon led to requests by allies, especially from the large Aegean islands, that Sparta be replaced by Athens as overall leader. The Spartans thought they could get away with merely recalling Pausanias and sending out another Spartan commander in his place, but the replacement too was rejected, and the Athenians under Aristides went ahead with setting up the Delian League during the winter of 478/7. Since naval warfare was hugely more expensive than land warfare and required enormous initial investment in ship-construction as well as very high day-to-day running costs, the Athenians required their allies to contribute either a predetermined number of ships or a predetermined amount of cash in lieu. This, as Thucydides was to note, was one of the major differences between the Delian and the Peloponnesian Leagues, and the growing unpopularity of tribute was a major theme of Athens' increasingly imperialistic policies throughout the rest of the fifth century.

However, as Thucydides then added, rather than ensuring their allies' subservience by means of exacting tribute, the Spartans

> *took care to ensure their compliance by establishing*
> *congenial oligarchies among them.*[1]

Whatever may be thought of the nature and workings of Sparta's own constitution – and some, both in antiquity and today, have wanted to emphasize its allegedly open, even democratic features – Sparta consistently, like most imperial powers throughout history, supported non- or anti-democratic regimes abroad, not shrinking from imposing them by force on unwilling majorities if that was the only way of ensuring its own security and gratifying foreign friends and adherents.

This was not a risk-free policy, by any means, at any time, and especially not in the early decades of the fifth century, when some of Sparta's allies quite close to home were showing unwelcome signs not just of independent-mindedness but even of wanting to imitate the Athenians' democratic experiment. For example, there is evidence that both Arcadian Mantinea and Elis introduced some form of democratic decision making during the 470s, and it was during this same decade that the great Athenian war-leader Themistocles – no longer interested in making war on Persia, but very interested in doing all he could to undermine Sparta – was most active in stirring up opposition to Sparta from his base of newly democratic Argos.

All this made Sparta's position within the Peloponnesian League alliance distinctly uncomfortable, and it puts in its true perspective the impact of the major earthquake in 465 or 464 that directly struck the town of Sparta itself and occasioned an equally major revolt by not only the Messenian Helots but also two Messenian Perioecic towns. A passage of Herodotus from his final, ninth book nicely illustrates the nature and the scale of Sparta's difficulties in the 470s and 460s. In it he tells briefly the contrasting stories of two diviners or seers (*manteis*), both originally from Sparta's key Peloponnesian League ally, Elis.

The first of these, Hegesistratus, Herodotus describes as:

the best-known member of the Telliadae descent-group.[2]

Being a *mantis* was clearly a hereditary, family business in Elis, as elsewhere. He had hired himself out to the loyalist Greeks' enemy, Persia, and served as principal diviner to Mardonius. It seems that, rather than being pro-Persian, he was on principle anti-Spartan, and this perhaps was because he was something of a democrat. Anyhow, he had once been captured by the Spartans and imprisoned in the stocks at Sparta, on the grounds of having performed a number of anti-Spartan activities. So determined was he to get away, knowing presumably that otherwise his days were numbered (perhaps he had heard of the fate of King Cleomenes), he actually hacked off part of one of his feet, so as to be able to withdraw it from the stocks and escape. Herodotus calls this 'the bravest action of all those we know', rather oddly, since it enabled him to serve Mardonius during the Persian Wars; but after the Wars the Spartans caught up with him again, on the island of Zacynthus off western Greece, and this time they left nothing to chance and executed him.

The other originally Elean seer was called Tisamenus, a distinguished, in fact royal (as in Orestes' son) name. Herodotus is careful to give details of his aristocratic ancestry and to add that he and his (unnamed) brother were the only two non-Spartans ever to be made Spartan citizens. All Classical Greek cities were jealous of their citizenship and did not extend it lightly to outsiders, but the Spartans were hypersensitive on the issue. It was not enough even to be born a Spartan, but one had to achieve Spartan citizenship by one's personal prowess and then to maintain it, or rather, not lose it for either economic or social reasons. In the late 470s Pausanias the Regent was accused of plotting to offer Spartan citizenship to Helots – an accusation that was enough to cause his downfall and death. Perioeci were, at best, second-class Lacedaemonian citizens, rather than Spartiatai, Tisamenus' – services. With his expert aid, Sparta proceeded to win five key victories over the next fifteen to twenty years.

TISAMENUS

Herodotus' version of how Tisamenus came to work for Sparta, and become a Spartan citizen, involves a typical Delphic story. He had gone to consult the oracle on an entirely personal and utterly normal matter (how to get children), when the priestess replied with an ambiguous utterance: that he was destined 'to win the five greatest contests'. He thought that meant he was destined to be a winner in the pentathlon event at the premier athletic games, the Olympics, and he in fact came within one victory of achieving that remarkable feat! However, really what Apollo had marked him down for was to play the role of official diviner in five separate military victories – because the Greek word *agônes*, 'contests', could be taken to refer equally naturally to battles as to athletic competitions.

There then ensued an almost comic bargaining process between the Spartans – who presumably heard about this consultation through their usual 'hot line' contacts with Delphi – and Tisamenus. They offered him a fee, cash plus expenses as it were, whereas he demanded the symbolic price – and prize – of Spartan citizenship. All this happened before 480, because it was only the impending threat of the Persian invasion, coupled with their deep reverence for Delphi's foreknowledge and support, that convinced the Spartans eventually to concede what Tisamenus demanded for himself – and presumably also for his brother.

So that was how Tisamenus became Sparta's official diviner, ahead of any local experts, advising the kings (or Regent) who commanded the relevant armies whenever they took the auspices through animal blood sacrifices. This military divination was for the Spartans no less a part of the technique of warfare than the more obvious physical and mental preparations and exertions. The gods' will had to be tried before, including immediately before, battle was joined, and tried again even while the conflict was in progress. Any unfavourable sign in the victim's entrails could be interpreted by a Spartan commander as a signal not to engage with the enemy or to break off an engagement – even when such action or inaction might seem on purely secular, 'rational' grounds to be wholly inadvisable. Seers were therefore key military personnel, and they always formed part of a commanding king's regular entourage or staff. It was notably because of this attention to the religious niceties of combat that Xenophon called the Spartans alone of all the Greeks 'craftsmen [professional experts] in warfare'.

Normally, the ranks of the Spartans themselves could have been expected to produce a steady supply of homebred religious specialist seers. Probably, as was the case with the sacrificers and heralds, the job was hereditary within certain family-lines, but for some reason the circumstances of the 480s were such as to persuade the Spartans to overlook their usual xenophobia and breach their usual citizenship rules by granting access to Tisamenus and his brother – though I suspect that the fact that they were aristocrats from Elis, a key but unreliable Peloponnesian League ally, may have had almost as much to do with this as their inherited mantic expertise.

The first of Tisamenus' five victories was the Battle of Plataea in 479, and the last was the Battle of Tanagra in 458 or 457, to the circumstances of which we shall return. Both of those were against external enemies of Sparta, the Persians and the Athenians, but his other three victories are in a way all the more interesting, and the more significant, because they were against Sparta's more or less internal enemies – more so in the case of the Messenian Helots and two Messenian Perioecic cities that revolted following the great earthquake of about 464, less so in the case of, first, the Tegeans (Peloponnesian League allies) and the Argives (perpetual enemies) and, second, all the Arcadians except the Mantineans. Let us leave the Helots and Perioeci on one side for the moment, and consider next the two battles involving different sets of Arcadian allies.

Arcadia was absolutely key to Sparta's control of the Peloponnese and so of the Peloponnesian League. Arcadian Tegea, the nearest *polis* to Sparta of any significance, had perhaps been the very first ally of what was to become eventually the Peloponnesian League, and Arcadia geographically controlled Sparta's egress from Laconia and Messenia to the northern Peloponnese and central Greece. One of the principal, out of many divide-and-rule, strategies practised by Sparta was to prevent any Peloponnesian League ally hooking up with Argos. The combination of Argos with Tegea, therefore, in the second of Tisamenus' series of five victories, spelled potential disaster for Sparta, almost as much as did the union of Argos with Corinth in the late 390s. We are told no more by Herodotus than that the battle between Sparta and the united Tegeans and Argives took place at Tegea, uncomfortably close to home. A date somewhere in the region of 470 would be plausible, and a causal link with the presence of Themistocles at Argos more than just possible.

The next of Tisamenus' victories was at Dipaea, alternatively called Dipaieis, again not too far from Tegea, in the disquieting southern border zone of Arcadia. The most hopeful sign for Sparta here was that Mantinea, the other major city of Arcadia, had decided either to remain neutral or fight on the Spartan side. This was especially remarkable as Mantinea, having recently become a democracy (possibly under the influence of Themistocles) and being further away from Sparta, much nearer to Argos, was the more likely of the two to have maintained the hostility to Sparta that may be inferred from its late arrival at the battle of Plataea. Here then, perhaps, we have a case of an internal Arcadian struggle for mastery, between Tegea and Mantinea, which the Spartans as past masters of divide-and-rule tactics knew very well how to exploit. At any rate, the Spartans' victory was safely done and dusted before Tisamenus was called upon for his fourth and, after the battle of Plataea, most testing intervention.

The earthquake that struck Sparta town in the mid-460s would have registered high on the Richter scale had the ancients possessed such a measuring device. Seismologists have detected its devastating impact over a wide distance from the quake's epicentre. Diodorus of Sicily, writing in the first century BC but reproducing the fourth-century general historian Ephorus, reported Spartan casualties at the huge, and presumably inflated, figure of 20,000 with the damage striking especially at the young (this, if true, would of course have had a serious demographic impact in the next generation). At any rate, the disaster did not prevent King Archidamus, who had taken over the Eurypontid throne from Leotychidas in time to lead the Spartans at Dipaea, from raising an army to foil any direct Helot attack on Sparta. Even he, though, was unable to prevent the Helots of Messenia, always a hotter property than their Laconian cousins, from revolting *en masse*, and being joined, moreover, by two Perioecic towns in south-eastern Messenia, Thouria and Aethaea. This was in a sense therefore a nationalist uprising as well as a revolt of the economically and in other ways exploited underclass.

The Helots took this as a literally heaven-sent opportunity to launch a major and prolonged revolt. The Spartans out of piety ascribed the earthquake to the wrath of the earth-shaker Poseidon, who was worshipped optimistically under the title of 'Earth-Holder' in several parts of Laconia as well as in Sparta itself. Why in their view had Poseidon been so angry with them? The view that gained most official credence – and perhaps this was the one that Tisamenus himself espoused – was that the Spartans had maltreated some Helots who had literally sought sanctuary at a shrine of Poseidon at Taenarum in the deep south of Laconia, at the foot of the central prong of the Peloponnese. Instead of respecting the conventionally agreed right of Helots to take asylum here (our word asylum comes directly from the Greek term meaning freedom from reprisals), the Spartans had torn them away from Poseidon's altar and put them to death in an act of gross sacrilege. Presumably they must have been feeling under abnormal pressure and tension to undertake such a risky act, so possibly that act of sacrilege should be associated with the alleged machinations of Pausanias the Regent in relation to the Helots (*see* biography in Chapter 3). At any rate, the earthquake clearly happened at a particularly bad time for Spartan–Helot relations, which would explain why it was not only the Messenian Helots but also the Helots of Laconia – or significant numbers of them – who rose up in revolt.

No ancient source gives us a proper account of the course of the revolt. Indeed, one notorious crux in the text of Thucydides leaves it uncertain how long it lasted in all – can we really believe those manuscripts that make Thucydides say it continued for as many as ten years? A simple palaeographical alteration would reduce that figure to the far more plausible figure of four, which would make the revolt come to an end in about 460, in round figures, but even a four-year revolt would have been bad enough for the Spartans, and one reported detail does ring wholly true, namely that it ended up with a prolonged siege of Mount Ithome in the Stenyclarus plain of Messenia. This was a natural stronghold, like the Acropolis of Athens for example, and it was where traditionally the Messenians had made their last stand much earlier, during the first Messenian Revolt or Second Messenian War of the seventh century.

After that revolt had been suppressed, it would appear that the Spartans tolerated or encouraged the development of a Perioecic town in the vicinity, and archaeology reveals that dedications, sometimes inscribed and sometimes quite impressive, were made by inhabitants of this nearby community to Zeus Ithomatas or Zeus of Ithome. In the 450s they did not join in the revolt, as did the Perioecic towns of Aethaea and Thouria farther south, but neither were they able to prevent the Helot rebels from seizing the peak of Ithome as their point of last resistance – their Masada, as it were. In fact, although one of the functions of the Perioeci in Laconia at least was precisely to act as a first line of deterrence and if need be defence against Helot unrest, the Perioecic settlements in Messenia were so few, so distant and so relatively weak that the Spartans felt obliged to summon help from allies outside their home territory.

This paradoxically was to cause even more lasting difficulty and damage than the earthquake and revolt themselves. For the Spartans did not summon help only from their Peloponnesian League allies, in accordance with the clause binding an ally to 'help the Spartans with all their strength to the limit of their capacity'. They also called for help from Athens, apparently on the basis of the anti-Persian 'Hellenic League' alliance concluded in 481. Athens, although it was not a member of the Peloponnesian League, and had a democratic constitution, and was more concerned with Persia and with spreading its influence in the Aegean and in northern Greece, nevertheless agreed to send help. Not just token help either, but a substantial force of 4,000 hoplites. This was thanks to the persuasive powers of Cimon, a known pro-Spartan who had gone to the lengths of calling one of his sons Lacedaemonius or 'Spartan'.

Since Themistocles had laid down the tiller in the aftermath of the expulsion of the Persian invaders, in order to concentrate on fomenting discord and dissension within the Peloponnese against Sparta, Cimon had been the principal helmsman of Athens' growing naval power, commanding allied fleets of the Delian League to a string of victories, of which the most prominent and decisive was the battle of the River Eurymedon in Pamphylia (southern Asia Minor) in about 466. He was therefore at the peak of his influence when the Spartan request for aid against the revolted Helots came through, but the decision to aid Sparta would lead to his political undoing.

Once the troops had reached Messenia, things went horribly wrong. Although one of the reasons the Spartans had specifically wanted the Athenians' help was their reputed expertise in siegecraft, this alleged skill in fact proved pretty useless in practice when pitched against a force as deeply entrenched as the Messenian rebels on Mount Ithome. Even more worrying, apparently, to the Spartans was the attitude of the Athenian soldiers. These were not the poorest of the poor or lowest of the low by any means – fewer than half the Athenians could afford to equip themselves as hoplites, so that these 4,000 Athenians were among the better off. Yet even they were citizens of a city that had by then lived under some form of democracy for almost half a century, and their surprise and shock at discovering that the Spartans' Helot 'slaves' were not barbarians but fellow Greeks with proud traditions of their own may well have been intense.

At all events, the Spartans claimed rather extravagantly that the Athenians' behaviour and attitude amounted to 'revolution', that is, creating some sort of social or political upheaval, and they therefore summarily dismissed the Athenians 'alone of all the allies', according to Thucydides, without giving any satisfactory explanation of this flagrant breach of diplomatic protocol. Cimon's authority at Athens was immediately undermined, and within a couple of years he had been discredited and exiled. His policy of co-operation and co-leadership of Greece between Athens and Sparta was in tatters. To rub salt in the Spartans' wounds, the Athenians settled the survivors of the Helot insurgents on Ithome at a new home, Naupactus, on the north shore of the Corinthian Gulf. Even if the Helot revolt was put down as early as 460, Sparta nevertheless found herself embroiled immediately after that in the First Peloponnesian War (c. 460–445), so called to distinguish it from 'the' Peloponnesian War, our Athenian War, of 431–404.

Some of Sparta's other allies too – such as the Mantineans, who were also democratically governed – may well have felt discomfited by their leader's highhanded action against Athens, and so Sparta will have needed to be able to demonstrate its capacity to enforce its will. This it did in the only field in which its pre-eminence was still undisputed, that of pitched battle. In either 458 or 457, Sparta led a Peloponnesian League army across the Isthmus of Corinth into central Greece, as far as Tanagra in Boeotia. Thucydides tells us tantalizingly that there was a group in Athens, with whom the Spartans were in touch, who hoped to exploit the presence of a Spartan army fairly nearby to bring about a coup such that the democracy would be replaced by an oligarchy, the sort of regime that the Spartans typically preferred to deal with among their subordinate allies. However, although the Spartans did defeat the Athenians and their allies at Tanagra, it was too close a victory for them to be able to exploit it politically, and they were relieved enough to be allowed to return unmolested to their Peloponnesian home.

This was the moment, I believe, when the Spartans decided, no doubt with considerable misgivings, to make a major change in their army organization. The earthquake had caused severe loss of Spartan life. Two Perioecic towns in Messenia had joined the Helot revolt. The Battle of Tanagra had been too close for comfort. These three facts, I suggest, prompted the Spartans to take the step of incorporating Perioecic hoplites in the regular Spartan regiments, in order both to ensure Perioecic loyalty and, more important still, to boost Sparta's flagging citizen numbers. This was not quite like incorporating Nepalese gurkhas into a regular regiment of the British army under the Raj, but it was still a pretty major breach of the Greek principle of the citizen militia army. For although the Perioeci could be called 'Lacedaemonians', just like the Spartans, they were not citizens on equal terms with the Spartans since they had not gone through the socializing discipline of the Agoge or been elected to a dining group. The change involving the incorporation of Perioecic hoplites took place some time after 479 and some time before the Battle of Mantinea in 418. It is only a guess of mine that it occurred in the 450s, after the Battle of Tanagra, but that does seem to me to have been the moment of military truth for the Spartans. It is also compatible with the fact that the Spartans did not perform too well during the First Peloponnesian War.

The Athenians, by contrast, were so encouraged by their side's relatively good showing at Tanagra that, within a few months, they had made themselves masters of almost all Boeotia, acquiring a kind of miniature land empire to add to their growing naval empire in the Aegean. One casualty of Sparta's relative failure was the loss of Aegina, a strategically vital island in the Saronic Gulf so visible from Athens that Pericles memorably called it 'the stye in the eye of the Piraeus'. Aegina was a Peloponnesian League ally that the Athenians now besieged and subjugated, punishing the population by expelling it and replacing it with colonists of their own. The most that the Spartans could do in the circumstances was offer the displaced Aeginetans a new temporary home within their own state territory, in Cynouria (also known as the Thyreatis) on their north-east frontier with the territory of their diehard enemy Argos. Temporary was to mean in practice more than half a century.

The so-called First Peloponnesian War dragged on for another decade, until Athens found it had overreached itself in attempting to maintain control of its central Greek land empire as well as the naval empire. In 446 Athens found itself faced with simultaneous revolts on either flank, in Megara (formerly also a Peloponnesian League ally of Sparta) to the west, and on the island of Euboea. Here, surely, was the chance for Sparta to make a decisive intervention, and King Pleistoanax, who had come of age since Tanagra, did indeed lead an allied force across the Isthmus as far east as to penetrate Athens' home territory; but when he was in the vicinity of Eleusis, he rather mysteriously decided to pull back. This allowed Athens the breathing space to re-establish its control at least of Euboea (strategically more important than that of Megara). Not long after, the two sides entered into negotiations that culminated in the swearing of a treaty known after its intended duration as the Thirty Years' Peace.

The essence of the treaty was that each side was to 'keep what it had': that is to say, the Spartans in effect 'recognized' the Athenians' empire, while the Athenians in their turn 'recognized' Sparta's hegemony of the Peloponnesian League. Much of mainland Greece was thus carved up into two great blocs between which was supposed to reign a sort of balance of power. Pleistoanax, however, for all that he may have been a principled believer in such a Cimonian 'dual hegemony' thesis, was punished with deposition and exile for what was construed by his domestic enemies as betrayal of Sparta's best interests, and he was destined to remain in exile, within a religious sanctuary in Arcadia, for almost twenty years.

It was these same enemies of his, presumably, who had had to be forced to acquiesce in the peace terms of 445, who within a mere four or five years were so keen to break the supposedly thirty-year peace. In 441 some Samians came to Sparta, following in the footsteps of those ancestors of theirs who had persuaded the Spartans to send a naval expedition to overthrow tyrant Polycrates in 525. These were no less successfully persuasive – so much so that one wonders whether there might not also have been at work some powerful personal connections between leading Spartans and leading Samians. At any rate, Herodotus says that he once met in Sparta one Archias, whose grandfather of the same name had been part of the expeditionary force of 525 and been given a state funeral by the Samians on account of his conspicuous gallantry. The younger Archias, presumably, was an influential voice calling for the Spartans to help those Samians, led by the oligarchs in power, who wished to revolt from the Athenian empire.

However, although the Spartans were persuaded, their Corinthian allies – unlike the situation in 525 – were not, and the Corinthians managed to persuade a majority of the other Peloponnesian League allies in this particular case not to 'follow the Spartans whithersoever they might lead them'. Surely that was a prudent decision. The Spartan alliance did not yet have anything like the naval force required to take on and defeat the Athenians at sea, even if the nearest Persian viceroy based at Sardis was prepared to supply them with money and perhaps material. All the same, the Samian revolt did necessitate for Athens a very long and very costly naval blockade, led by Pericles, and did provoke extreme measures of exemplary reprisal and punishment after it had finally been put down. Indeed, looking back from a vantage point of 411 BC, some Samians observed that the revolt of 440–439 had nearly cost the Athenians their control of the sea, that is, of the eastern Aegean.

That, certainly, was how the great historian Thucydides saw it in retrospect, though he was probably not yet of age when the event itself occurred. In writing a brief narrative of events that occurred between the Persian Wars of 480–479 and the outbreak of the Peloponnesian/Athenian War in 431, he chose to end with the revolt of Samos. This left a gap of some four years before the political unrest on the island of Corcyra (Corfu) that broke out in 435, which he considered the War's most immediate antecedent and its most important precipitating cause. Despite the importance of the Corcyra unrest, Thucydides believed the main cause of the outbreak of the Peloponnesian/Athenian War to be the growth of the Athenian empire and the fear this caused the Spartans: that the Athenians would encroach upon and eventually diminish or destroy their own power. The reduction of revolted Samos in 439 was a sure token and confirmation of Athens' imperial power.

So threatening in fact did the growth of the Athenian empire quickly come to seem that, in 432, the Spartans declared that the peace of 445 was at an end, wrongly accusing Athens of having broken it. In fact it was the Spartans who made the crucial move towards open warfare – and they did so against the express advice of their senior king, the man who would inevitably lead them into battle, Archidamus II.

KING ARCHIDAMUS II
(REIGNED c. 469–427)

Archidamus, the second king of that name (which meant 'leader – or ruler – of the people'), belonged to what was considered the junior of the two Spartan royal houses, that of the Eurypontids, and reigned for over four decades. He was born in about 500 to a father called Zeuxidamus; the -*damus* suffix that runs in the family suggests a deliberate attempt to advertise their connections to the people (*damos*) and to curry favour with the ordinary Spartans, perhaps because the descendants of Eurypon were conscious of their juniority to the even more elite Agiads. Zeuxidamus, however, never reigned, and presumably therefore had predeceased his own father Latychidas II (who died in about 470, though he had been disgraced and lived in exile for almost a decade). Archidamus, by contrast, enjoyed one of the longest historically authenticated reigns of all, and enjoyed it in the fullest sense. For it was, on the whole, a reign of success, against increasing odds.

He first comes to the attention of the sources in the mid-460s, as the commander of the Spartan forces that suppressed some serious intra-Peloponnesian League disaffection at the battle of Dipaea (or Dipaieis) in Arcadia. Soon after, he was called to be the saviour of Sparta from the double blow of a major earthquake and an equally major Helot, mainly Messenian, revolt. Then, so far as Sparta's public history is concerned, he fades entirely from view until 432, when his is the major voice in the Spartan Assembly advocating caution over the proposal to declare war on Athens. Thucydides uses him somewhat as Herodotus had used a Eurypontid predecessor, Demaratus, as a wise adviser figure, to illustrate the true nature of the situation and to foreshadow the actual course of events. This mark of respect had been fully earned, it would appear.

We shall consider later the key role Archidamus played at the end of his long career. First, let us retrace our steps to the 470s, when he married Lampito, daughter of Leotychidas by a second wife and so his own step-aunt. This is unlikely to have been a marriage of passion. It was rather a match of political and, no less important, economic convenience, ensuring that inherited paternal property was kept firmly within the patriline. Aristophanes chose 'Lampito' as the name of his forceful Spartan character in the *Lysistrata*. Perhaps he had heard something about her real namesake to justify that choice. With Lampito, Archidamus had the one son, Agis, who in due course succeeded him in 427/6, but after Lampito's death he married again, a very short woman (or perhaps one who was unusually short for a Spartan woman). With this second wife, Eupolia (literally 'well-colted', a reference to the ownership of horses, always a superior aristocratic status symbol in ancient Greece), he had two more children, Agesilaus (later Agesilaus II) and a daughter Cynisca ('Puppy' or 'Little Bitch').

The other interesting fact about Archidamus' personal connections is that he was a *xenos* of Pericles of Athens. The word *xenos* in this sense is often translated 'guest-friend', since the relationship involved mutual hospitality (like French *hôte*, the same word *xenos* served to mean both 'host' and 'guest'), but this is a considerable under-translation. The root meaning of *xenos* was 'stranger', 'outsider', 'foreigner'; and *xenoi* in the sense of 'guest-friends' were always foreigners, that is members of two different political communities. *Xenia* was, moreover, an ancient and aristocratic or at any rate elite institution. Typically both partners were Greek, but the institution was extended also to non-Greek communities; for example, it was possible even for a non-royal Greek citizen to establish a relationship of *xenia* with the Great King of Persia (as did the Spartan Antalcidas with Great King Artaxerxes II, for example, in the early fourth century). Then again, 'friendship' is in English rather too tame a word for a relationship that was morally and spiritually so binding that it might induce or require one of the *xenoi* to prefer his *xenos* to his country. (This anticipates E. M. Forster's famous dictum that, if faced with the choice between betraying a friend or betraying his country, he hoped he would always choose the latter.) Both the contracting and the maintenance of *xenia* relationships were expressed in powerful ritual observances. So, for all those reasons a translation of *xenos* in this sense as something like 'ritualized guest-friend', clumsy though that is, is required.

Finally, the relationship was not simply between two individuals, but between two families, since it was hereditary – even if the existence of a *xenia* was not necessarily known to one or both partners. This was the point of the famous story in the *Iliad* of the encounter between the Greek Diomedes (from Tiryns in the Peloponnese) and Glaucus the Lycian (Lycia was in the southern coastal region of western Asia Minor). Diomedes had to remind, or rather tell, Glaucus that they were hereditary *xenoi*. As were King Archidamus of Sparta and Pericles of Athens. We do not know when the hereditary relationship between them was first contracted, but a plausible guess is that it was when Archidamus' grandfather Latychidas II and Pericles' father Xanthippus were serving jointly as commanders of the united Hellenic fleet against Persia in 479 that the tokens of *xenia* were given and accepted, with all due ritual and ceremony.

Nor was this by any means the only such top-level Spartan–Athenian *xenia* on record. A contemporary of Archidamus was called Pericleidas, and he named his son Athenaeus ('Athenian'). It was Pericleidas who on the Spartan side was most responsible for persuading the Spartans to appeal to Athens for help against the revolted Helots in the 460s, while the chief co-operating actor on the Athenian side was Cimon, who in the 470s had named a son of his Lacedaemonius ('Spartan'). Pericleidas and Cimon no doubt both believed in Spartan–Athenian co-operation on principle, but their separate connections with families in the other city will have reinforced their desire for collaboration rather than confrontation between their two states.

The same was less true of Archidamus and Pericles. That is, Pericles seems early on to have decided, regardless of any personal relationships or connections, that Sparta, rather than Persia, was Athens' principal potential enemy and he did everything in his power to develop Athenian might even at the cost, ultimately, of a major war with Sparta. Thus one of the more intriguing sidelights on the origins and outbreak of the Peloponnesian/Athenian War is the familial relationship of these two leading figures. It accounts probably for at least two episodes in the fierce propaganda campaign surrounding the War's outbreak.

By 432 diplomatic relations between Sparta and Athens were at a breaking point, and most Spartan citizens had already made up their minds that Athens was in the wrong and that the right decision for them was to go to war at once. Matters came to a head at a meeting of the Spartan Assembly at which representatives from Corinth, Sparta's chief ally, and from Athens, the enemy party, were invited to speak. According to Thucydides, only two Spartans, both leading figures, spoke – but he may have suppressed mention of other, less influential speakers for artistic reasons. Those two were Archidamus and the powerful Ephor Sthenelaidas.

Archidamus, as represented by Thucydides, did not actually speak outright against a decision for war, let alone defend Athens' record. What he did argue was that, before the Spartans declared and joined war, they should reflect further and use the time thus gained for diplomatic exchanges. His speech was balanced, measured, and relatively lengthy. Sthenelaidas' rejoinder was a classic of laconic brevity and inartistic bluntness: the Athenians are guilty of breaking the peace (of 445), he stormed, so let's go to war. Probably because the experienced Archidamus was the senior reigning king (his co-king Pleistoanax had been in exile, convicted of treason, since 445) and would therefore inevitably lead any Peloponnesian League force against Athens, his views commanded respect, and the first round of voting – by shouting, in the usual Spartan way – was not entirely conclusive. Or so Sthenelaidas claimed, since he then called for a vote by division and, by playing on Spartans' fears of appearing unwarlike, secured a thumping majority for War Now.

Even so, the Spartans did in fact continue to engage in diplomatic exchanges with Athens after this vote, and indeed even after securing the approval of Apollo of Delphi for their decision to go to war. This suggests that Archidamus was by no means a spent force, a suggestion that would seem to be confirmed by one of the ultimata that the Spartans sent Athens. If, it said, you expel 'the accursed ones', then there need be no war. That phrase was code for the Athenian family of the Alcmeonids, who laboured under a curse inherited from an act of sacrilege committed two centuries earlier in the late seventh century, but the Alcmeonid against whom this ultimatum was really aimed was Pericles, whose mother belonged to that patriline. No one will have known more than Archidamus about Pericles' family liabilities.

Conversely, when the diplomatic offensive on either side was over, and hostilities were about to commence with an invasion of Attica by a Peloponnesian League army commanded by Archidamus, Pericles so feared what his *xenos* Archidamus might do to undermine his authority, whether deliberately or not, that he 'nationalized' his own major landholdings, that is, he handed them over to public ownership. This was in case Archidamus should order his troops to spare them the ravaging that other Athenians' land would suffer. In practice, it appears that Archidamus was more interested in avoiding having to ravage any Athenian land whatsoever, since even after his army was on the march in 431, he still sent out peace feelers to Athens; and when he did finally get to Attica, he seems to have spent a long time doing remarkably little. He seems hardly to have been serious about prosecuting the war.

In 430, nevertheless, he again led a Peloponnesian League force into Attica in the early summer, at the start of the conventional campaigning season for hoplite armies. The outbreak of the great plague (which could have been typhus) in the city of Athens caused him to withdraw very soon, and in 429 he led a Peloponnesian force that concentrated on laying siege to Athens' ally Plataea, not on ravaging Attica and menacing Athens. In 428 he returned to the pattern of 431 and 430, and 427 saw the end of the Plataea siege, but in 426 the Peloponnesian invasion force for Attica was under the new command of Archidamus' elder son and successor, Agis II. By then, Archidamus himself was dead.

Already, just as Archidamus had predicted in 432, and partly of course because of his own conduct as leader of the Spartans, the Peloponnesian/Athenian War was proving to be no pushover for Sparta, and in fact after his death it took several turns for the worse, utterly falsifying the prediction of the hotheads who opposed him that it would be over in a couple of years, three at the outside. It is therefore somewhat ironic, to say the least, that the first, ten-year phase of the War should be routinely named after Archidamus II, as the 'Archidamian War'. Even more so, in fact, given that he died before fewer than half of those ten years were over. In this book we shall speak strictly and descriptively, as did Thucydides, of the Ten Years' War, and give Archidamus the benefit of the doubt as to his true intentions and aims.

* * *

Thucydides chose to write up a full-dress account of this momentous decision of the Spartans. He describes the scene in which the Spartans held an Assembly meeting addressed first by foreign delegates and then by selected Spartan speakers, including Archidamus. He writes, in his own words, four set policy speeches. First, a delegate from Corinth, representing Sparta's single most important ally, urges war, chiefly on the grounds that the Athenians have already broken the peace agreement of 445 and anyway have to be stopped sooner rather than later. Next, an Athenian delegate urges maintenance of the still – he claims – existent peace. Then, King Archidamus, with all the weight of his inherited authority and acquired prestige and influence, urges the Spartans cautiously against at any rate an immediate declaration of war. Finally, conclusively, one of the five Ephors of that year, presumably the most influential of them, delivers a classically laconic speech to the effect that the rights and wrongs of the case are crystal clear, Athens is entirely in the wrong, and besides the Spartans have a moral duty to their allies.

To be strictly accurate, that Ephor's speech was not by itself decisive. The Spartans, remarkably enough, normally voted by means of shouting – those who shouted loudest 'yea' or 'nay' won the day. On this occasion, the presiding Ephor claimed he was not absolutely certain which of the shouts, 'yea' (war) or 'nay' (peace), had been the louder, so he ordered the citizens to divide and be counted individually. Perhaps he genuinely had been uncertain; perhaps the authority of Archidamus was so great that a significant number of Spartans had stifled their naturally – or rather culturally – bellicose instincts and voted 'nay' (peace – for now). Just as likely is that he wanted to get the biggest majority possible, and so he exploited the Spartans' culturally induced notions of patriotism and bravery to get them to – literally – stand up and be counted. Which Spartan would want to seem, or even run the risk of seeming, a coward, a 'trembler' in official parlance?

Predictably enough, the majority for war was now seen to be

massive, and in the following spring, 431, Sparta and Athens and their respective allies embarked on what was to prove a generation-long conflict of increasingly desperate and desolating character. Perhaps the underlying cause was indeed the growth of Athenian power, but it was the Spartans who started the war.

5

WOMEN AND RELIGION

Females are, and always have been, more or less half the human race, but they have usually received nothing like half the due care and attention in historical sources and historical accounts that their roles and functions in society and history really merit and require. One great exception to that rule – there are always exceptions – was the women of ancient Sparta. So far from being silent or silenced, they had a lot to say for themselves, and there are even sayings attributed to them by name in ancient texts. Let us not forget the truly laconic rejoinder allegedly made by Gorgo, daughter and wife of Spartan kings, to the non-Spartan woman who, marvelling at the Spartan women's apparent control over their men, asked her how come only Spartan women ruled their men: 'Because we are the only women who give birth to (real) men!' What gave that no doubt apocryphal reply its special charge was that even the most sober and acute outside observers of the Spartan scene could seriously believe in the literal factual truth of women's power, or rather domination, in Sparta.

One of the acutest and most sober of such observers was Aristotle. He came originally from an elite family in northern Greece (his father was court physician to King Amyntas III of Macedon, father of Philip

II), but he spent most of his adult life at Athens. Here he was first the star pupil of his day at Plato's Academy, where he arrived at the age of seventeen in 367, some twenty years after its foundation; and then the founder of his own school of higher learning, the Lyceum, which he opened in the mid-330s. Between them, he and his pupils compiled, among much else, accounts of the laws and main constitutional developments of 158 political entities, mostly Greek cities, including of course Sparta. These in turn informed the most brilliant work of political analysis that has come down to us from the ancient world, Aristotle's *Politics* or 'Matters Concerning the *Polis*'. In the second book of that work he did a pretty devastating job of pointing out all the major weaknesses, as he saw them, of Spartan society and Sparta's political system.

In a sense, this wasn't too difficult to do, since by the time the work was being composed, in the 330s and 320s, Sparta had long since ceased to be a major Greek power, though it remained something of an icon to those who for political or philosophical reasons were unhappy with their own cities' social or political arrangements, and still looked to Sparta to provide some kind of ideal alternative. My present interest in the relevant passage of the *Politics* stems from the fact that Aristotle here explicitly subscribes to the view that in Sparta the women ruled the men, and that this gynecocracy (rule of women) was, for him, a key part of the explanation for Sparta's political – and moral – failure. How could that possibly have been right?

The basis for Aristotle's view was twofold, one part intellect, one – almost equal – part sheer prejudice. Consider the prejudice first. Aristotle fully shared the absolutely standard Greek male (chauvinist) view of women's inferiority to men, but to that conventional attitude he added a powerful dose of Aristotelian 'science'. He thought he could prove scientifically that women's bodies and women's minds ('souls', as he called them) were categorically, naturally, that is unalterably, inferior to men's. Women were, in other words, the second sex in the fullest sense: physically, they were deformed males, and intellectually they lacked the capacity to make their reasoning powers, such as they were, authoritative. This 'theory' applied generically to all women, of course, not only Greek women, and it applied generally to all women, not only to some. In these respects Aristotle went beyond the views of his master, Plato, who was prepared to concede that some very few women might be the intellectual equals and genuine partners of the elite philosopher-rulers of his ideal state.

So, how come Spartan women, despite these inherent feminine defects, were able to, had got themselves in a position to, rule their menfolk? This would surely be, as Aristotle of all people ought to have realized, a contradiction or, at best, a paradox. Yet Aristotle firmly believed it, so firmly that he spent a good deal of time trying to figure it out. In the end, he came up with a sort of historical explanation on the following lines. The besetting sin of Spartan women was, for Aristotle, the characteristic female vice of lack of self-discipline and self-control. The way he accounted for that was by supposing that, whereas the Spartan men had become disciplined by submitting themselves voluntarily to the iron laws of Lycurgus and the consequent Lycurgan regimen, the women had refused to submit to Lycurgus and no one since then had been able to control them, with the result that they wallowed in every sort of luxury and self-indulgence, aided and abetted by their complaisant, uxorious husbands. However, this seems a little hard to accept as a properly historical explanation. For in fact Spartan girls too, even if they did not live in communal barracks from the age of seven like their brothers, did undergo some form of public educational instruction, with tellingly unusual results by general Greek standards of womanly behaviour, as we shall see.

It is easier, on the other hand, to see what it was about the Spartan women's status and entitlements that should have led Aristotle to imagine Sparta to have been a gynecocracy. Two socio-legal facts above all – on top of their formal education – differentiated them from women in all other Greek states. First, they were entitled to own and manage property, including landed property, in their own right,

This sprightly figurine of a young female in athletic pose originally decorated the rim of a large bronze vessel (somewhat like that in Ill. p. 97). Found at Prisrend in Albania, it illustrates the wide distribution achieved by bronze and other artefacts manufactured in Laconia in the sixth century. The athlete's off-the-shoulder shift was a Spartan peculiarity, appropriate for the athletic exercise that we know was part of a Spartan girl's public education. Every four years at Olympia Greek women, including Spartans, raced in honour of Hera. Alternatively, the figure is being depicted in the act of dancing, a form of ritual activity for which Spartan girls and women were widely celebrated.

probably without the necessary legal intervention of a male guardian. Heiresses in Sparta – that is, daughters without legitimate brothers of the same father – were called *patrouchoi*, which means literally 'holders of the patrimony', whereas in Athens they were called *epiklêroi*, which means 'on (i.e., going with) the *klêros* (allotment, lot, portion)'. Athenian *epiklêroi*, that is, served merely as a vehicle for transmitting the paternal inheritance to the next male heir and owner, that is to their oldest son, their father's grandson, whereas Spartan *patrouchoi* inherited in their own right. Such heiresses in Sparta were highly prized commodities, much sought after by eligible Spartan men, since they could be married to any Spartan, not only to the nearest male kin on the father's side.

The second point of sociolegal differentiation was that Spartan wives might have sex with a man other than their husband without falling afoul of any adultery laws – because in Sparta, unlike in the rest of Greece, there apparently were no such laws. Indeed, their husband might actually 'lend' them to another man for the specific purpose of procreating legitimate offspring – for that other man's household and lineage. As for the wives in these cases, they are said to have welcomed such an arrangement, so Xenophon assures us in his fourth-century essay on Spartan society and its mores, since it gave them the chance to manage more than one household. This reminds us that all Spartan wives, like only the wives of rich men elsewhere in Greece, were freed by servile (Helot) labour from domestic drudgery. They did not have to prepare and cook food, make clothes or do the housework: Helot women did all that for them. Possibly they did not even breastfeed their own infants; at any rate Spartan nurses, presumably Helot women, had a high reputation outside Sparta, so high that Alcibiades of Athens, for example, was reared by such a Spartan Helot nurse.

In these circumstances it was easy to twist the fact of Spartan women's ownership of land and other property, and their apparently open and easy sexual congress with men other than their husbands, into a picture of immoral depravity, of a world turned upside down. 'When the female rules the male' – so began a Delphic oracle, meaning when everything is at sixes and sevens and nothing is right with the world. 'In Sparta the female rules the male' – so believed many non-Spartan men, including Aristotle, who wrote in that same Book II of the *Politics* that:

> at the time of the Spartans' domination [archê] *many things were accomplished by the women.*[1]

What he seems to have been claiming is that, at any rate in the early fourth century, Spartan women did not only control their men within the confines of the household, but also somehow exercised a decisive influence over affairs of state. Yet the only actual instance of female intervention in the public sphere during the period that he chooses to give, seems to tell in the exact opposite direction. When in 370/69 the Spartan women saw a mighty Thebes-led army of invasion actually on Spartan home territory and devastating land within sight of Sparta itself, the women allegedly caused more consternation and uproar even than the enemy, through their manically panicky reaction. Again, that looks uncomfortably like sheer male prejudice, since courage in war was deemed to be a peculiarly masculine quality and virtue. Also, the women's panic would in any case have been wholly understandable, since seeing Spartan land, including land that they themselves owned, destroyed in front of their very eyes was hardly something they had been schooled for by the national curriculum.

In short, what Aristotle and other conventionally minded non-Spartan men feared subconsciously and perhaps sometimes consciously was feminine power. One expression of that Greek male fear was the invention of the mythical race of Amazons, but at least the Amazons had the decency to live apart from men, whereas the Spartan viragos apparently exercised their power from within the heart of the community. In the grip of such fear, the male sources often distorted the facts they had access to, usually only at second-hand at best, about Spartan women. Let us instead try to redress the balance and paint a picture of what life, or rather a lifecycle, might have been like for the average Spartan girl and woman, from the womb to the tomb.

Spartan laws as well as social mores privileged reproduction, 'children-making' (*teknopoiia*). Apart from the standard desire of individual Spartans to have a son and heir to continue the family line, there was an overwhelming pressure for the state to maintain the strength of the adult male Spartan citizen community, a community of warriors for defence against the enemy within, the Helots, as much as attack on enemies without. Hence a number of features of Spartan society that would have struck other Greeks as distinctly odd, such as public penalties, including ritual humiliation by women at a religious festival, imposed upon adult men for late marriage, and, conversely, public benefits for fathers of three or more sons; the exemption of women who died in childbirth from the general prohibition against tombstones bearing the names of men or women; and, as we have seen, the absence of laws against adultery.

However, although adultery was not punished or even legally recognized, marriage was nevertheless considered a prerequisite for legitimacy of offspring, and only marriage between two Spartans was legally acceptable. Courting happened in the usual Greek way; that is, fathers of nubile girls were approached by interested potential husbands or their representatives. Heiresses whose fathers had failed to make provision for their marriage before they died were supposed to have their interests looked after by the kings, a sure sign of their crucial social importance. The actual marriage ceremony, however, was not at all normal by common Greek standards.

In the first place, it began with a rape – normally a purely symbolic and ritualized rape, no doubt, but the symbolism in itself was revealing of the potential for masculine violence and violation. In one famous case, we heard of a future Spartan king, Demaratus, who got his rape in first, as it were, by carrying off a girl already betrothed to another man, his distant cousin and future replacement as king, Leotychidas (*see* p. 103). Next, after the bride had been seized and somehow conveyed to the marital home of the husband, she was prepared by her female bridal attendant to receive her husband on the wedding-night. Preparation began with the shaving of the bride's head; thereafter as a married woman she had to keep it close cropped, and perhaps also was obliged to wear a veil in public. She was then clothed in a simple shift fastened by a belt, which the husband would unfasten before deflowering her. If the husband was under thirty when he married, as he perhaps normally would be, he was required still to live in barracks under full military discipline and could visit his wife only by sneaking away at night under cover of darkness. It was said that a Spartan husband might father several children before he saw his wife in daylight!

The ideal outcome of marital sex in Sparta was (to use the language of Mario Puzo's *Godfather*) a masculine child. This ideal was based partly on the traditional peasant patriarchal view of the superiority of the male and the desire of the father to reproduce himself as faithfully as possible, but it was also a tribute to the overriding military imperative in the peculiar conditions of ancient Spartan society. In a later age, the inhabitants of the Mani (the central southern prong of the Peloponnese) would refer to their sons as 'guns' for the same reason, so that male Maniotes were literally sons of a gun. Elsewhere in ancient Greece there are reasons for suspecting a quite high rate of female infanticide, but it is not possible to generalize that expectation to Sparta automatically. We do know, at any rate, of one very ill-favoured girl baby who was reared – though we hear of her because she grew to be extremely beautiful and eventually became the mother of King Demaratus. Her parents will not have been odd, on the other hand, in praying fervently to Helen that their daughter should grow up to be as beautiful as she.

Unlike their brothers, as we have noted, Spartan girls did not go to boarding school from the age of seven. They were educated, rather, at home, by their mothers and domestic Helots, but by no means exclusively so. For uniquely in Greece, they too experienced some sort of public educational programme, which – like that of the boys – focused heavily on the physical dimension. They ran, they jumped, they threw,

Spartan women had a lot to live up to in the awesome standard of physical beauty set by Helen. A series of fine Laconian-made bronze mirrors of the sixth century, found outside Laconia as well as inside (as here), suggests that they paid considerable attention to their looks. Such mirrors were typically dedicated in sanctuaries as offerings to a female divinity. One exceptional feature of the series is that some of the women were depicted completely naked, as Spartan females actually appeared in public in real life, whereas everywhere else in Greece it was the norm for respectable women at this period to be shown in art fully clothed (and seen in public as little as practically feasible).

and they wrestled, allegedly naked and with the boys, but that may well be more non-Spartan male fantasy than Spartan actuality. They also sang and danced, in distinctive and competitive ways. Dance competitions for girls are attested elsewhere in Greece too, but the Spartans cleverly turned girls' dancing to political ends. Selected girls, for example, were sent to dance for Artemis in Caryae, a Perioecic town on Sparta's north-eastern border.

At home in Sparta, competitive girls' choruses led to the invention of a new genre of Greek poetry, the *partheneion* or maiden-song. Its inventor was Alcman (*c*. 600 BC), a poet with deep lyric sensitivities and an unusually wide range of geographical reference (his mentions of Lydia prompted the ill-informed guess that he had been born in Sardis). The longest *partheneion* fragment we have by Alcman was found in Egypt written on papyrus. In this extract, the singers compete in singing the praises of their leaders, Hagesichora (which means simply 'chorus-leader') and Agido (a name suggesting a female member of the royal family of the Agiads):

> *Our purple finery is not*
> *the treasure that defends us,*
> *no coiled snake-bangle of solid gold,*
> *nor Lydian headband splendid upon girls*
> *with big dark eyes,*
> *nor Nanno's hair, no, nor nymphlike Areta,*
> *nor Thulacis, nor Clesithera...*
> *No, it's Hagesichora –*
> *she is my heart's desire.*
> *For her beauty of ankles is not here in the dance:*
> *she bides by Agido, commends*
> *our ceremonial.* [2]

Presumably such a song as this was sung originally at some religious festival, in honour of a specific goddess; though the precise identity of the goddess in question here remains uncertain, she is most likely to have been some version of Artemis, perhaps the local variant called Orthia, since *parthenoi* were virgins on the threshold of marriage, and Artemis was the goddess who oversaw the crucial transition from girlhood and virginity to marriage and motherhood. After marriage, a *parthenos* became first a *numphê* ('bride'), then a *gunê*. *Gunê* may be translated 'wife', but, like French *femme*, it also meant 'woman': the point was that every Spartan girl was expected to become a wife – and mother. Wifehood and motherhood were every Greek female's social as well as anatomical destiny – and nowhere was that emphasized more than in Sparta. The divine recipient of worship in connection with pregnancy and childbirth was Eileithyia, closely associated in Sparta as elsewhere with Artemis (Orthia).

So why the public educational cycle with its emphasis on the physical? There were probably two main reasons for it. One was pragmatic and secular: it was thought that the fittest mothers were, well, the fittest mothers – in other words, that physical fitness conduced directly to eugenic fitness. The other main reason was

In the sanctuary of Orthia, besides dedications to Orthia herself, have been found dedications to the local version of Eileithyia, a Greek divinity of childbirth. It is probably she who is depicted here, in the squatting childbirth position, accompanied on either side by two fertility spirits. Her left hand draws attention to the birth canal. For Spartan women, reproduction was a necessity not an option, and their education was geared to producing maximum eugenic fitness.

sociological and symbolic: Spartan females were not regarded as categorically inferior in the way that male outsiders such as Aristotle would ideally have wished. Young girls were given comparable food rations to those of the boys, adolescent girls went through a process of public education and socialization that imbued them with the society's ideals, to the realization of which their adult behaviour was absolutely crucial, and women could inherit, own and manage property in their own right. It is even possible that they had some say in their father's or guardian's choice of marriage partner, as they certainly did in the running of their home – or homes.

In many societies, women play a key religious role. The women of Sparta were no exception, but Sparta as a society was an exception in terms of Greek religious practice and attitudes, in several ways. The Spartans had the reputation for being unusually pious, even by ancient Greek standards, and they worked hard at maintaining that reputation. They were what we – or an ancient Athenian even – might call monumentally superstitious. Thus they were said, twice, by Herodotus to honour the things of the gods more highly than the things of men: since that was true of all Greeks, what he meant was that the Spartans took their piety and religious devotion to exceptional heights and lengths. He was prompted to this repeated observation by the fact that Sparta failed to turn up at all for the Battle of Marathon in 490, because the phase of the moon was deemed inauspicious, and did not send a full force to Thermopylae in 480, ostensibly because they were celebrating the Carneia festival.

Again, when Xenophon described the Spartans as 'craftsmen of war', he was referring specifically to military manifestations of their religious zeal, such as the animal sacrifices performed on crossing a river-frontier or even on the battlefield as battle was about to be joined. The Spartans were particularly keen on such military divination. If the signs (of a sacrificial animal's entrails) were not 'right', then even an imperatively necessary military action might be delayed, aborted, or avoided altogether. Xenophon records one Spartan commander as taking the omens no fewer than four times before the signs came out 'right'.

In addition to their exceptional piety or religiosity, the profile of the Spartans' religious observance was significantly skewed in comparison to what would have been considered normal practice elsewhere, in two key respects above all. Spartan women, like women elsewhere in Greece, played a leading role in Spartan public and private religion or quasi-religious manifestations. However, there were, apparently, no citizen women-only festivals at Sparta, not even the Thesmophoria in honour of Demeter, the fertility-giving earth mother goddess. Although Demeter did have her own shrine, an Eleusinion, on Spartan territory, it was not located in the town of Sparta itself, nor yet in Amyclae, but a notable distance further south. The nearest local equivalent to the Thesmophoria perhaps was the Tithenidia, a festival celebrating the nursing and nurturing of infants, but this was not a festival confined to Spartan women. A possible explanation for this de-emphasis on Demeter worship in Sparta was that the fertility of crops and animals was in the hands, not of Spartans, but of Helots. A similar explanation could be advanced for the second obtrusive religious abnormality, the curious lack of prominence of Dionysiac worship in Sparta – a staple of religious expression elsewhere in Greece, for both men and women. Again, this absence was presumably somehow connected to the fact that the fruit of the grapevine was produced by Helot labour.

Yet, as we have seen, young Spartan girls on the threshold of marriage sang and danced in competitive choruses, and as adult married women sang songs of scorn around an altar to shame reluctant Spartan bachelors into obeying the laws and taking a bride. The women seem also to have occupied an especially important place in the annual Hyacinthia festival in honour of Apollo and Hyacinthus. Xenophon in his biography of King Agesilaus II says that Agesilaus made a point of sending his daughters to the festival, which was celebrated at Amyclae several kilometres south of Sparta, in the usual public carriage used by the daughters of ordinary citizens, in order to minimize the social distance between his family and the rest of the citizens. The importance of making such a gesture at this major religious festival is the underlying message.

It was not, however, for their piety that Spartan women were best known outside Sparta. Apart from their shameful – or rather shameless – sexuality, what most transfixed outsiders' attention was the fact that they did not perform the absolutely standard Greek female role of weeping and wailing following a death in the family. In 371, in circumstances we shall describe in a later chapter, Sparta finally suffered a defeat in a pitched battle, a catastrophic defeat, at Leuctra in Boeotia. This is how Xenophon, who may actually have been present, reported the way that the Spartans back home reacted to the news:

> *It was on the last day of the Gymnopaediae festival that the messenger sent to report the catastrophe arrived in Sparta. The men's chorus was in the theatre at the time. When the Ephors heard what had happened, they were deeply grieved, as indeed they were bound to be. Yet instead of closing the performance, they allowed the chorus to continue to the end. When they gave the names of all the dead to the respective relatives, they instructed the women to bear their suffering in silence and to stifle any cries of lamentation. On the following day you could see those women whose relatives had been killed going about looking bright and cheerful, whereas those whose relatives had been reported as still alive were not much in evidence, and those few who were out and about were looking gloomy and sorry for themselves.*[3]

In other words, they did not weep and keen and beat their breasts in lamentation, they did not put on sackcloth and ashes, and they did not enter into a period of mourning, retreating to the innermost recesses of their houses. On the contrary. The show must go on. This is how

Spartan women ought to behave, and presumably had behaved, without needing to be told, for many years, possibly even centuries, before that.

The inconsistency, or contradiction, between Xenophon's picture here of Spartan women's behaviour and Aristotle's negative picture of their non-conformity need not be laboured. It is even tempting to follow the novelist Steven Pressfield in applying the Xenophontic line to the situation at the time of Thermopylae in 480. It is Pressfield's entirely original – and unfortunately entirely unsupported – notion that one of the major considerations guiding the choice of Leonidas' special bodyguard of 300 was the known character of their wives. Those men who were selected were those whose wives could be counted on to not just grin and bear the inevitable death of their husband but laugh and make a happy song and dance about it.

Let us conclude this chapter with the paradigmatic example of an individual, named Spartan mother. Among the so-called *Apophthegms* attributed to Spartan women, in a collection of that title that has come down to us in the works of Plutarch, the first is credited to Argileonis ('lion-bright'), mother of Brasidas. It makes this precisely same point about Spartan women's dutiful subservience to their society's norms, if in a rather different way:

> *Argileonis, mother of Brasidas, when her son had died, and some of the citizens of Amphipolis came to Sparta to visit her, asked them whether her son had died finely and as befitted a Spartan. When they praised him to the skies and told her that he was the best of all the Spartans in such deeds of valour, she replied: 'My friends, it is true that my child was a fine and good man, but Sparta has many men better than he.'* [4]

The full force of that alleged remark derives from the fact that, unlike his self-abnegating mother, the Amphipolitans literally worshipped Brasidas as their founder-hero after his death, as something more than a mere mortal man.

There is not enough evidence, unfortunately, to write any sort of biography of Argileonis (as there is of Gorgo – *see* Chapter 3, and of Cynisca – *see* Chapter 7), since apart from this anecdote we know nothing about her except that she was married to one Tellis. Given that he was part of the official Spartan delegation to Athens in 421 that concluded first a general peace and then a separate treaty with Athens, Tellis may well have been a member of the Gerousia and thus a man of distinguished aristocratic family. However, Argileonis, like King Agesilaus when he insisted on his daughters travelling to a major religious festival in the regular public carriage, was concerned rather to de-emphasize any special difference or distinction that her family undoubtedly bore. She can therefore stand as an emblem of Spartan womanhood.

Other *Apophthegms* flesh out the ancient picture of Spartan mothers, attributing to them colourful language and equally colourful gestures. We can thus well imagine Argileonis urging Brasidas, as he set off for Amphipolis in 422, to return from battle, 'With your shield – or on it!' Or, supposing Brasidas had *per impossibile* proved to be a coward and returned home alive but defeated, we can visualize Argileonis pointing to her womb and asking her son publicly and humiliatingly if he wanted to crawl back inside there. Of such awesomely stern stuff were Spartan mothers made.

6

THE ATHENIAN WAR
432–404 BC

This chapter will deal with what, seen from the Athenian standpoint, is conventionally called the Peloponnesian War, but it will be viewed and described here from the Spartan side. Hence the unfamiliar title, 'the Athenian War', which is the ancient Greek way of saying 'the war against the Athenians'. The conflict was begun by the Spartans with high but misplaced hopes, and was ended finally, twenty-seven years later, only when the Spartans came to an arrangement for financial reasons with the Greeks' old enemy, the Persians. However, the latter had their own quite separate motives for wanting to destroy the power of Athens and they used the Spartans merely as a cat's-paw. This cynical manoeuvring, of which all parties concerned were equally guilty, was to poison Greek inter-state relations from then until the conquest of Greece by Macedon under Philip II and his son Alexander the Great, who then went on quite extraordinarily to conquer all the Persian Empire as well.

The Spartans' strategy for winning the Athenian War was in a sense null and void from the start. Imprisoned in their hoplite mentality, which had after all served them exceptionally well for over two centuries, they imagined that straightforward application of more of the same would do the trick. They believed that, simply by invading Athens' home territory of Attica by land in the early summer shortly before the grain harvest, they either would compel the Athenians to come out from behind their city walls to fight for their grainland, and be inevitably defeated in pitched hoplite battle, or would destroy the Athenians' harvest, thereby threatening them with starvation and compelling them eventually to sue for peace on humiliating terms. Or, to be more exact, the vast majority of Spartans believed that. King Archidamus, who tried to dissuade them from an immediate declaration of war in 432, almost certainly did not. How right he was proved to be.

For, as Pericles, following his mentor Themistocles, had long ago foreseen, such a Spartan strategy would by itself be inconclusive, because Athens was in effect a sort of island and not dependent for its population's survival on home-grown grain. It was isolated and insulated, thanks to the so-called Long Walls that linked the city of Athens to its port – virtually a second city, in fact – of Piraeus and to Phaleron; and it was not dependent entirely, or indeed for the most part, on home-grown grain, because Attica could feed at best only about 75,000 people (chiefly with barley, less desirable and nutritious than wheat), and Attica's population was then in the range of 250–300,000. The remaining 200,000-plus were fed on grain imported both directly from the Athenian-controlled north Aegean island of Lemnos and, above all, through the trade in grain from what are today the Ukraine and Crimea, supplemented by supplies from Cyprus and north Africa as necessary, available and affordable. In other words, as long as Athens through its overwhelming sea-power retained control of the vital bottlenecks of the Bosporus and the Hellespont (Dardanelles), its principal supply of wheat from the north shore of the Black Sea was safe and Athens was not in imminent danger of starvation, even should the Spartans manage to destroy all the grain-crops of Attica in any one campaigning season.

Actually, the destruction of grain-crops was not all that easy a task. The grain had to be dry enough to be combustible, and the ravaging Peloponnesian troops both had to be equipped with sufficient tinder and firewood, and protected from counter-attacks from the Athenians. They also had to be able to live off the land while they were doing the ravaging, to eke out the relatively meagre food supplies they were able to bring from home. This formidable combination of technical obstacles meant that the longest stay of any Peloponnesian expedition in Attica during the Athenian war was in fact a mere forty days. That was not enough time to ravage significantly, let alone entirely destroy, anything like all the grain crops of Attica, not to mention the grape-vines and olives (olive-trees are anyway virtually indestructible). Far more successful a strategy would have been for the Spartans to occupy a position permanently within Athens' home territory, garrison it, and then use it both to conduct raids there from on to surrounding land and even to prevent local Athenian farmers from farming at all. Eventually, that strategy was indeed adopted by the Spartans, but not until 413, and then only after taking advice from a renegade Athenian (Alcibiades). As we shall see, this strategy had one further devastating effect on the Athenians' economy, though even so it did not by itself end the war in Sparta's favour.

So, with the Spartans' only strategy to begin with pretty much ineffectual, the Athenians were free to respond offensively and heavily in other ways, both by land and by sea. Thucydides, because he wanted to emphasize the foresight and wisdom of Pericles, and to exonerate the Athenians from any blame for starting this disastrous international conflict, represented their counter-strategy as overwhelmingly defensive. Being the good historian he was, Thucydides did also mention the fact that twice each campaigning season the Athenians made hoplite forays by land into the territory of neighbouring Megara, an important member of Sparta's Peloponnesian League, and he did describe the large naval expeditions that the Athenians launched against the eastern Peloponnese in the early years of the war. By 428, therefore, when the Spartans sought to lead their allies for a second time into Athenian territory in the same season, war-weariness had already begun to set in among the Peloponnesians. The Spartans should not have needed the Mytilenaeans (seeking Spartan help for their projected revolt from Athens) to tell them during the Olympic Games in 428 that the war would not be won in Attica, but in the lands (the Crimea, Ukraine and so on) by which Attica was supplied with foreign wheat, etc. Yet they apparently did need to be told that, as they certainly failed to act on the advice.

Instead, the Spartans found the boot uncomfortably on the other foot. They had started the war in 431, having first confirmed with Apollo at Delphi that they would be in the right if they did so, and it was therefore for them to be seen to win the war and defeat the Athenians convincingly. So far was that from being the case after six years of conflict that, in the summer of 425, the Athenians under Demosthenes established a base camp actually within Sparta's own home territory of Messenia, at Pylos on the west coast (near what was later to be called Navarino, site of the great sea-battle of 1829).

In 425 the Athenians accepted the surrender of 292 Lacedaemonians, 120 of them Spartans, on the islet of Sphacteria near Pylos in western Messenia and then held them as hostages in Athens until 421. Along with the men they took captive their arms and armour, and of these the bronze facing of one shield has been excavated in the Agora (civic centre) of Athens, not far from where the men were held prisoner. On the shield was traced this message: 'The Athenians [took and dedicated this] from the Lacedaemonians at Pylos'.

Demosthenes cunningly had brought with him Messenians, or rather soldiers of Messenian descent, from the city of Naupactus that the Athenians had helped to establish as a refuge for liberated ex-Helots during the great post-earthquake revolt of the 460s. These Naupactian Messenians, together with new Messenian Helot escapees attracted to the Athenians' Pylos base, managed to cause havoc and destruction on the Spartans' Messenian farms, not least because they could speak the language – that is, they could all pass as loyal Helots in order to murder any Helots who preferred to stay genuinely loyal to their Spartan masters, and to do damage to their crops and other possessions.

The Spartans of course reacted instantly to this devastating news. They recalled the army of invasion from Attica, and they sent a roving task force of elite soldiers immediately to the Pylos area. They also, after some delay, sent a fleet. Included in this was a trireme war-ship commanded by Brasidas, who according to Thucydides was the combatant who 'most distinguished himself' in a fruitless seaborne assault on the Athenians' stockade. For the next three years until his death in 422, Brasidas was to be the major source of Athens' difficulties both in the Peloponnese and as far north as Amphipolis in Chalcidice. So influential had he become by then that it required his removal from the scene by death before the Spartans were willing or able to proceed with vigour along the path of peace-making.

BRASIDAS

Brasidas is, thanks above all to the keen interest taken in him by Thucydides, one of the very few non-royal Spartans to whom any sort of proper biographical treatment can be given. His name may be derived ultimately from that of the town of Prasiae, on the north-east coast of Laconia, which before it became a Perioecic city was a member of an amphictyony, or religious league, based on the island of Calaurea (modern Poros). That would have been back in the seventh century BC. Brasidas' parents' names are, unusually, both known. His father Tellis was one of the distinguished Spartans chosen to negotiate the terms of peace and alliance with Athens in 421, to conclude the Athenian War. His mother Argileonis we have also already met, since she is exceptionally attributed with an apophthegm in the Plutarchan collection of *Apophthegms*.

Her saying as quoted there (*see* Chapter 5), whatever its literal authenticity, was designed to make two points: that even a citizen as distinguished as her son Brasidas was by no means a rarity in Sparta, and that exemplary Spartan mothers such as Argileonis were more interested in the common good of Sparta than in glorifying their own immediate family members. Yet in reality there were few if any Spartans more able and effective, or more respected outside Sparta, than Brasidas, both in his lifetime and after his death. Had he lived longer, he might well have qualified for a biography by Plutarch, as did the only non-royal Spartan to make the grade, Lysander.

Brasidas was one of the board of five Ephors in 431, when the Athenian War broke out. This can hardly have been accidental or coincidental. Would-be Ephors were not supposed to canvass for office, but it would have been odd if the men who chose – or were permitted – to stand for election at that crucial time were not known to be 'hawks', that is, rock-solid opponents of the Athenians and advocates of immediate hostilities against them. Everything known of Brasidas' subsequent career confirms that profile. He next turns up in 430 in Methone on the western coast of Messenia where he led a mobile defence force. The following year, 429, he seems to have been promoted, since he is found serving as a fleet commissioner in Cyllene in the northwest Peloponnese; he was still there in 427. Guarding the 'northwest passage', that is, preventing the Athenians from sailing round the Peloponnese to link up with the Naupactian Messenians and other potential or actual allies in the Ionian islands, or resisting them if they did, was clearly regarded as a high priority by the

Spartans. Brasidas thus found himself assisting the Spartan admiral of the fleet in connection with the particularly vicious fighting, including the civil war memorably described and analysed by Thucydides, on Corcyra (Corfu) that summer.

This precautionary action nevertheless did not foreclose the Athenian initiative under Demosthenes in seizing and garrisoning Pylos in Messenia in 425. Brasidas predictably was dispatched to this critical scene, by now the commander of a trireme. His conduct was said to be the most distinguished of any, but Pylos as a whole was a disaster for the Spartans, and there was a desperate need for diversionary measures that would restore the Spartans' flagging morale at home and reputation abroad. The problem of Megara, where there was a strong pro-Athenian and possibly democratic tendency, was a suitable case for treatment by Brasidas, who in 424 did indeed prevent the city from slipping over into the Athenian camp, but he had far fatter fish to fry further north.

In 426 the Spartans had established a new military colony in central Greece, Heraclea in Trachis. The mainly military and strategic purpose of this new settlement was clear from the start. From here, the Spartans could put pressure on Athens' control of Euboea. Through here, the way led to the north from allied Boeotia into Thessaly, Macedonia and the Thracian Chalcidice. Brasidas was allowed to recruit an army of distinctively new composition, which reveals his peculiar genius and gives the lie to the claim that all Spartans were by definition, and social habituation, immovably conservative in their thinking. To supplement the Peloponnesian League allied hoplites, he was given money to recruit mercenaries; these had been present in Greek warfare from early times, but it was only during the Athenian War and more especially immediately after it that they began to take centre stage. Then, on top of the Peloponnesians and mercenaries, he was provided with a force of 700 Helots, armed as hoplites by the Spartans. Those who survived were eventually manumitted on their return to Sparta, but their distinct status is signified by their collective tag 'the Brasideans' or 'Brasidas' men'. This seems also to betoken a special bond between men and commander, and it was as 'Brasideans' that these soldiers fought later in the ranks of the regular Spartan army at the Battle of Mantinea in 418, four years after Brasidas' death.

Brasidas interestingly is said to have had special friends among the cities and communities of Thessaly. These contacts enabled him to make a safe passage through Thessaly and on into Macedonia and Chalcidice. The latter was his real objective, since it was here that Athens had as recently as 437 established a wholly new colony called Amphipolis. Amphipolis both guarded key land routes across the northern Aegean littoral and also gave Athens access to timber and metals that were vital to its naval war-effort. Imagine therefore the consternation in Athens as Brasidas succeeded in winning over to his support, first King Perdiccas of Macedon and then a succession of the Greek cities along the northern Aegean coast. He accomplished this partly by threat of force but also, surprisingly for a Spartan, by his oratorical eloquence. Thucydides pays tribute to this quality not only by referring to his skill explicitly but also by writing for him two brief (suitably laconic!) set speeches. The historian had, however, a rather embarrassingly personal reason for not wanting to diminish Brasidas' image unduly: Thucydides in 424 was one of the ten elected Athenian generals, and his special brief was to prevent Brasidas from getting hold of Amphipolis. This, alas, he signally failed to do.

So greatly did the 'liberated' Amphipolitans respect Brasidas that after he was killed in battle there in 422 they made him their new oecist, or founder-hero, and paid him the due religious honours that his station in death merited. To put it another way, they disinherited their true oecist, Hagnon of Athens, in a gesture that perfectly illustrates the complete solidarity of religion and politics in ancient Greece. Nor were the Amphipolitans the only Greeks in the region to feel so strongly towards Brasidas. The men of Scione (in the words of Thucydides)

welcomed Brasidas with all possible honours. They crowned him publicly with a wreath of gold, as the

*liberator of all Greece, and private citizens crowded
round him and decked him with garlands as though he
had been a victorious athlete.*[1]

Only Potidaea, which the Athenians had succeeded in preventing from
seceding after a long and bitter siege from 432 to 429, remained impervious to Brasidas' blandishments, but that was enough to halt Brasidas'
victorious progress in the region, and that setback, coupled with envy
from rivals back home, led to a switch of Spartan policy from aggression
to peacemaking.

Brasidas, however, was having no truck with the armistice concluded
in 423, any more than would Cleon of Athens, the politician who had
most contributed to and most exploited Sparta's humiliation at Pylos in
425. So in 422 the two of them, like Homeric champions, squared up
to each other on the battlefield outside the walls of Amphipolis. They
did not actually kill each other, but both did die in the conflict and that
opened the way to a renewal of peacemaking. Amphipolis, however,
never returned to the Athenian fold, and that was perhaps Brasidas'
most lasting monument.

What Brasidas saw was the Spartans' need to open a second front, in
the north, to destabilize Athens' alliance from within. Already in 426
the Spartans had planted the new colony of Heraclea in Trachis, which
lay *en route* to Athens' important allies in the Thraceward region,
Amphipolis chief among them. After the Pylos affair of 425, with Pylos
still firmly in Athenian hands, the need for a second-front initiative
was all the greater. It was a mark of Sparta's desperation that Brasidas
was allowed to recruit the mixed force of allied hoplites, mercenaries,
and Helots.

It is important to stress that these Helots were recruited and fought
as Helots, as had their predecessors such as those who fought at Plataea
in 479. However, such was the effect of the Pylos crisis that from 424

onwards the Spartans for the first time resorted to a deliberate policy of offering manumission as an incentive for loyal military service. Those of Brasidas' Helots who survived to return to Sparta were therefore liberated and joined other ex-Helots who had been granted the new status of Neodamodeis, or 'New Damos-men', who appear in the sources between 424 and 370. No doubt these were mainly if not wholly drawn from the Laconian as opposed to the Messenian Helots, in line with the Spartans' traditional divide-and-rule policies, but their recruitment marked a significant new twist to Spartan–Helot relations, as well as providing the Spartans with an entirely new kind of troops for overseas service, whether fighting in the field or on garrison duty. Indeed, Neodamodeis were far easier for the Spartans to cope with abroad than they were at home, where they formed a sort of undigested lump, being neither still unfree Helots nor yet fully integrated as free and equal citizens into the ranks of the Peers.

Brasidas at first prospered in the north, most signally by winning over Amphipolis from Athens and garrisoning it in the Spartan interest, but Brasidas' success also excited both envy from rivals within the ranks of the Spartan elite, and genuine concern that his initiative might be inaugurating a new style of overseas imperialism for which Sparta was ill suited. There was, besides, a group around King Pleistoanax (who had finally been recalled to the Agiad throne in 427/6 from an eighteen-year exile in Arcadia) who were peacemakers on principle. They either believed in the 'dual hegemony' thesis of Athens–Sparta relations espoused by Cimon in an earlier generation, or they were non-interventionist – or at least more *laissez-faire* – in their attitude towards Peloponnesian League allies. It was a combination of these forces that led to the conclusion of an armistice in 423.

This was an armistice that Brasidas and his bellicose counterpart at Athens, Cleon, did all they could to undermine, and successfully so, up to the point when both men were killed in renewed fighting around Amphipolis in 422. The way was then open for the conclusion of what is conventionally known, after its principal Athenian architect, as the

Peace of Nicias, but which could just as accurately be called the Peace of Pleistoanax. The Peace of course affected all the allies on either side, but it was concluded essentially by the two principals without much serious attention to the special needs or desires of individual allies. That led to some of Sparta's most important allies, Corinth and Elis among them, not only refusing to ratify the Peace but joining in an anti-Spartan *entente* to try to compel the Spartans to take their interests into account too. In the wings, as ever, the Argives waited to see how this disaffection could be turned to suit their perennial urge to be number one in the Peloponnese.

The Spartans' response was to conclude a fifty-year non-aggression pact with the Athenians, separately from all the allies on either side. The chief motivation of this new treaty was to try to secure two of the most pressing immediate objectives of the Peace agreement, the return of Pylos and some 300 Spartan and Perioecic hostages from Athens, and the return of Amphipolis to Athens. This pact, however, only increased the suspicion of the Corinthians and Eleans, though the Boeotian cities led by Thebes refused to join the *entente* since it seemed to their governments that they stood a better chance of remaining in power under the wing of traditionally pro-oligarchic Sparta. On the other hand, they remained steadfastly opposed to the Peace of Nicias, and received rather surprising support from two of the new board of Ephors for 420, who belonged to the bellicose tendency represented by the late Brasidas.

The Athenians did hand back the hostages, but they did not receive back Amphipolis in return; so Sparta did not get back Pylos. The Spartan warhawks were in the ascendancy, aided and abetted by the new kid on the Athenian block, Alcibiades. By his very name, Alcibiades exhibited his links with Sparta, since the name was originally a Spartan one that had been introduced into our Alcibiades' aristocratic patriline via a cross-state *xenia* relationship. Alcibiades had been born about 450, but his father had died when he was very young and he had been brought up in the household of his father's friend Pericles and the latter's new partner Aspasia. In such a politicized home environment, Alcibiades' public ambitions will have been kindled early, and in his late twenties, the earliest age considered suitable in Athens, Alcibiades made his first, botched attempt to cut a figure on the public stage. This involved him in trying to resume the *proxenia*, or public representation, of Sparta that had been held by his grandfather, but the ageist Spartans had rebuffed him, and in angry response Alcibiades had, for the time being, promoted a vigorous anti-Spartan line, persuading the Athenians to do all they could against Sparta short of openly breaking the Peace, and the alliance, of 421 and actually fighting Sparta.

In 418, however, the logical conclusion of this anti-Spartan activity was reached at the Battle of Mantinea, where Athens with its democratic allies of Argos and the rebel Peloponnesian city of Mantinea took on the might of Sparta and her Peloponnesian League hoplites. Thucydides, the Athenian War's historian, properly devoted a large portion of his work to this encounter, adding a number of telling explanatory details for his non-Spartan audience or readership. For example, as the battle was about to commence, the Athenian side started edging to the right – as was typical of all hoplite armies, Thucydides says:

> *because fear makes each man do his best to shelter his*
> *unarmed right side with the shield of the man next to him,*
> *thinking that the closer the shields are locked together*
> *the better will he be protected.*

Then, when the two sides advanced to begin the fighting, whereas the Argives and their allies advanced in a headlong rush full of sound and fury, the Spartans moved forward slowly and to the music of many *aulos*-players. This, Thucydides adds, was:

> *a standing institution in their army, that has nothing to do*
> *with religion. Rather, it is intended to make them advance*

evenly, and in time, without breaking their order, as large armies customarily do at the moment of engagement. [2]

The Spartans, as we have seen from a reading of Herodotus' account of their behaviour at the time of Marathon and later in the Persian Wars, were known to be exceptionally pious. The *aulos*, a reed instrument something like our oboe perhaps, was used by the Greeks in the performance of religious rituals and ceremonies, for example to accompany performances of tragic drama at Athens. It would therefore have been easy for observers of the scene at Mantinea in 418 to put two and two together and make...five, assuming that the Spartans used *aulos* accompaniment for religious reasons. Not so, retorts Thucydides: its use was purely functional – just as functional, he might have added, and adopted for precisely the same reason, as the music played on an Athenian trireme warship by the *trieraulês*, the member of the supernumerary crew who played the *aulos* to help the rowers keep their oarstrokes in time.

What Thucydides does not add, because he did not need to in the context, was that these Spartan *aulêtai* were members of an honoured hereditary guild, 'the sons of fathers who followed the same profession', as Herodotus had phrased it. As such, they were on a par with the hereditary Spartan citizen heralds and ritual sacrificers. In fact, music in general occupied an honoured place in Spartan culture and society. Among the early composers and poets named by Plutarch, in his essay *On Music*, as having achieved fame outside their immediate locality, was one Xenodamus of Perioecic Cythera. The finds from the sanctuary of Artemis Orthia include fragments of *auloi* made out of animal bone, some inscribed, and dedications of humble lead figurines representing both *aulos*-players and players of the *kithara*, a form of lyre. The conservative Spartans were supposed to have been very strict with *kithara*-players who played around with the canonical number of strings. Besides playing instruments, the Spartans were also particularly keen on choral singing; Pratinas of Elis amusingly likened every Spartan to a cicada – always seeking a chorus. Also, as we have seen, Alcman of Sparta invented one particular form of Greek choral singing, the *partheneion*, or maiden-song.

The word *choros* in Greek originally meant dance, so the Spartans were often to be found literally making a song and dance. In fact, they were credited with a number of peculiar local dances, including some that were frankly obscene. When, in about 575 BC, an Athenian aristocrat got a little too emotional during a contest for the hand of the daughter of a Peloponnesian tyrant, he is said to have lapsed into performing some Spartan dances on a table-top, perhaps becoming the original table dancer. All such performances were considered within the sphere of the divine Muses, so formally they contradict the ancient myth-image of Sparta according to which the practical Spartans would have no truck with the higher arts. However, it is only fair to end this digression by mentioning the handsome bronze figurine of a trumpeter, dedicated to the state's patron goddess Athena on the Spartan acropolis in about 500 BC. He clearly was intended to represent a figure who, in the real situation of hoplite warfare, after the *aulos*-players had piped their men into battle, played a vital role in signalling the wishes of the Spartan commander.

The Battle of Mantinea was hard-fought and close, 'the greatest battle that had occurred among the Greeks for a very long time' in the words of Thucydides. In the end it was a decisive victory for the Spartans:

> *The aspersions cast upon them by the Greeks at the time,*
> *whether of cowardice on account of the disaster at Pylos*
> *or of incompetence and slowness generally, were all erased*
> *by this one action. Fortune, it was thought, might have humbled*
> *them, but the men themselves were the same as ever.* [3]

That was strictly not quite accurate. First, the Spartan citizens, the men of the messes, had for the first time been tried and tested in a major pitched battle fighting in mixed regiments brigaded alongside Perioecic hoplites. Second, apart from the mixed Spartan–Perioecic regiments the Spartans had relied on a special force of Perioeci drawn from the northern frontier district of Laconia called Sciritis. Perhaps they had been recruited and deployed before, but this is their first mention in the literature and their recruitment probably speaks for a newly awakened concern for frontier security. Then, third and by no means least, the Spartans for the first time made use in regular line of battle of ex-Helot hoplites, the Brasideioi and the Neodamodeis. So it was really a new model Spartan army that had won the Battle of Mantinea, however much the Spartans might have wanted the outside world to think otherwise.

Defeat here was sufficient to compel a strategic rethink on the part of the Athenians. Again led by, or under the spell of, the maverick Alcibiades, the Athenian Assembly in 415 was persuaded to open a whole new front, or rather embark on a separate war from the Athenian War, though the two were to intersect in due course, fatally for the Athenians. In 415 the Athenians launched an armada to conquer as much of the island of Sicily as they could, taking the city of Syracuse as their principal enemy and target. Syracuse had been founded in the third quarter of the eighth century, by settlers from Dorian Corinth. It had experienced a period of rule by tyrants and then, since the 460s, gone democratic. One of the leading themes of Thucydides' memorable account of the Sicilian campaign of 415 to 413 is the similarity between the two major antagonists, Syracuse and Athens.

Again, like the Battle of Mantinea, the contest in Sicily was desperately close, and the result went against Athens. A leading player in Athens' catastrophe was Alcibiades, first as the expedition's prime advocate and then, once the Athenians had been persuaded to recall him to face a charge of sacrilege, as his city's betrayer, for Alcibiades escaped from the ship sent to bring him back to stand trial in Athens and made his way to, of all places, Sparta. Colourful anecdotes were spread of his going native and becoming more Spartan than the

Spartans, even to the extent of allegedly seducing the wife of King Agis II in his absence and fathering a son by her, but the sober truth was colourful enough for the Athenians' taste. Alcibiades, in the best position to advise the Spartans how and where to exploit Athens' weak spots, had gone for the jugular. It was on his advice, reportedly, that the Spartans first sent out an enterprising Spartan commander, Gylippus, to bolster the Syracusans' ultimately successful resistance to the Athenian siege, and then in 413 permanently occupied and garrisoned a position at Decelea well within the frontier of Athens' home territory.

The *epiteichismos* (hostile fortification) at Decelea in 413 under King Agis represented the opening of the final phase of the Athenian War by land. It was, however, by sea, paradoxically for the normally landlubbing Spartans, that the War was to be decided, and thanks, crucially, to funds supplied by Athens' old enemy Persia through Great King Darius II's two western satraps, Pharnabazus in the north, and Tissaphernes in the south. With Persian gold, the Spartans built up a fleet that could at first match and later even outmatch the hitherto invincible Athenian navies.

Alcibiades, tiring of Sparta (or perhaps hounded out by friends of a cuckolded King Agis), turned up in the eastern theatre, once more causing harm to his native city's cause at first, but by 411 he seems to have preferred to be a prophet with honour again in his own country. Athens in that year underwent an internal revolution, from democracy to extreme oligarchy, masterminded by an intellectual called Antiphon for whom Thucydides expressed unusual respect. The hoplites of Athens were at first in favour of this oligarchic counter-revolution, but the fleet, which was manned by the poorest and most democratically minded Athenians, remained resolutely opposed. The fleet's main Aegean base was the island of Samos, and it was here that representatives of the new oligarchic regime at Athens came to try to persuade the fleet to sail away back to the Piraeus. Alcibiades happened to be on Samos, realized that such a departure would cost Athens its control of the sea, and persuaded the fleet's commanders to remain at their Samos base. This, Thucydides comments acerbically, was the first real service that Alcibiades had done for his city.

Even so, despite a number of successes which enabled Athens to retain control of the all-important Hellespont narrows, the Athenian fleet was powerless to prevent a number of rebellions and defections within the Athenian naval alliance. Prominent among these were the revolts of the island cities of Euboea, Chios and Thasos, in 411, and, though the Athenians did bring Euboea for the time being back within their alliance, they were unable to restore either Chios or Thasos. Eventually, of its major allies, only Samos itself, firmly in the hands of a militantly pro-Athenian democracy, remained loyal. However, that was not enough to counter the crucial combination forged in 407 of the Persian prince Cyrus, younger son of Darius II (reigned 425–404), and the remarkable Spartan Lysander.

LYSANDER

Lysander – *Lusandros* in Greek – is the first, and almost the last, of the Spartans selected for individual biographical treatment in this book who was already the subject of a biography in antiquity. However, this was not a contemporary biography, or anything like contemporary: Plutarch wrote his *Life of Lysander* some five centuries after Lysander's death, in the almost unimaginably different conditions of the early Roman Empire. Plutarch's general biographical project was to make the new Roman world comprehensible, for his now humble or rather humbled Greek countrymen, by writing a series of parallel lives of great Greeks and Romans. The Greeks chosen as subjects were all more or less 'ancient' to Plutarch's immediate audience and readership, but some of his Roman subjects were a lot more contemporary than that. Julius Caesar, for example, had been assassinated in 44 BC, less than a century before Plutarch's birth (in AD 46).

Plutarch paid Lysander the handsome compliment of not only select-ing him as a suitably great and exemplary biographical subject but also paralleling him with Sulla, the Roman dictator of the late eighties and early seventies BC. Sulla was a larger-than-life figure who had trans-formed the map of the Roman Empire and the shape of the Roman republican constitution, both mainly to fit in with his own desires and self-image. He acquired the nickname 'Lucky' and somehow managed to die of natural causes after voluntarily resigning his dictatorship and retiring to spend more time with his family. Lysander, by contrast, never became a dictator of any empire and died rather ingloriously on cam-paign in Boeotia (Plutarch's own native region).

Plutarch had his reasons for writing his *Life* as a parallel to that of Sulla, but they do not in any way advance our understanding of Lysander's career. Apart from Plutarch, our other main source on Lysander is the contemporary historian Xenophon of Athens, who knew him personally, but Xenophon was a partisan of King Agesilaus, who as we shall see fell out very viciously with Lysander at the end, so that his account – which Plutarch of course also used – has to be read with no less caution.

Lysander was, according to tradition, a *mothax*; that is, he was said to have been a Spartan citizen by adoption, brought up in the house-hold of a Spartan other than his father and put through the Agoge with the son or sons of that other Spartan. If that tradition is correct, Lysander could have had a Helot mother rather than being the son of his father's Spartan wife, or his father could have been too poor to raise him, though he was legitimately born. The latter seems the more likely to me, since Lysander's father Aristocritus is reported to have been

Lysander (who died in 395 BC) belonged, just, to the age of genuine Greek portraiture, but no portrait of him has reliably survived from antiquity, though he was vain enough to have a bronze statue of himself included together with Olympian gods led by Poseidon in a massive triumphal group at Delphi in or soon after 404. Therefore this frontispiece by J. Chapman to a book published in London in 1807 by J. Wilkes is, alas (or perhaps fortunately), sheer imag-inative fantasy. The gross anachronism of the armour is palpable, even without the addition of a curiously tailed lion on the top of the helmet.

J. Chapman sculp.

poor, although he was a member of the Heraclid aristocracy and his other son was named Libys, 'Libyan', in honour of a high-status *xenia*-relationship with a Libyan prince. On the other hand, in aristocratic and slave-societies births 'on the wrong side of the blanket' are hardly unknown, so Lysander's mother could well have been a Helot woman belonging to his father's household.

The details of Lysander's childhood and adolescence, apart from his alleged *mothax* status, are a blank to us. But when he first makes his appearance as more than just making up the numbers of full Spartan citizens, it is within a peculiarly Spartan context of erotics and pedagogy. Somewhere around 430 BC, when Lysander was in his mid-twenties perhaps, he managed to become the lover of one of the most eligible of Sparta's adolescents then going through the Agoge, none other than Agesilaus, the younger son of reigning King Archidamus II. Agesilaus as the son of Archidamus' second marriage was not expected to succeed to the Eurypontid throne and therefore was not exempted from the Agoge, as the crown prince Agis (the future Agis II) had been. In fact, it was something of a surprise, in two senses, that Agesilaus was able even to go through the Agoge: he had been born lame, which might have qualified him only for exposure as an infant and thus an early death, and yet despite his lameness he performed all the demanding physical tasks set by the Agoge with triumphant success.

Lysander therefore, who presumably had needed to win and keep Agesilaus' favours against fierce competition from other possibly more distinguished suitors, considerably enhanced had in doing so, both his own immediate prestige and his future political leverage.

Lysander presumably had a 'good' Athenian War. We know absolutely nothing about what he did in it until 407, by which time he was probably in his late forties. This was old enough by age-worshipping Spartan standards to qualify him for the supreme command by sea, an office open to all Spartans that was judged to be on a par with the generalship by land for which only Spartan kings were eligible. In 407 Lysander was appointed Nauarchos, or Admiral of the Fleet, a fleet that by then was very far from being just the usual puny flotilla that Sparta by itself could or would muster. Lysander's assurance, political acumen and general indispensability in overall naval command were such that, although the law forbade it, in 405 he was once again dispatched to the Aegean theatre as *de facto* Admiral of the Fleet. In this capacity, with crucial financial aid from his personal friend the Persian prince Cyrus, Lysander finally brought the twenty-seven-year Athenian War to a crunching end.

However, according to the traditional rules of the Spartan political game, it was the kings, not even a commander as powerful as Lysander, who held the key cards. So, although Lysander at first had his way in the postwar settlement with Athens, seeing to it that it was shackled by a pro-Spartan oligarchic junta backed by a Spartan garrison, while others of Athens' former allies and subjects were placed under the control of very narrow regimes of his own partisans, within a couple of years of Athens' defeat the new Spartan Empire was no longer being ruled on precisely his terms. This was thanks above all to the opposition of the Agiad King Pausanias, son of the peacemaking Pleistoanax, and notwithstanding the support Lysander could have expected to receive from Pausanias' rival and hostile co-king Agis II. In 403 Pausanias was put on trial in Sparta, on a charge of treason brought no doubt by Agis, but he was acquitted, largely because all five Ephors supported his relatively more liberal policy of minimal interference in the internal affairs of the former member states of the Athenian Empire, above all Athens itself.

Lysander's failure to dominate counsels at home will have been all the more galling by comparison with the paroxysm of personal success and hero-worship that he enjoyed abroad, above all on the island of Samos, where his partisans took a step unprecedented in all Greek history. They paid him divine honours, worshipping a living mortal man as though he were an immortal god, and renaming the Heraea, their principal religious festival (held for their patron goddess Hera), the Lysandrea in his honour. At Delphi, the very epicentre of Greek religion, Lysander went as near as he dared to having that quasi-immortal status enshrined permanently in a public monument. He commissioned – and paid for out of his huge naval spoils of war – a vast sculptural feature, to be sited prominently near the entrance to Delphi's Sacred Way, consisting of a forest of bronze statues, both human and divine. All the twelve Olympian gods and goddesses were represented there, and at the centre of them Poseidon god of the sea, depicted in the act of awarding Lysander a victor's crown.

Lysander would have done well to recall the sage advice of the praise-singer Simonides to another Spartan panhellenic military victor, Regent Pausanias: never forget that you are a mortal man. From that height, there was only one way for him to go, down, but he was by no means an entirely spent force yet. In about 400 a further opportunity arose for him to assert himself again at the head of Spartan affairs. By then, his Persian friend Cyrus was dead, having got himself killed in an attempt to usurp the Persian throne from his older brother Artaxerxes II; and Sparta was again at war with Persia, this time as heir to Athens' Empire and position of imperial champion of Hellenism against the oriental barbarian. There was plenty of scope therefore for throwing his weight around on the international stage, and the death of Agis gave Lysander the idea that he might regain power, vicariously, by championing the claim to the Eurypontid throne of his former beloved Agesilaus and in effect ruling Sparta through him.

His support for Agesilaus did indeed prove decisive in the unseemly contest for the throne. Lysander was able to persuade the relevant Spartans that the dire consequences for Sparta of a lame kingship prophesied by some oracle would not come from appointing the physically lame Agesilaus as king but from appointing his rival Leotychidas, the presumed son of Agis, whose legitimacy was seriously in question (one rumour was that he was actually the son of Alcibiades – presumably the date of his birth fitted that hypothesis). Since the purity and authenticity of the kings were crucial to the perceived effectiveness of the office, this was a brilliantly effective ploy on the cunning Lysander's part, and Agesilaus duly ascended the throne – to rule for some forty years.

However, if Lysander had thought Agesilaus would be as wax in his hands, he was soon cruelly undeceived. Agesilaus had gone through the Agoge, knew how ordinary Spartans thought, and proved a past master of political patronage within the elite. Agesilaus actually had himself appointed as leader of the anti-Persian expedition in 396, and once he had taken over the command in Asia, Lysander soon found himself demoted to a purely ceremonial role and returned to Sparta with his tail between his legs. Again, though, despite this setback he was by no means finished, and in 395, when Sparta found itself with wars on two fronts – against the Persian Empire in Asia and against a powerful coalition of Greek cities including Athens and Thebes in central Greece – Lysander was dispatched to the Boeotian front as one of the two principal commanders, the other being Regent Pausanias.

Partly no doubt through the sheer difficulty of military communication using ancient means, but also surely because of his burning desire for personal glory, and his rivalry with Pausanias, Lysander failed to link up his forces with those of the king as planned and instead charged on ahead against the Boeotian town of Haliartus. There he was killed, in a rather tame end to an extraordinary career, but, though dead, he still remained a potent legend, and he had numerous personal followers, not only abroad but in Sparta itself. It was the latter that Agesilaus felt he had to contend with on his return from Asia in 394, and he did so in the most interesting way.

He claimed that, in Lysander's house after his death, there had been found a papyrus text containing an undelivered speech written for him by a non-Spartan intellectual. The theme of the speech was the Spartan kingship, and the proposal that Lysander would allegedly have made was that the kingship should cease to be hereditary and confined to the two houses of the Agiads and Eurypontids, but should rather be thrown open more widely – at least to all 'descendants of Heracles' (of whom Lysander was one) and possibly to all Spartans. Agesilaus' accusation, tellingly, was believed and proved effective in weakening the influence of Lysander's known friends and partisans in Sparta. I per-

Elsewhere in what had been their empire, Lysander saw to the installation of decarchies, regimes of ten partisan and extreme oligarchs. Athens was too big to be governed by so small a group: instead, under the leadership of the pro-Spartan Critias (a follower of Socrates, and a relative of Plato), a junta of thirty took control, in conjunction with a supplementary decarchy to look after the port city of Piraeus. In order to ensure the stability of the rule of the Thirty, Lysander saw to it that the Spartans despatched a garrison consisting of ex-Helot Neodamodeis, to provide the necessary muscle. Yet such were the morale and democratic spirit of the majority of Athenians, and such the brutality of the Thirty who deservedly acquired the nickname of Thirty Tyrants, that within little more than a year democratic government had been restored to Athens – under the strict supervision of the Spartans, it is true, but also with their acquiescence.

PART III

A
CRIPPLED
KINGSHIP

7

THE SPARTAN EMPIRE
404–371 BC

Thanks to Persian funds, and to the Athenians' own strategic and tactical mistakes, the Spartans ran out victors in the Athenian War. Spartan counsels were then dominated by Lysander, and Lysander peddled a maximalist, strongly imperialist line. What is sometimes called the 'second' Spartan Empire, to distinguish it from the Empire Sparta wielded in the Peloponnese and mainland Greece, was the old Athenian Empire, but in a more extreme imperialist version. The Spartans also levied tribute and maintained a navy, but whereas the Athenians' Empire had been conceived and largely maintained as anti-Persian, the Lysandrean version of the Spartan Empire was mainly anti-democratic and pro-autocratic. Soon, though, Lysander antagonized the more conservative members of the Spartan hierarchy, including those like King Pausanias who believed in a policy of dual hegemony, or peaceful coexistence, between Sparta and Athens. Lysander found himself quickly set aside but attempted to bounce back by supporting the contested claims to the kingship of his former beloved Agesilaus, who succeeded his half-brother Agis in about 400.

The next thirty years of Spartan – and indeed to some extent all Greek – history are the years of Agesilaus. Since his career is so inseparably intertwined with the fate of Sparta as a whole, more so even than that of Cleomenes I, he will not be given a separate biography here by me, as he was by both Xenophon and Plutarch. Not expected to become king, he had undergone all the usual manhood trials and tests of an ordinary Spartan's education and, despite his congenital lameness, come through them *summa cum laude*. He therefore embodied the characteristic Spartan virtues – and vices. Intolerant of alternatives to Spartan-dominated oligarchy, he ended by having to endure the crumbling of Spartan power on the battlefield of Leuctra in 371, and its consequences. Yet who could have predicted confidently that that would be the case, from a vantage-point of about 400 BC, the time of his succession to the Eurypontid throne?

The succession itself, however, was not a simple matter. In the normal course of events Agesilaus' older half-brother Agis II's son Leotychidas would have been expected to succeed his father, but in 400 very little was normal in Sparta. A suspicion of illegitimacy hung over Leotychidas, compounded by the rumour that his true father was Alcibiades of Athens. Leotychidas, besides, was barely into his teens when Agis died, and he lacked a male relative who would take over as regent until he himself reached his majority. Or rather, the man who might have so acted, Agesilaus, instead put himself forward as his rival for the throne, prompted perhaps and certainly backed by his former lover Lysander, and then won the succession contest.

Agesilaus had a great deal going for him, in that he had been successfully through the Agoge, was a citizen of proven Spartan valour, and had shown himself utterly devoted to Lycurgan values. Yet he had been born lame, and had had to contend with the production of an oracle that prophesied doom to Sparta if the kingship were to 'go lame'. Lysander had managed to allegorize that oracle harmlessly away, but the literal interpretation was to come back to haunt Agesilaus and Sparta. Hence the title of this third and final Part.

Not long after Agesilaus' accession to the Eurypontid throne, to rule jointly with the Agiad Pausanias, a public seer announced the illest of ill omens after consulting the entrails of a sacrificed animal. It was as though, he said, Sparta were in the midst of enemies. Interpreted in one way, that was nothing short of the bald truth: every year the incoming board of Ephors declared war on the Helots and thereby officially turned them all into public enemies. However, the seer's announcement was soon shown to have an even more wide-ranging and threatening application, because the enemies involved ran from the bottom to almost the top of the social classes into which the denizens of the Spartan state were divided. What was uncovered, allegedly, was a conspiracy led by one Cinadon, either a full Spartiate degraded for economic reasons, or a mixed-birth Spartan. The former associate of Cinadon who turned state's evidence and informed on him to the Ephors, extravagantly claimed that his supporters included all the Perioeci, Neodamodeis, Helots, and a shadowy group referred to as 'Inferiors' (Hupomeiones); and he said they all hated the full Spartan citizens so much that they were itching to cannibalize them, even raw.

There is a great deal of sheer speculation, innuendo and exaggeration in this report, which is faithfully if not disinterestedly retailed by Xenophon, a personal supporter and client of Agesilaus. However, it does graphically reveal just what an odd society Sparta was, since in no other Greek city could even the vaguest possibility of a conspiracy between free and unfree, ex-citizens and half-citizens be entertained for a moment. In the event, nothing came of the conspiracy, beyond the fact that Cinadon received exemplary and typically cruel public punishment, being dragged through the streets of Sparta, wearing a halter, until presumably his body was broken to bits. Aristotle later picked up on the significance of this potential challenge to the established order, and in Agesilaus' defence it would probably be fair to say that his extreme and ultimately counterproductive conservatism was in part a reaction to such serious internal provocation.

During the 390s, Sparta was at its most expansionist. It conducted not just foreign, but overseas, campaigns, on the continent of Asia as well as in mainland Greece. At first, Sparta did at least seem to be fighting for a just cause: that of Greek liberty. Indeed, the liberation propaganda used against Persia was an echo, if a faint one, of the propaganda used by the Athenians in order to develop and maintain their Empire – the Empire that the Spartans had just destroyed in the Athenian War. However, it never had quite the same favourable effect on Sparta's fighting capacity that it did on Athens', no doubt because it was widely perceived as hypocritical from the start.

A succession of Spartan commanders struggled to make headway against the wily satrap Tissaphernes, based on Sardis, and his more straightforward colleague, Pharnabazus, based on Dascylium near the Hellespont to the north. Eventually, in 396 Agesilaus persuaded the authorities of the day to grant him the power of supreme command in Asia. He thereby became only the second Spartan king after Leotychidas II to venture so far east as commander, and in 395 he became the first king to be put in charge of both the land army and the fleet simultaneously. The year 396 was also a momentous one for Agesilaus in another respect, since it witnessed his sister Cynisca's unprecedented first Olympic victory.[1]

CYNISCA

Cynisca sounds like a childhood nickname, because it means (female) puppy; an ancestor of hers had been given the equivalent masculine nickname Cyniscus. It may rather have been intended as a tribute to the particular type of hound bred in Sparta, the female of which species was renowned as a scenter in the hunting of the fearsome wild boar. If, as is probable, Cynisca was the full sister of Agesilaus, and daughter of Archidamus III and Eupolia, she was probably born some time around 440 BC. She would then have been in her forties when she became the first woman ever to win a victory in the Olympic Games, a feat that she repeated at the immediately succeeding Games of 392.

Cynisca was thus no ordinary Spartan girl, but a royal princess. Spartan marital relations could be complex enough in ordinary circumstances, as we have seen; royal marital arrangements were always so, since as in all such dynastic regimes economic and above all political considerations were involved. A possibly apocryphal story retailed by Aristotle's pupil Theophrastus and quoted later by Plutarch said that the Ephors wanted to fine Archidamus for marrying too small a woman. Spartan women do seem to have been unusually tall by general Greek standards, perhaps because they were relatively well-fed. Presumably therefore Eupolia, his second wife, held some other attraction for Archidamus than her height.

The relative equality between the sexes enjoyed by adult Spartans was prepared for and reinforced by giving the Spartan girls something like an equivalent to the physical part of the Spartan boys' state-run upbringing. There is even evidence that there was a female counterpart to the system of male pederastic pairing relationships that was a required component of the educational curriculum once a boy attained his teens. Presumably Cynisca will have taken part in this female curriculum, just as her brother Agesilaus went through the boys' Agoge. Some very fine bronze figurines made in Sparta showing adolescent girls or young women in athletic poses are a powerful illustration of this social phenomenon, unique in Greece. However, this was a source of shock rather than admiration to most other Greeks, who insulted Spartan girls as 'thigh-flashers', because they were wore revealing mini-tunics, and who regarded all Spartan girls and women as little better than whores.

The point of the male Agoge was to prepare a youth to become a citizen warrior, ready to fight against not only external enemies but also the Helots, the enemy within. A Spartan citizen's life was not all fighting or play-fighting, however. Religion was of paramount importance to the Spartans, and line-dancing was a useful way of both honouring the gods and enhancing the communal rhythm and cohesion needed by hoplites fighting in the phalanx formation. As for the girls, they danced not only in Sparta but in a number of other towns in the vicinity. For the Hyacinthia festival, for example, held in honour of Apollo at Amyclae a few kilometres south of Sparta, girls were taken down by carriage, and a passage in Xenophon's biography of Agesilaus tells of how even the king's daughters travelled down in the ordinary public carriage like any other girls. Presumably Cynisca had not received any special treatment from her father Archidamus, either.

Another form of religious celebration that appealed especially to the competitive and martial spirit of the Spartans was athletics. Traditionally, the first panhellenic (all-Greek and only Greek) athletics festival was the Olympic Games, established – according to the traditional chronology – in what we call 776 BC. Possibly that date should be lowered somewhat, and in any case 'games' is a rather grand term for what was for a long time just a single running race, the equivalent of our 200-metre sprint. However, over the years other events were added, equestrian as well as athletic, and competitors in the athletics were divided by age into Men and Boys categories. So by the time the administration of the Games was overhauled by the managing state of Elis in 472, the festival had grown to occupy five days.

Competition for an Olympic prize was fierce, but the prize itself was always a purely symbolic olive wreath. An Olympic victory was considered to be sufficient reward in itself, since it was paid in the most valuable currency of all – undying fame. The original religious dimension of the Games was never forgotten. The central act of the festival was a communal procession and sacrifice to the patron god Zeus of Mount Olympus. On the other hand, competition for the prizes was not always conducted in what we would consider a particularly religious spirit. In fact, the competitive atmosphere was more like that of a paramilitary exercise. One reason for this was that athletics, like so many other fundamental aspects of Greek culture, was radically gendered. So strictly male-only were the Olympics that women (apart perhaps from an official priestess) were not even allowed to watch the men compete.

However, apart from the running events and the combat sports, which took place in or around the main stadium at Olympia, there were also equestrian events which were held in a separate hippodrome (literally, a course for horses). In these events alone could women compete – though only by proxy: not as riders or drivers (who were always men or boys), but as owners of the chariots and teams. In 396 Cynisca entered her four-horse chariot team, and won. In 392 she competed, and won, again.

We happen to be quite well informed about these two successive victories of hers, because they attracted the attention and caught the imagination of a much later traveller, Pausanias, an Asia Minor Greek who visited Olympia in about the middle of the second century AD. Still legible then – and today – was the inscription set into the base of the commemorative monument that Cynisca had had erected:

> My fathers and brothers were Spartan kings,
> I won with a team of fast-footed horses,
> and put up this monument: I am Cynisca:
> I say I am the only woman in all Greece
> to have won this wreath.[2]

That assertive 'I' might by itself suggest that our Cynisca was not modest about coming forward. However, we happen also to possess Xenophon's biography of her brother, written no doubt with Agesilaus' full knowledge and approval as a work of propaganda for publication immediately after his death (in about 359). In this work we are told that it was not Cynisca's own idea that she should breed chariot racehorses and compete with them at Olympia, but Agesilaus'. His aim, moreover, was to demonstrate that victories won in this way were a function merely of wealth, unlike victories in other events and spheres (above all battle) where what counted decisively was manly virtue. What man, he implied, would want to win a prize that a woman could win too?

It is of course conceivable that Agesilaus and his publicist were try-ing to cover up the fact that Cynisca had gone her own way without official approval, but in either case we are bound to ask why Agesilaus should have sought to diminish in this manner his sister's pioneering achievement and conspicuously panhellenic glory. Probably several fac-tors and motives were in play. At one level, Agesilaus was seeking to maintain his society's possibly flagging devotion to success in warfare through communal endeavour as against the increasingly seductive individual glory that might accrue from a victory in this most expensive and glory-bringing of Olympic events. The success of Spartans in the Olympic and other chariot-races in the fifth century is certainly very noticeable indeed, and Xenophon reports that Agesilaus made a special point of the fact that, whereas Cynisca merely bred racehorses, he bred warhorses. At another level, perhaps, he was seeking to diminish Cynisca as a woman, in a period of Spartan history when, so Aristotle later reported, 'many things were accomplished by the women'. If so, this was a dangerously two-edged game to play, and it may not be just coincidence that later in his reign Agesilaus reportedly found it necessary to execute two high-ranking Spartan women, the mother and aunt of a disgraced commanding officer.

In the end, anyway, Cynisca had the last laugh. After her death, to complement her lifetime monument at Olympia, she was awarded a heroine's shrine in Sparta, and the religious veneration that went with that. It is true that all Spartan kings were so venerated posthumously, but Cynisca is the only Spartan woman on record as having achieved this highly desirable status.

Agesilaus' unprecedented joint command by land and sea in 395/4 was to no avail. Despite some successes, rather exaggerated in Xenophon's *History*, Agesilaus could never make decisive headway without an effective siege train nor was he willing or able to venture far from the Aegean coast to make serious inroads into the heartland of the Persian Empire, where the Ten Thousand mercenaries had shown the way half a dozen years earlier. In 394 a major defeat at sea, inflicted by a Persian fleet under the command of an Athenian admiral, led to his recall to Sparta to face a seriously menacing Persian-financed coalition of Greek enemies, a quadruple alliance comprising Athens, Boeotia, Corinth and Argos. The fortunes of the alliance had waxed during 395, when their successes included the death of Lysander and the consequent exile (for the second and last time) of King Pausanias. They waned in 394 as Sparta won two major land battles, the first at the River of Nemea near Corinth, the second at Coronea in Boeotia.

In command at Coronea was Agesilaus, supported by among others Xenophon and the remnant of the Ten Thousand mercenaries who had been recruited into the Spartan army to fight Persia some years earlier. For his part in Sparta's victory against his own city of Athens, Xenophon suffered exile for treason, but Agesilaus saw to it that he was suitably rewarded for his loyalty to him, with a pleasant country retreat near Olympia. Here he laundered his Asiatic spoils by building a temple to Artemis, patroness of his favourite sport of hunting. Agesilaus too had spoils to dedicate, in his case to Apollo of Delphi. If the tithe that Agesilaus dedicated means literally a tenth, Agesilaus brought back to Sparta from Asia booty worth almost 1,000 *talents* (when three *talents* would have been enough to make a man the equivalent of a millionaire today). This ingress of coined and uncoined wealth, like the previous influx occasioned by Lysander's victory over Athens and its empire in 404, caused serious destabilization of Sparta's moral values.

Later sources quoted a convenient oracle to the effect that 'Love of money, and nothing else, will destroy Sparta.' That love was perhaps nothing very new in about 400, but the practical expression of it certainly was, and the consequences were not favourable to the maintenance of the rigid Lycurgan code. Lysander himself, like Agesilaus, was apparently personally impervious to the charms of riches, but most Spartans unfortunately were not. Both Plato and Aristotle commented unfavourably on the proneness to luxury of the Spartan women, and the proneness of their menfolk to indulge their tastes. Perhaps that is part of what Aristotle meant by alleging that 'at the time of the Spartans' Empire many things were accomplished by the women'.

For the time being, though, the Spartans' empire at least in mainland Greece was pretty secure, as the River of Nemea and Coronea victories of 394 underlined. However, still their enemies persisted in resisting them, achieving occasional successes like the destruction of a Spartan regiment near Corinth in 390, and still Persian money underpinned their resistance – until in the early 380s a major swing in Spartan foreign policy could be observed. Just what role Agesilaus or his much younger and generally complaisant co-king Agesipolis (son of the exiled Pausanias) played in this swing is unclear. The Spartan who spearheaded it at any rate was Antalcidas. Like Lysander, it was through holding the office of Nauarchos, and holding it *de facto* for more than one year, that Antalcidas achieved the feat of transforming Sparta from Persia's principal Greek enemy to Persia's number one Greek friend. Like Lysander, again, Antalcidas had considerable diplomatic as well as military skills. With Persian money flowing to him and his reinforced fleet from 388, Antalcidas first wrested control of the Hellespont from Athens, thereby threatening Athens again with starvation, and then prepared the way for a negotiated peace settlement in which Sparta with Persian backing would carve up all Aegean Greece, both the Greek mainland and the islands, leaving control of 'Asia' to Great King Artaxerxes II.

ANTALCIDAS

In the modern world we name peace treaties after the places where they are negotiated and signed – Utrecht, Versailles, and so on. The ancient Greeks did these things differently. They did not sign treaties but swore them, in the name of the gods who would act as their guarantors; to break a peace treaty or a treaty of alliance was in ancient Greece an act of sacrilege liable to be punished by or in the name of the god or gods directly invoked. Typically they named treaties after their principal negotiator, or one of the principal negotiators. In the fifth century BC, the men whose names marked key diplomatic watersheds were Callias, an Athenian aristocrat who appears to have moved to the left over the course of his career, and Nicias, another Athenian politician but one who could never remotely be called left-wing.

The Peace of Callias in the early 440s, between Athens and the Great King of Persia, symbolized the rise of Athens to supreme power in the eastern Mediterranean. Whether or not the Great King formally swore the oaths, the effect of the Peace *de facto* was to end hostilities between any Greeks and the Persians for over a generation. The Peace of Nicias in 421 between Athens and Sparta and their respective allies (or most of them) merely interrupted rather than finally terminated the Athenian War, but it remained the most salient diplomatic instrument governing Greek–Greek relations until the Peace of Antalcidas.

That latter Peace carried the alternative name, the King's Peace, since the Great King of Persia liked to imagine that he had sent down the clauses for ratification by the Greeks on his terms, and his alone. Actually the Peace was a bigger thing than that; it was also the first of what came to be called Common Peaces, because they applied to all Greeks whether or not they were directly involved in the swearing of the oaths. For that major diplomatic development, a significant potential contribution to the cause of peacemaking in a notoriously war-ridden world, Antalcidas must deserve the lion's share of the credit. If only we knew a good deal more about him than we do...

His very name has been transmitted under alternative forms – both Antalcidas and Antialcidas, but the former is certainly the correct one. It means 'the counterpart (or replacement) of Alcidas', and coincidentally a predecessor of his in the post of Nauarch, or Admiral of the Fleet, was called Alcidas, who served, ingloriously, during the first phase of the Athenian War. Exactly forty years later, in 388, Antalcidas was appointed Nauarch with a twofold mission: first, to nip in the bud the control of the area around the Hellespont that Athens through Thrasybulus was beginning to exercise again, and, second, to use Sparta's control of the Hellespont to bring Athens once again to its knees, as Lysander had done in 405/4.

Both of these objectives he accomplished with aplomb, not least because, just like Lysander, he had the capacity to enter into a *xenia* relationship with a high-ranking Persian – in his case, with Ariobarzanes, who had succeeded Pharnabazus as the satrap of Hellespontine Phrygia. Actually, Xenophon says that he was an 'old', that is longstanding, *xenos* of Ariobarzanes, which tantalizingly suggests either that Antalcidas had inherited this *xenia* relationship or that he had been active in the eastern sphere possibly even as early as the concluding phase of the Athenian War. As it is, he first emerges into the light of history in 393/2, when he was sent as official Spartan ambassador to the court of Persian satrap Tiribazus at Sardis. Our ignorance of Antalcidas' early career before 393 is therefore all the more frustrating. That he belonged to the Spartan elite might have been guessed anyway, but there is also enough evidence to suggest that his father Leon was the Leon who married Teleutia (a name that recalls Teleutias, half-brother of Agesilaus) and with her produced Pedaritos, who died holding a high command in 411, as well as Antalcidas, who presumably therefore was the younger son, born perhaps around 435.

His mission to Tiribazus in 393 eventually proved abortive, though Antalcidas did receive substantial Persian financial support. His naval command five years later, as we have seen, was completely successful, but his crowning achievement was diplomatic and followed an audience actually with Great King Artaxerxes II himself at Susa. Hence the Peace 'of Antalcidas'. The terms of the Peace coincided entirely with the wishes and policy aims of King Agesilaus, but the source used by Plutarch believed that the two men were at odds over it. However, that is probably to be explained as an anachronistic inference from the better documented and more plausible claim that in later years the two men did indeed fall out over foreign policy towards, not Persia, but Thebes.

So at least an anecdote also preserved by Plutarch seems to indicate. It is repeated in the Plutarchan collection *Sayings of Spartans*, in a shorter and a longer version. The longer one goes like this:

[Agesilaus] *was making war constantly on the*
Thebans, and when he received a wound in battle

against them, it is said that Antalcidas remarked
to him: 'What splendid payment you are getting
from the Thebans for your instruction of them,
since you have taught them how to fight when
they had neither the wish nor the capacity to do
so.' In fact at that period the Thebans are said to
have excelled themselves in battle because of the
Spartans' many campaigns against them. This was
why Lycurgus of old in [one of] *the so-called rhetras*
[pronouncements, laws] *forbade frequent campaigns*
against the same people, so as to prevent them from
learning how to fight.[3]

This anecdote seems to imply a difference of attitude towards the Thebans, during their rise to power in the 370s. This is not the only anecdote, though, in which Antalcidas is represented as a champion of the good old days and ways, somewhat ironically so, as Agesilaus liked to represent himself in precisely the same way. Agesilaus, the hammer of the Thebans, would settle for nothing less than all-out assault and total victory. Antalcidas, apparently, favoured a less blunt and more subtle approach, as befitted a consummate diplomatist. It is at least interesting that, just when Agesilaus was working up to the paroxysm of aggression that culminated in 371 in the catastrophic defeat of Sparta by Thebes at Leuctra, Antalcidas was away again in Susa, negotiating for further diplomatic and financial support from Persia.

The year after Leuctra, Antalcidas was elected to the office of Ephor. This is doubly interesting. Unless the normal rule of a single term of office was waived in these exceptional circumstances for the benefit of an elder statesman, it means that Antalcidas had not previously stood for the office, or at least had not previously been elected. Second, it implies that, at this moment of deep crisis, even Agesilaus had to tolerate a critic and possibly an enemy holding high office. It was to be Antalcidas' last hurrah. Three years later, in 367, he made the long trek east to Susa for a third and last time, on this occasion to compete with the Thebans led by Pelopidas for the Great King's favour. He – and Sparta – lost the contest, hands down.

This extraordinary diplomatic *volte-face* by Sparta meant, so far as the Greeks of Asia were concerned, abandoning the liberation propaganda of 431, 404 and later years, and turning the clock back to 481, when the Persian Empire in the west had extended as far as the Aegean shoreline. In return for handing these Greeks to Persia on a plate, the Spartans – and that means above all Agesilaus – were given a free hand to 'settle' mainland Greece as he and they wished. The buzzword of the new Spartan order was 'autonomy', in the sense that every Greek city great or small was henceforth to be autonomous from every other – except of course the Perioecic cities in Laconia and Messenia over which Sparta wished to retain direct control. The Spartans in other words imposed autonomy as and where it suited them. Thus Athens was forcibly separated from the towns and cities of the eastern Mediterranean and Hellespontine region over which it had begun to reassert something like a proto-empire, Argos was disaggregated from Corinth and their interesting experiment in co-partnership was terminated, the federal state of Boeotia was reduced to its atomized elements to the detriment of Thebes' overall control, and even the unified city of Mantinea was broken up into its constituent villages, as a way of getting rid of the hated democratic regime.

Opposition to democracy was indeed the theme of Sparta's Agesilaus-driven policy and conduct for the next half-dozen years. Perhaps the most striking and brutal case was Sparta's treatment of its Peloponnesian League ally Phlius. In 381 Agesilaus began to lay siege to the city on the grounds that it had been disloyal during the Corinthian War. At least as important a consideration for Agesilaus was to restore to power some oligarchic exiles who were personally connected to him and to Sparta. This rank favouritism and infringement of Phlius' autonomy on any normal definition provoked dissent and criticism even among the Spartans themselves. Xenophon, usually a warm friend of both Sparta and Agesilaus, could not resist including mention of this criticism of Agesilaus even in his posthumous hagiography of the king, but it was only in his general *History of Greece* that he spelled out exactly what was at issue:

> *There were many Spartans who complained that for the sake of a few men* [the oligarchic exiles] *they were incurring the hatred of a city of over 5,000 men.*[4]

Xenophon cannot quite bring himself to state that Phlius was then a democratic city, but here and elsewhere in his account the inference is unavoidable.

The siege of Phlius was eventually successful after almost two years, in 379. However, this success paled beside the Spartans' triumphant intervention in Boeotia in 382, when a Spartan force had seized control of the acropolis of Thebes and, as at Athens in 404, followed this up with the imposition of a narrow pro-Spartan oligarchy propped up by a garrison under a military-political officer called a *harmost*. In fact, the *harmost* system was extended to the whole of what had until 386 been the independent Boeotian federal state, and indeed had been widely used by the Spartans whenever they could throughout the Greek mainland, in the islands and on the Asiatic littoral since the end of the Athenian War. In the same year that the Spartans reduced Phlius, 379, they achieved the feasible limits of their territorial ambitions in mainland Greece by bringing under their control Olynthus in the Chalcidice and dissolving the Chalcidian federation that Olynthus had dominated. It might therefore have seemed that, by the summer of 379, Sparta had an empire every bit as impressive and powerful as the Athenians had enjoyed in the fifth century. In the winter of 379/8, however, all that was to begin to change.

Those whom the gods wish to destroy they first make mad – so a character in a play of Euripides had once said. The behaviour of Sphodrias, Spartan harmost of Boeotian Thespiae, in early 378 can be described as nothing other than an act of lunacy. Perhaps seeking to achieve some exceptional personal renown, perhaps because he had been bribed by the Thebans, or perhaps because he had acted on what he understood to be the orders or wishes of Agesilaus' co-king Cleombrotus, Sphodrias tried to capture Athens' port of Piraeus. The attempt was a fiasco. If the Athenians had needed any spur to persuade them to support actively and vigorously the liberation of Thebes from Spartan control, this was it. One night, with a suitably dramatic mixture of tragedy and farce, Pelopidas and a handful of other Theban exiles succeeded in inveigling themselves into Thebes and capturing, killing or driving out the Spartan garrison and overthrowing the pro-Spartan junta.

Back in Sparta, Sphodrias was put on trial for high treason, but the trial had to go forward without the presence of Sphodrias himself. So convinced was he that he would be found guilty and executed that he in effect condemned himself to death in advance by refusing to return to Sparta to face the music. Yet even so he was found not guilty, in what Xenophon rightly describes as one of the most egregious miscarriages of justice in all Greek history. His acquittal was thanks to Agesilaus, who controlled a majority of the votes on the Spartan supreme court (composed of the Gerousia, sitting probably together with the Ephors of the day). One factor that ordinarily might have influenced a man in Agesilaus' position was that his son and heir Archidamus was the lover of Sphodrias' son, and Xenophon tells a pretty tale of Archidamus seeking to intercede on behalf of his beloved's father, but Agesilaus was not to be swayed by merely sentimental considerations. What he allegedly told his son was that, though Sphodrias was undoubtedly guilty, yet he would vote for his acquittal on the pragmatic grounds that Sparta needed soldiers like Sphodrias. There was a dire shortage of Spartan military manpower, to be sure; but to be more accurate and honest, Agesilaus should have said that he needed leading Spartans who, like Sphodrias after his acquittal, would be unquestioningly and unswervingly loyal and obedient servants of his will. Seven years later, Sphodrias was to die on the battlefield of Leuctra – a melancholy witness to Agesilaus' deadly influence over Spartan counsels.

The newly liberated Thebes in 378 first reconstituted itself politically as a – moderate – democracy and then reconstituted the Boeotian federal state, now for the first time as a democratic system. A dynamic military reform was set in place by the returned exile Pelopidas in tandem with the even more brilliant general and philosopher Epaminondas. Among the innovations they presided over was the creation of an elite hoplite force of 300, consisting of 150 homosexual couples, known as the Sacred Band. The number was the same as that of the normal royal bodyguard in the Spartan army and of the Spartans' specially chosen Thermopylae force, so probably this was a deliberate echo of a Spartan idea, though in the Spartan army homosexual couples were not stationed next to each other in the phalanx. The Sacred Band was to be the Boeotians' principal strike force over the next decade, during which Boeotia both built up a formidable military alliance on land in central Greece and lent its support to the foundation and development of an essentially naval alliance led by Athens, the Second Athenian League. The target of both these alliances was Sparta, which, they reasonably claimed, had not merely exploited but flagrantly broken the terms of the Peace of Antalcidas in pursuit of its own selfish and reactionary aims.

Active military co-operation between Thebes and Athens was very limited. Events showed that it did not need to be more so, in so far as defeating Sparta was concerned. The first sign that Sparta was no longer the force it had once been declared itself in 375, at the Battle of Tegyra in Boeotia. It was not a full Spartan or Peloponnesian levy that Pelopidas and the Sacred Band defeated, only a Spartan detachment, but the victory was loaded with significance in as much as it was the first Spartan defeat in regular hoplite fighting since the one-off disaster at Lechaeum in 390 during the Corinthian War. Sparta nevertheless refused to give up its claim on central Greece, and it was ostensibly in aid of allies in Phocis that Cleombrotus was finally despatched in 371 to head a regular Peloponnesian levy against the full Theban-led alliance, against which Agesilaus and Cleombrotus had failed to make any significant inroads in 376 and 375.

The ensuing Battle of Leuctra was the decisive battle of the first half of the fourth century. Xenophon tried to make light of Agesilaus' ultimate responsibility for Sparta's calamitous defeat by saying that Cleombrotus and the high command had gone into the battle more than a little tipsy. What really did for the Spartans were the discipline and tactical innovativeness of Epaminondas and Pelopidas. Regardless of whether the Spartans had been the Thebans' teachers, as Antalcidas allegedly claimed, the Thebans were by now more proficient in the field than the Spartans – something as extraordinary as the fact that by the latter stages of the Athenian War the Spartans' fleet was superior to that of the Athenians. In places, Epaminondas massed his Theban hoplites fifty deep – compared with the usual depth of eight ranks employed in hoplite battle. He positioned his crack troops, the Sacred Band under Pelopidas, on the left of his line, whereas conventionally the superior wing in hoplite battle was the right. He advanced his troops slantwise, not head-on as would have been normal. He was faced, moreover, only by a demoralized and shortweight Spartan army.

By 371 there were not many more than 1,000 adult male Spartans citizens, all told. Various causes – above all, the earthquake of *c.* 464, losses in battle, and the Spartan property and inheritance regime – had operated to bring about this *oliganthrôpia*, this shortage of military manpower, which Aristotle rightly considered to be the determining factor in Sparta's ultimate failure as a great power. A significant proportion of these few remaining citizens fought, and lost, at Leuctra; some 400 out of the 700 died, including King Cleombrotus and, as mentioned above, Sphodrias. Even Xenophon could not resist pointing out that some of Sparta's Peloponnesian League allies were not displeased by this outcome. The effect on Spartan morale was such that the surviving king, Agesilaus, was reduced to decreeing by fiat that the usual punishments should not be applied to those Spartans who had been guilty of shirking or cowardice at Leuctra. This was a tacit admission that the Lycurgan regime had decisively failed.

8

FALL AND DECLINE
371–331 BC

This chapter will chart the catastrophic decline in Spartan fortunes during the decades following the disaster on the field of Leuctra. The Messenian Helots, with vital help from democratic Thebes led by the philosopher and general Epaminondas, revolted once more, but this time for good. Their new capital Messene was the outward and very visible sign of Sparta's humiliation. Within a few years, the Peloponnesian League too had dissolved as an effective instrument of Spartan power abroad. The fact that Sparta during these years felt compelled to make alliance again with Athens indicates how desperate the city had become. The hollowness of Agesilaus' crown was thus glaringly exposed.

The final liberation of the Messenians could not have happened without outside intervention, and intervention of the specific kind undertaken by the Greek world's most brilliant general who was also a man of a philosophic cast of mind. Epaminondas achieved fame chiefly on the battlefield, but Sir Walter Raleigh had good reason for rating him the greatest of the ancient Greeks, not just the greatest of ancient Greek generals. He was a liberator on a hitherto unprecedented scale. In late 370, encouraged by divisions within Arcadia, uneasily close to Sparta, he at last was in a position to exploit his stupendous victory at Leuctra and press home the full implications of Sparta's historic defeat.

He invaded Laconia with an allied force of between 30,000 and 40,000 men. It helped that many of the Perioeci of northern Laconia had already defected, but had they resisted, they could merely have slowed up not prevented his ingress. He approached close to Sparta, close enough for the fires of burning crops and buildings to be seen and smelled by the inhabitants of unwalled Sparta. Aristotle rather unchivalrously claimed that the Spartan women caused more tumult and confusion in the Spartan ranks than the enemy themselves, but that was probably just a loaded way of saying that the women were terrified by the utterly unfamiliar sight of a massed enemy army actually destroying property, including their own, under their very noses. Epaminondas, however, was not interested in taking, let alone destroying, Sparta. He marched on down through the Eurotas valley as far as Sparta's port city of Gytheum, which he probably did destroy, for military as well as political reasons. He then retraced his steps northwards through Laconia before marching west into Messenia, his principal objective.

The Messenian Helots had already risen in revolt, at about the same time as the northern Laconian Perioeci; presumably some at least of the Messenian Perioeci joined the revolt too, as their ancestors had almost exactly a century earlier following the great earthquake. Epaminondas' task was to see that the revolt was not quashed and that the liberation of the ex-Helots was made permanent. This he achieved through overseeing the construction of the city of New Messene, buttressed by its massive enceinte walling that cleverly took advantage of its site against the flank of Mount Ithome. The remains of these walls, which so flagrantly contradicted wall-less Sparta, are still mightily impressive to this day. As citizens of the New Messene, first in line were of course the adult males among the resident ex-Helots, but they were soon joined by people of Helot descent from the Messenian diaspora, including some from as far afield as north Africa.

Ever since the renaming of Sicilian Zancle as Messana in about 490, and the foundation of Naupactus by the Athenians in about 460, there had been 'Messenians' who were proud to call themselves that and, in the case of the Naupactians, to make in-your-face dedications at Olympia under that name to spite their former Spartan masters. The most conspicuous of these offerings is the still largely extant Victory monument sculpted by Paeonius of Mende in the late 420s, but from 369 onwards 'the Messenians' *par excellence* were the citizens of New Messene, and as such they were the subject of much excited comment among intellectuals elsewhere in Greece.

Alcidamas, the rhetorician and sophist from Asia Minor, wrote, in support of their liberation, that 'God has made no man a slave' – implying that all slavery was purely a human convention without divine warrant and possibly therefore unwarranted. Plato did not go anything like that far – indeed, slavery crucially influenced his own mode of thought; but he did report that the Helot system of the Spartans was the most controversial slave system in all Greece, presumably because the Helots were Greeks, not foreign barbarians like most of the unfree in the Greek world. However, the most telling comment on the ex-Helot Messenians was made by Isocrates, a professional rival of both Alcidamas and Plato, in a pamphlet dressed up as a speech by crown prince Archidamus in a dramatic context of about 366 BC. What upset Isocrates' Archidamus the most was the Spartans having to put up with their former slaves lording it as free and independent citizens, in what had lately been their own back yard.

ARCHIDAMUS III

Archidamus was the son of Agesilaus and his wife Cleora, born probably in the late 400s. His own marriage took place in the later 370s or early 360s to Deinicha, daughter of Eudamidas, a prominent commander in pursuit of policies known to have been favoured by Agesilaus and brother to the late Phoebidas (died 378) who had likewise enjoyed Agesilaus' protection and favour. The marriage was presumably dynastic.

He first makes an appearance in the historical record in 378 as the lover of the son of Sphodrias, pleading with his all-powerful father for the life of his beloved's father. Sphodrias was spared then but soon to be killed at the Battle of Leuctra in 371. Archidamus did not take part in that deadly conflict, perhaps because he had not yet fathered a son and heir. His purely auxiliary role was to meet the survivors in the Megarid and escort them home. Three years later, he was given the first of his attested commands, in effect deputizing for his now elderly father, in Arcadia. Here he won what was labelled the Tearless Battle, because it was won at the cost of no Spartan lives, so precious and scarce had those lives now become. No less revealing of Sparta's dire condition is an anecdote preserved under the name of Archidamus in the Plutarchan collection of *Sayings of Kings and Commanders*:

> *Archidamus, the son of Agesilaus, when he saw a*
> *missile bolt shot from a catapult then for the first*
> *time brought over from Sicily, exclaimed:*
> *'By Heracles! A man's valour is dead!'* [1]

In the post-Leuctra crisis the Spartans had willingly allied themselves to Dionysius I, tyrant of Syracuse from 405 to 367 (so much for their principled opposition to tyranny...), in return for his sending mercenary troops and the latest equipment to their aid in the Peloponnese. Among his other successful innovations Dionysius had patronized improvements in artillery, which had enabled him, for example, to take Motya in western Sicily by siege in 398. Archidamus' comment on the catapult missile he saw in the early 360s is the exact counterpart of the remark attributed by Thucydides to one of the Spartans captured on Sphacteria in 425 and held hostage at Athens, to the effect that arrows ('spindles') were women's weapons and not a true test of manly courage in face-to-face, hand-to-hand hoplite battle. *A fortiori* that was true of bolts fired by a torsion catapult, but Archidamus' horrified response also nicely emblematizes one of the major reasons for reactionary Sparta's military failure in the changed conditions of fourth-century warfare.

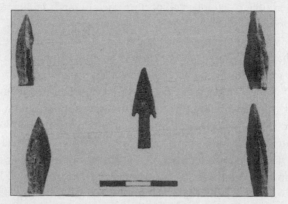

A hoplite's weapons were the spear and the sword, and hoplite ideology tended to make light of the contribution of arrows, which could be sneered at as 'spindles', that is, peculiarly feminine implements. But archers were in fact a regular part of Spartan composite armies, performing support and covering rather than decisive strike roles. These arrowheads were excavated at a sanctuary site near Sparta, where they had presumably been dedicated by Perioecic or at any rate sub-Spartan archers.

Archidamus is said to have distinguished himself again during Epaminondas' incursion of 362, when the Theban penetrated the town of Sparta itself. He was not given his head fully until the death of his father in 360 or 359, whereupon apparently without a contest he ascended the Eurypontid throne as Archidamus III. His Agiad co-king Cleomenes II was a mere cipher, on the throne (he could hardly be said to be ruling) from 370 to 309 without troubling the historical record. However, even the able and active Archidamus could do little to resist the tide of the Macedonian advance southwards under King Philip II (359–336) or even to restore Sparta's position in the Peloponnese, despite an attack on Megalopolis in 352. In 346 he occupied Thermopylae briefly on behalf of the Phocians in their decade-long war with Philip, but the ghosts of his heroic ancestors slain in the pass will not have been comforted by his ignominious withdrawal.

The climax of Philip's triumphant progress in subduing all mainland Greece came at the Battle of Chaeronea in Boeotia in 338, but by then Sparta was too enfeebled even to take part. When Philip followed his victory up by invading Laconia, as Epaminondas had done, he likewise did not trouble to conquer or occupy the city and deliberately left it outside the diplomatic framework of his new League of Corinth. Corinth, site of the famous Hellenic declaration of resistance to Persia in 481, had once been the leading ally in Sparta's Peloponnesian League, but that organization too had quietly folded up and gone away in the mid-360s. The Corinthians, like other former Peloponnesian League allies, like the new cities of Messene and Megalopolis, and like Argos, preferred to side with Philip rather than with Sparta. The ultra-skilled diplomatist Philip, for his part, knew that, by excluding Sparta from the League, he would ensure the loyalty of these anti-Spartan cities.

Philip's son and successor Alexander the Great rammed home the message of Sparta's international impotence in two pithy statements. First, in 334 after the Battle of the River Granicus, he sent back to Athens precisely three hundred panoplies (suits of hoplite armour) for dedication on the Athenian Acropolis with the following inscription:

Alexander son of Philip and the Greeks – except the Spartans – dedicated these spoils from the barbarians of Asia.[2]

The phrase 'Except the Spartans' – for whom the number 300 was indelibly seared on their collective national consciousness – was a calculated insult and publicly humiliating reminder that they were no part of the panhellenic anti-Persian crusade led by Alexander. Second, three years later, in 331, Archidamus' son and successor Agis III led an attempted revolt against Macedonian domination but was defeated comprehensively and definitively at Megalopolis. Alexander referred to the affray contemptuously as a 'Battle of Mice'.

What, to return in conclusion to the momentous events of 338, was Archidamus then up to? He was over the seas and far away, fighting and dying as a mercenary on behalf of Sparta's one true colony, Taras (Tarentum), against the neighbouring native Lucanians. Shades of his father Agesilaus (p. 237) and to equally little avail! Yet even so a portrait statue of Archidamus was set up at Olympia, of which we have perhaps a copy from the Roman period. Agesilaus would have been appalled. For him, it was a man's deeds, and only a man's deeds, that should be left behind him as a memorial, rather than any worthless counterfeit graven image. *Sic transit gloria laconica.*

The foundation of New Messene was not the only post-Leuctra blow that Epaminondas was able to inflict on Sparta. Turning the screw, he supervised, also in 368, the construction of Megalopolis ('The Great City') in southern Arcadia, a blend of forty previous communities, some of them formerly Laconian Perioeci. There had been federalist tendencies visible in Arcadia since at least the early fifth century, but it took Epaminondas, himself a citizen of the Boeotian federal democratic state, to bring them to fruition by making Megalopolis the new federal capital of Arcadia. The size of its theatre, the largest in the Peloponnese, was an index of Megalopolis' importance as a central federal gathering-place. Sparta of course had resisted federal states tooth and nail, and disbanded them whenever it could (the Boeotian in 386, the Chalcidian in 379, for instance). The siting of Megalopolis, moreover, was such that it directly threatened the passage northwards of any Spartan army wishing to intervene either elsewhere in the Peloponnese or in Greece north of the Isthmus of Corinth. It was a permanent bone lodged in Sparta's throat.

Not surprisingly, when it came to the composing of Epaminondas' funerary epigram (attached to his statue erected on the Theban acropolis), these two new Peloponnesian cities featured most prominently:

This came from my counsel:
Sparta has cut the hair of its glory:
Messene takes her children in:
a wreath of the spears of Thebe
has crowned Megalopolis:
Greece is free.[3]

The reference to Sparta's cutting its hair was a brilliant conceit; hair-cutting was a universal Greek token of mourning, but Spartan men had an exceptional amount of hair to cut. The maternal image of Messene was counterposed implicitly to Sparta's murderous and emphatically non-familial attitude to its enslaved Helot workforce. Megalopolis, finally, is presented as a victor in the crown games, thanks to the spears of Thebe, eponym of Thebes. Once, it had been Sparta's glorious 'Dorian spear' (Aeschylus's fine phrase) that had kept Greece free – from the Persians. Now the Laconian shoe (a rather fancy kind of slipper, apparently) was on the other foot.

Epaminondas' funerary epigram was composed only six years after the foundation of Megalopolis, for Epaminondas died, victorious, at the second major battle to be staged at Mantinea in northern Arcadia (the first had been in 418). He had invaded the Peloponnese, for the fourth time, in the summer of 362. To ensure that Sparta would not be present at the coming decisive battle in full force, he had conducted a second invasion of Laconia, but this time he penetrated the unwalled settlement of Sparta itself. Apologists for the Spartan cause preferred to divert attention to an individual act of heroism, performed by an adolescent of eighteen or nineteen, rather than dwell on the impotence of Agesilaus' Spartans to resist Epaminondas and on the outbreak of significant dissidence within the Spartan ranks.

ISADAS

Reliably attested information about Isadas is confined to a single passage in Plutarch's *Life of Agesilaus*. The context of the passage is Epaminondas' penetration of Sparta itself in 362, but, though the context is clearly critical, it by no means exhausts the passage's interest and importance:

*Isadas, the son of Phoebidas, in my view provided
a superb spectacle of bravery not only for his fellow-
citizens but also for his enemies. For he was outstanding
both in good looks and in size, and he was at that stage
of life between boyhood and adulthood when people
bloom exceedingly sweetly. He was stark naked, bereft
entirely both of weapons and of protective clothing, since
he had just oiled himself, yet he seized a spear in one
hand and a sword in the other and rushed out of the
house. He hurled himself into the very thick of the enemy,
striking down one opponent after another. He was
wounded by none of them, whether this was because some
god was watching over him on account of his bravery or
because he seemed to the enemy to be something greater
and more powerful than a mere mortal man. The Ephors
reportedly first crowned him and then fined him 1,000
drachmas, because he had foolhardily risked his life
fighting without any protective gear.*[4]

Phoebidas, Isadas' father, was no ordinary Spartan, and even for a
Spartan was inordinately ambitious. In 382 he had illegally occupied
and garrisoned Thebes, in peacetime, and yet Agesilaus had backed his
action retrospectively, whether or not he had also prompted or ordered
it in advance. Phoebidas' brother Eudamidas, Isadas' uncle, was likewise distinguished as a commander in Sparta's campaign against Olynthus
(381–379); and, perhaps in the late 370s or early 360s, Agesilaus' son
Archidamus married a daughter of Eudamidas, no doubt for the usual
financial and political reasons. Phoebidas, however, was killed in 378,
while holding a high command in Boeotia, so that Isadas, born in the
late 380s, grew up fatherless but with the conscious memory of a father
who had been a Spartan hero.

In 362, when Epaminondas invaded Sparta, Isadas was at the stage
of life for a male that the Spartans called technically *paidiskos*, 'boy-ish',

that is, between the status of a boy (*pais*, from age seven to eighteen) and that of a full adult warrior (*anêr*, twenty-plus). This was the intermediate stage at which certain especially distinguished youths were selected for the Helot-hunting Crypteia or secret service brigade, when they were sent out into the countryside armed only with a dagger and with no rations other than what they could glean or steal for themselves. As a sort of manhood test or initiatory ritual, they were required to 'blood' themselves by killing any Helots they happened on – or perhaps rather Helots who were known troublemakers. Isadas' nakedness corresponds to this pre-adult, ephebic stage of his life, but the fact that he had just anointed himself with oil perhaps is meant to suggest that he had been taking exercise. It was the Spartans, Thucydides tells us, who introduced this practice of oiling down in Greece, no doubt partly because of the abundance of olive oil produced in the favourable Laconian and Messenian conditions, and we recall the astonishment of Xerxes' scout when he saw the Spartans at Thermopylae taking vigorous gymnastic exercise as they prepared to fight and die (p. 125).

It was perhaps therefore with the memory both of his father's heroic career and of other Spartan heroes such as those of Thermopylae to inspire him that Isadas behaved as he did. Yet his behaviour was also crucially un-adult Spartan in that he fought alone, rather than as a member of a disciplined phalanx, and he fought with a kind of frenzy – somewhat like Aristodamus at Plataea in 479, perhaps, who had not been awarded the prize for valour by the Spartans because he seemed to them to have been acting out of a death-wish rather than showing properly self-controlled bravery. That presumably is why the Ephors, in a characteristically Spartan mixture of legalism and pragmatism, both crowned Isadas, as though he were a victorious athlete in the games, and then imposed on him a hefty – and, revealingly, monetary – fine.

After tying down Agesilaus in Sparta, Epaminondas returned north. A preliminary cavalry skirmish occurred, in which Gryllus, a son of

Xenophon who had been brought up within the Agoge as an honoured foreign guest, was killed. The main feature took place shortly thereafter. As a set-piece hoplite engagement, the second Battle of Mantinea followed along similar lines to the Battle of Leuctra, and had the identical outcome, though on this occasion the Spartans were aided by their allies from Athens.

What followed was a Common Peace concluded actually on the battlefield – or was it rather common confusion? The latter was the view of the period's historian, Xenophon, one-time client of Agesilaus and pro-Spartan exile, by then perhaps again reconciled with the city of his birth. As for Agesilaus, in these dire straits for his city he could envisage no more useful action than setting off for north Africa, though well into his eighties, to serve as a mercenary commander. His main objective was to gain a heap of cash quickly in Egypt in order to refill Sparta's depleted war-chest, but he died on his way back home at a site known as the Harbour of Menelaus, in what is now Libya.

The name of the deathplace was apt enough for a Spartan king, but the manner of his passing marked a sorry end to a reign that had begun when Sparta seemingly occupied a pinnacle of power and success both at home and abroad. The jury of modern scholarship is still out on the degree of personal responsibility that Agesilaus ought to bear for Sparta's demise, but my own view is that both positively, because he pursued too vigorously a consistently wrong line of imperialist foreign policy, and negatively, because he failed seriously to address Sparta's underlying and long-standing economic, social, political and military problems, he deserves a large share of the blame. His was indeed a crippled kingship.

9

REVIVAL
AND REINVENTION
331 BC–AD 14

S parta in 331 was down, but not yet quite out. Alexander died at
Babylon in 323 before he could return to Greece and settle the
Spartan question for good, if indeed he had any intention of either
returning or altering his father's cleverly contrived non-settlement of
Sparta's position. In the wars of Alexander's Successors, as they came
to be known, that disturbed the Aegean Greek world for over twenty
years (the Battle of Ipsus in 301 marked some sort of a conclusion),
Sparta was very much a bit player, and more often than not sat waiting
in the wings, separated from the main action. Notably, Sparta took no
part in the Athens-led revolt against Macedon of 323–2, the so-called
Lamian War; and in 315, when Cassander of Macedon intervened in
the Peloponnese, it was to seize control of Messenia.

Instead, Sparta played the mercenary game. The city both supplied
mercenaries itself and provided at Taenarum, in southern Mani, one of the
major centres for the recruitment of the ever more ubiquitous mercenaries
with whom the Successors fought their interminable wars. Indeed in 315,
another Spartan royal, the Agiad Acrotatus (son of the prodigious nonen-
tity King Cleomenes II, who 'reigned' from 370 to 309), followed in the
footsteps of the Eurypontids Agesilaus II and his son Archidamus III in
choosing to embark in person on mercenary service abroad. But he
achieved little in Sicily and, having returned to Sparta, he predeceased his

father. By his high-handed behaviour he had shown himself to be a Spartan of the old school. His son Areus, however, who was to succeed his grandfather as Agiad king, proved to be the very reverse of traditional.

In about 300, Archidamus IV succeeded his father Eudamidas I as Eurypontid king. It was under him that Sparta was for the first time drawn directly into the Wars of the Successors, some years after the main division of the spoils following the Battle of Ipsus. In 294 Demetrius Poliorcetes, son of Cassander, invaded the Peloponnese, seeing it as a counter in the higher game he was playing for the prize of the throne of Macedon, of which defeat at Ipsus had robbed him. At Mantinea he was met by Archidamus IV, who promptly lost not only the battle but his own life and those of perhaps as many as 700 others including fellow-Spartans. Demetrius pressed on south to Sparta and would no doubt have taken it and done violence to it, had he not been diverted by more pressing business in the north of Greece. Laconia had by now been invaded four times since 370, but still, remarkably, Sparta remained untaken by a foreign conqueror. Just over a decade later, in 281, Areus made his debut on the international stage, a genuinely ruling king at last. With him, Sparta may be said to have fully entered into the Hellenistic Age of Greek history. This was an age, not so much of cultural fusion between Greek and oriental custom and practice, as of cultural approximation and alignment, as Greeks and orientals mingled with each other and borrowed from each other, but without entirely effacing or totally transforming the culture of either.

AREUS I

Areus I, son of the late Acrotatus, succeeded his long-lived grandfather Cleomenes II on the Agiad throne in 309, though to begin with, since he was under-age, control nominally rested with his uncle, regent Cleonymus. Soon, however, Cleonymus chose to follow the same mercenary path

as his brother to south Italy, with equally small success. Areus, however, belonged to a different thoughtworld from that occupied by his
immediate ascendants. His vision was that of a new-style Hellenistic
monarch.

In 307 the chief rivals for Alexander's inheritance declared themselves kings of their respective territories. Areus took them for his
models and, some time after coming of age and assuming his role
as Agiad king, he issued the first-ever Spartan silver coinage, using
types of Alexander the Great, with his own image and superscription
boldly engraved thereon. But to call himself sole 'King of the
Spartans', as if the Eurypontid dynasty was no more, was a grave
breach with Lycurgan tradition. Not that he was alone in effecting
such a breach. Some time in the 270s, his uncle and erstwhile regent
Cleonymus married a Eurypontid heiress, across dynastic lines. But
Areus was equal to the situation, and the dangerous liaison that
developed between his son (and future Agiad king) Acrotatus and
Cleonymus's Eurypontid spouse surely owed a good deal to his cunning diplomacy.

That diplomatic skill was even more in evidence on the grand scale
of Hellenistic inter-dynastic quarrelling. Early in the third century, he
was the supposed recipient (under the spelling 'Areius') of a letter from
the High Priest in Jerusalem, appealing to the common ancestry of the
Spartans and the Jews with a view to procuring Spartan aid against the
Seleucid king Antiochus. In 280 he invaded Aetolia after organizing a
Peloponnesian coalition against the Greeks' Macedonian suzerain. In
the late 270s, having switched sides, he received a timely infusion of
mercenary support from Macedon's king Antigonus II Gonatas, to help
him successfully beat off an attack on Sparta from Pyrrhus king of
Epirus. Shortly thereafter he concluded an alliance with Ptolemy II
Philadelphus of Egypt that enabled him to consider intervening across
the Isthmus of Corinth in the so-called Chremonidean War of 267–262
as part of a Spartan–Athenian–Ptolemaic axis. But it was also in his
reign that the famed 'Lycurgan' regime began seriously to disintegrate,

and in 265 he failed to breach the blockade imposed by the Macedonian garrison occupying Acrocorinth and was killed nearby.

Areus's initial mission was to liberate Delphi from the control of the Aetolian League. This goal no doubt owed as much to Areus's desire for personal power and prestige as it did to piety, though Sparta's traditional regard for Delphi was probably genuine enough. At any rate, though Areus's failure was costly in military terms, it was by no means a completely inglorious one, not least because he had managed to persuade Megara, Boeotia, some Argolic towns and four towns in Achaea in the northern Peloponnese (which were to form the nucleus of the Achaean League founded in 280) to join his cause. Rebuffed here, Areus resorted later in the 270s to a by now familiar Spartan regal ploy, recruiting mercenaries from Crete. But he was recalled from Crete posthaste in 272 to face yet another invasion of Laconia and assault on Sparta, this time by King Pyrrhus of Epirus. With his own 2,000 mercenaries, reinforced by mercenaries sent to his aid from Corinth by Antigonus II Gonatas of Macedon, Areus was able to raise the siege. Allegedly, too, an important contribution had been made by the extraordinary bravery of some aristocratic Spartan women, including the widow of Eudamidas I. This presaged the undoubtedly central roles certain Spartan women were to play in Sparta's history during the third quarter of the third century.

Areus's bid for a place in the Hellenistic world's premier division came unstuck during what is known, after one of its chief Athenian protagonists, as the Chremonidean War in the early 260s. Despite achieving some kind of link-up with one of the seriously big Hellenistic players, Ptolemy II of Egypt, Areus was himself killed near Corinth. Spartan fortunes were now about to hit their lowest ebb ever, lower even than in the immediate post-Leuctra decade of the 360s. For not only was Sparta's intended territorial reach abroad considerably shorter than its actual grasp, but at home the time-honoured 'Lycurgan' customs were foundering on the reef of gross and increasing social inequality among the supposedly 'equal' Spartiates, of whom there were by now only about 700 left. Cue the entrance of two reformist kings, one from each of the two royal houses, whose fame is owed, not least, to the fact that they were selected for the full biographical treatment by the ancient world's most distinguished biographer, Plutarch of Chaeronea in Boeotia, who flourished in the decades on either side of AD 100.

When Plutarch sat down to write his *Parallel Lives* of the great Greeks and Romans, he could hardly overlook the fame of the brothers Gracchus, Tiberius and Gaius. They had both held the office of tribune of the plebs (in 133, and 123 and 122, respectively). And both had been murdered amid bitter civil strife, punished for trying to introduce necessary reforms into a Roman Republican system of government that was still dominated by a deeply conservative and largely cohesive Senate. To which Greeks could Plutarch compare the stirring lives – and even more stirring deaths – of the Gracchi? Ideally, they should be a pair of brothers, but, failing that, at any rate a pair in some sense. His slightly awkward answer was: the Spartan kings Agis IV and Cleomenes III of Sparta. This choice explains why there are no separate biographies of these two remarkable kings in the present book. Their life-stories are at the same time the story of Sparta during the third quarter of the third century BC.

Any parallel between Agis and Cleomenes and the Gracchi brothers was, at best, inexact and far less than total. For a start, Agis and Cleomenes were not brothers, though they were at least related posthumously: Cleomenes married Agis' widow Agiatis. Nor were Agis and Cleomenes official representatives of the people of Sparta in the way that Tiberius and Gaius Gracchus had been elected tribunes of the Roman plebs on reformist tickets. They were hereditary kings, succeeding to the thrones of the Eurypontid and Agiad royal houses and ruling from *c.* 244–241 and 235–222 respectively. Yet, as Plutarch was surely not the first to see, there was indeed more than a little in common between the two Spartan kings and the two Roman Republican tribunes. The Spartans too were both killed in the course of bitter civil strife, and both had explicitly espoused a radical, if not revolutionary social programme, which they had sought to implement through manipulation of the powers of their office.

So, why did Agis IV and Cleomenes III live and die as they did? It is not enough, of course, simply to rely on Plutarch's joint *Life* for possible answers to that complex question. First, we must enquire into the nature and especially the reliability of the sources that Plutarch chose to follow. One writer above all, the contemporary third-century historian Phylarchus of Athens, was his preferred source. But how reliable was Phylarchus's account? If we are to believe his fiercest critic, Polybius, the great Arcadian historian of the rise of Rome, we would have to answer – not at all. Phylarchus was in fact singled out by name by Polybius as a paradigm of how not to write good history. What seems to have upset Polybius as much as anything else was Phylarchus' style, since he made the category error of confusing pragmatic historiography with the fictional, emotive literary genre of tragedy.

But there was also a serious ideological issue between them, and Polybius cannot be exonerated of the charge of partiality. He was born at Megalopolis in about 200 into the aristocratic elite that dominated the Achaean League in the later third and early second century (*see* p. 250). So far as the writing of history was concerned, he explicitly held the view that patriotism justified bias in favour of one's own country or city. Now, Cleomenes III of Sparta was a determined, and for a considerable time very successful, enemy of the Achaean League, who had actually sacked and dealt very savagely with Polybius' own Megalopolis just a generation before the historian's birth. Polybius therefore could not accept and indeed felt he had to demolish the generally very favourable picture of Cleomenes that he found in the work of Phylarchus.

Where does the truth lie? Plutarch's choice to follow Phylarchus for interpretation as well as the facts does not, unfortunately, decide the issue, since he was a moralizing biographer rather than the best kind of historian. The most we can claim therefore for our own account is that it will not be inconsistent with such facts as Phylarchus, Polybius and Plutarch between them preserve relatively unadorned, and that our interpretation of those facts at least makes consistent sense of one of the most intriguing as well as most important episodes in Spartan history.

One reason this episode is so fascinating is that it is one of those very rare occasions in all ancient Greek (or Roman) history where we can say for sure that the role of women was not only unusually prominent but actually decisive. Aristotle in the Politics had written a century earlier:

> at the time of the Spartans' domination (archê) many things were accomplished by the women.[1]

That referred probably to the period from 404 to 371 especially. It was, however, in the years between 244 and 221 that that rather controversial claim acquired real substance and substantiation. I have mentioned already that Cleomenes III married the widow of Agis IV, Agiatis. Plutarch tells us moreover that it was Agiatis, burning for revenge for the murder of her husband and no less keen than he to carry out the reform programme for which he had been murdered in the first place, who converted her second husband Cleomenes to the reformist cause. Then there were the mother and grandmother of Agis, Agesistrata and Archidamia, whom Plutarch confidently labelled 'the richest of all the Spartans' (including men as well as women), and who likewise gave Agis their unequivocal support; and, last but by no means least, Cleomenes's redoubtable mother Cratesicleia, who preceded her son into exile as a hostage at the court of Ptolemy III and was also murdered there in a bout of bloody faction fighting.

The Greek word for civil strife, faction-fighting, or civil war was *stasis* (it's now the modern Greek word for 'bus stop'...). Since *stasis* could sometimes threaten the very existence of a Greek *polis*, Aristotle had made its prevention or avoidance the main subject of Book V of his

Politics. But to little or no purpose, it would seem: at any rate, *stasis* continued to rack the Greek world in the third century as it had in the fifth and fourth. One apparent novelty, however, was that now Sparta too – the city famed in the preceding era for its *eunomia* (orderly good government) and social stability – was as disturbed by *stasis* as any other Greek city. The root of the condition here as elsewhere was extreme and increasing inequality in the distribution and ownership of landed property.

Sparta once had prided itself on precisely the opposite. Its boasted political equality among the Homoioi or 'Similars' was supposed to be based on a foundational economic equality among the citizens that went back originally to the supposed legislation of Lycurgus, which had included an allegedly equal distribution of land in Laconia and Messenia. Actually, Spartan land was not at all equally distributed, and never had been. There were always rich Spartans and poor Spartans, as there were in other Greek cities. The sharp and increasingly sensitive difference between Sparta and some other Greek cities was this: if a Spartan became too impoverished to contribute a legally fixed minimum of natural produce to his common mess (*suskanion, syssition*), he forfeited his status as a Homoios and became a member of the sub-citizen class of Hupomeiones ('Inferiors'). This automatic demotion, in turn, more and more weakened Sparta's effective military strength, which had guaranteed its great-power status inside and outside Greece down to the battle of Leuctra in 371.

However exactly the mechanism of land-concentration in Sparta operated (modern scholars are as divided on this issue as the ancient sources were), this factor was probably the main reason for the growing shortage of Spartiate military manpower (*oliganthrôpia*), whereby between 400 and 250 the citizen body fell from a figure of about 3,000 to only 700, of whom just 100 held a substantial stake in landed property-ownership. It was this dire situation that Agis IV set out to remedy, and he did so by proclaiming the time-honoured rallying slogans of an oppressed peasantry – cancellation of debts and the redistribution of land. This in itself was, paradoxically, a sign of Sparta's increasing 'normalization'. It was becoming less and less of a special case in social and economic terms, even if it remained politically very odd indeed by general Greek standards.

Apart from a handful of rich individuals who were either relatives of Agis or otherwise bound to him, the rich Spartans as a group predictably combined to resist his measures of reform, and in the usual Spartan way they turned to Agis's fellow-king, the Agiad Leonidas II (reigned *c.* 254–235), to champion their cause. Agis was initially a match for them. Leonidas was exiled, debts were indeed cancelled, and written mortgage-deeds (known as *klaria* from *klaros*, meaning a lot or plot of land) were symbolically and publicly burned. But that was the extent of Agis's success. Before he could turn seriously to the planned land-redistribution, he suffered a humiliating reverse abroad, at the isthmus of Corinth, and on his return to Sparta was murdered by his enemies, together with his immediate relatives.

The cause of reform, necessary though it was pragmatically and equally justified on ethical grounds, had to be put on hold for almost fifteen years. It was taken up, somewhat surprisingly, by Leonidas' son Cleomenes, who succeeded his father on the Agiad throne in 235. Unlike Agis, Cleomenes realized that foreign policy mattered as much as domestic, and he prepared the way for internal reform by a series of remarkable military successes, most conspicuously against Aratus of Sicyon and the Achaean League that he dominated. His sack of Megalopolis (in 223), mentioned above, was the culmination of this successful enterprise, which for a time had even made it look as though Cleomenes might restore Sparta to something like the position of international dominance the state had enjoyed down to 371.

Cleomenes, however, was not just a proficient military leader. He was also a highly effective domestic reformer, even possibly a social revolutionary. Agis, so far as we can tell, had merely proposed a radical land-redistribution. Figures of 4,500 land lots for Spartans and 15,000 for Perioeci are mentioned as his ultimate targets, but he had made little or no progress towards achieving them. Cleomenes, however, beginning in 227, actually carried out a land-redistribution in Laconia on something like that scale. Moreover, he did not include just the poor Spartans in his scheme but also poor Perioeci. He additionally set free some 6,000 of the remaining Laconian Helots, in exchange for a manumission fee payable by them in cash. The fact that they had the cash to pay the fee is in itself interesting as another sign of the changing nature of Sparta's economy. These ex-Helots presumably thus became the owners of the land on which they had previously worked under compulsion. They also became full citizens, not just Neodamodeis like the Helots liberated by the Spartans for military purposes between the 420s and 370s. Also included in Cleomenes's package were numbers of his mercenary soldiers. These formed a key part of Cleomenes's military reforms, whereby he had tried to bring the decadent and outmoded Spartan army up to the best Hellenistic standards set by Antigonid Macedon or Ptolemaic Egypt.

To make absolutely sure that his political enemies could not prevent or overturn his reforms, he first had them murdered and then took decisive personal control of the political institutions and structures that might be used to thwart him. Ephors were killed, the dual monarchy was effectively abolished when he placed his brother Euclidas on the Eurypontid throne, and the Gerousia of hoary antiquity (mentioned in the Great Rhetra) was bypassed and downgraded by the creation of the office of Patronomos. Nor were Cleomenes's reforms confined to the economic and political spheres. He also embarked on major social reform, aiming to restore the Agoge, the supposedly 'Lycurgan' regime of comprehensive and uniform public education for all prospective male citizens, and reinstate communal living in messes and constant training for the adult citizen-warriors. It is in this regard, above all, that the question must be asked whether Cleomenes was not merely a reformer but also a social revolutionary, possibly an ideologically or even philosophically motivated revolutionary.

Sphaerus, of Borysthenes on the Black Sea, is reported to have visited Sparta when Cleomenes was in power and conducting his reforms; and Sphaerus was a noted Stoic philosopher with an unusually practical concern to change the world as it was and to see Stoic ideas implemented in practice. Andrew Erskine is the most convinced and forceful recent exponent of the view that behind Cleomenes' practical social reform package lay the ideas and inspiration of the Stoic Sphaerus.[2] Perhaps. If Cleomenes really had been so philosophically motivated and inspired, it would certainly be another clear indication of the massive cultural change that Sparta had undergone since the heyday of, for example, King Agesilaus II (c. 445–360). But that connection cannot unfortunately be demonstrated. In any case, the reforms had only a very short shelf life. In 222 Cleomenes was decisively defeated at Sellasia just north of Sparta by Antigonus III of Macedon. His reforms were annulled and reversed. Three years later, Cleomenes himself met a less than glorious death in exile at the Ptolemaic capital Alexandria. This brought to an end a remarkable and possibly unrepeatable political and social experiment.

For the next period, Sparta's fortunes ran again at a low ebb. A couple of individuals, first Lycurgus (significant name!) and then Machanidas, raised themselves above the crowd and figured briefly in military and political roles that earned them the designation of 'tyrant' from unfriendly sources. But it was only following Machanidas's disastrous and costly (4,000 'Spartan' dead allegedly) defeat at the Battle of Mantinea in 207, twelve years after Cleomenes's death, that Sparta again experienced a significant renascence, under yet another 'tyrant'. For the next fifteen years, Sparta's destiny was to be associated with the name of Nabis son of Demaratus.

NABIS

Nabis' name has been thought to be semitic rather than (Indo-European) Greek, and, despite his claim, based on his father's name, to lineal descent from the deposed Eurypontid king Demaratus who was exiled in about 490, he was probably a mere upstart usurper. He was born somewhere around 250 to 245. In 207 he seized the crown – now a single crown –

on the perhaps suspiciously well-timed death of his royal ward with the evocative name of Pelops. In the manner of Greek tyrants of old, he formed a personal bodyguard of mercenaries and summoned in aid also some Cretan pirates. Once in power, he did nothing to avoid the associations of royalty. On the contrary: he lived in a palace, the first time southern Greece had seen such a building since the Mycenaean Late Bronze Age, kept a stable of parade-horses, and of course had himself styled 'king' on coins, official brick-stamps and other inscribed documents.

Nabis is said to have tortured and then exiled his Spartan opponents and forced their wives to marry ex-Helots whom he had both liberated and made Spartan citizens. His own wife was a foreigner, a Greek woman from Argos called Apia; such dynastic marriages were commonplace among Hellenistic rulers. But this was the first time a Spartan ruler got away with marrying outside Sparta in this way. A predecessor, Leonidas II, had been temporarily ousted in 244 precisely because he had married a non-Spartan wife.

For fifteen years, Nabis managed to remain at the helm, but in 192 he was assassinated in a coup carried out by the Aetolian League, the main Greek rival of the Achaean League. The sources we have are uniformly hostile to him, so it is difficult to judge the significance of the claim that he sought to revolutionise the state in his own dictatorial interests by restoring a version of the drastic reforms of Cleomenes III that had been overturned on that king's overthrow in 222. Perhaps it would be nearer the mark to say that he set in motion the necessary modernization of Sparta that would finally bring it out of its particularistic and parochial Lycurgan shadow and into the sunlight of the more cosmopolitan late Hellenistic Greek world.

Whereas Cleomenes III had liberated 6,000 Helots only as a last-ditch military manoeuvre, probably with no long-term social implications for the end of Helotage in general in mind, Nabis liberated Helots as a set policy, as part of an economic modernization package. He encouraged a more flexible, market-oriented outlook, giving a boost to artisanal and trading activities, such that by the end of his reign Sparta could plausibly for the first time be depicted as economically dependent on the outside world. In foreign affairs, though, his fortunes were mixed, and finally Rome in the shape of Titus Quinctius Flamininus put an end to any pretensions to independence in 195, when he was forced to surrender control of not only Argos but also the Laconian ports of the Perioeci. An attempt to regain these in 193 was subdued by Flamininus in association with Philopoemen, general of the Achaean League, and in the following year Nabis himself was assassinated.

Nabis's legacy was most tangibly apparent in the city-wall that Sparta finally completed not later than 188, though it had probably been conceived or at least most determinedly forwarded under the regime of Nabis. In the good old days of the Classical era, the very idea of throwing a defensive girdle round Sparta had been scorned as effeminate – though there were also sound practical reasons for not doing so, both positive (Sparta already had adequate defences, both environmental and human) and negative (the physical separation of Sparta's fifth constituent village, Amyclae). Now, at the turn of the third and second centuries, Sparta desperately needed the protection a city-wall could afford, and besides, a ruler like Nabis could make political capital out of building an exceptionally large and powerful enceinte. In the event, Sparta's new city wall measured some 48 *stades* (about six miles) in circumference, and was constructed out of tile-capped mudbrick placed on top of a stone base, interspersed with lookout towers at regular intervals. At the same time as the wall was going up, in *c.* 200, one of Sparta's four core villages, Cynosura ('Dog's Tail'), publicly thanked its official water-commissioner, another sign both of Sparta's urbanization and of heightened concern over urban security.

Rome's decisive intervention, whatever its precise motivation, redounded principally to the immediate benefit of the Achaean League, which since its formation in 280 had become one of the two most powerful Greek groupings of cities, the other being the Aetolian League.

Sparta and Achaea had been enemies since the time of Cleomenes III, and on the familiar principle that my enemy's enemy is my friend, Sparta and Aetolia had been allies. Yet it was an Aetolian-sponsored hand, ironically, that dispatched Nabis in 192, since Aetolia feared that Nabis was unreliable. But that too merely played into the hands of Achaea, which through Philopoemen forcibly incorporated Sparta in the Achaean League in 192. This was a humiliation and shock for Sparta on an unprecedented scale. Once – and not all that long ago – still a force to be reckoned with, at least in Peloponnesian politics, Sparta, was now on a par with the humblest constituent member of the Achaean League. Its autonomy, a prized component of the Greeks' cherished value of freedom, was at an end. Four years later, in 188, Philopoemen completed the humiliation by a thoroughgoing internal reform – in the exact opposite sense to the reforms carried out by Agis, Cleomenes and, to some extent, Nabis. He abolished the laws of 'Lycurgus', whatever precisely that now meant, and – consistently in a way – destroyed Sparta's un-Lycurgan new city wall.

Sparta now in a sense had two masters, Achaea and Rome. The next near-decade saw a series of diplomatic toings and froings between southern Greece and the city of Rome, as various groups of Spartan exiles attempted to persuade the Roman Senate, against fierce Achaean opposition, to restore both them and some semblance of 'Lycurgan' Sparta (but including the city-wall). Eventually in about 180–179 the exile problem was solved, and the city-wall rebuilt, but any sort of restoration of a supposedly Lycurgan Sparta had to wait much longer than that, at least until after Rome's general settlement of southern Greece in 146. Meanwhile, in the winter of 168/7, a most significant event occurred. The leading Roman general L. Aemilius Paullus had, in the summer of 168, defeated King Philip V of Macedon at the Battle of Pydna. In the following winter, he undertook a large-scale progress through Greece, at least part of the purpose of which was what we might call cultural tourism. As a key stop on his itinerary he called in at Sparta, since he wished, as it was reported, to pay his respects to

Sparta's ancestral way of life. Actually, there was not much left of that beyond a peculiar style of clothing and way of wearing the hair for the men. But it may well have been Paullus' visit that gave crucial impetus to the Spartans' subsequent determined efforts to turn their city into a kind of theme park, a museum of their once glorious past, precisely as a way of attracting cultural tourists like Paullus and claiming a place in the Hellenistic sun, on cultural rather than military or political grounds.

Sparta smarted under its subjection, as it was viewed, to Achaea. Achaea for its part smarted under Rome's punishment for Achaea's having sided with Philip's Macedon in the war with Rome; this involved the forcible transfer to Rome and Italy of 1,000 leading Achaeans, including Polybius, as hostages. It was the issue of Spartan independence from Achaea that brought Achaea into conflict again with Sparta and, thereby, into conflict with and final defeat by Rome, during the period between 152 and 146 that Polybius (repatriated finally in 150, and by then a partisan of Rome) contemptuously labelled 'confusion and disturbance'. In 148 Sparta, now under the strong leadership of Menalcidas (suitably named – from a combination of the Greek words for 'might' and 'strength'), finally seceded from the Achaean League, leaving it on the sidelines as the Achaeans in turn revolted against Rome in what, from the Roman point of view, was the Achaean War.

That war was terminated drastically in 146 by L. Mummius's victory and savage reprisals against the rebels. Sparta, by contrast, came out of it all rather well. Independence from the now defunct Achaean League was of course exchanged for subordination to the overall suzerain of Greece, Rome, but the city had its rebuilt wall left intact, and it was probably now that a limited restoration of 'Lycurgan' institutions was accomplished. This affected above all the Agoge, and it is to this post-146 Agoge that most of the extant evidence, especially inscriptions from the sanctuary of Orthia by the Eurotas, relates. However, Sparta was now just one city-state like any other, confined more or less to its immediate hinterland in the Spartan plain, since it had been certainly deprived of the last of its Perioeci, with the possible exception of those in the Belminatis area at the head of the Eurotas valley, and even in the Spartan plain was probably soon also bereft of any remaining Helots. Roman Sparta may properly be said to have begun life here, and a very different Sparta it was too, another city altogether compared to its Hellenistic, Classical and Archaic forebears.

Antiquarianism was the keynote of the new Sparta, and appropriately enough the city, never before famed as a centre of written culture, at last produced its own homegrown antiquarians to record the processes of fossilization. Contact between Sparta and Rome intensified, to the extent that Sparta built a special hostel for visiting Roman officials. Nothing much of note happened in Sparta's recorded public history between 146 and 88, the outbreak of the first war of Rome against the Pontic king Mithradates, into which the Spartans were reluctantly drawn. This seems to have involved a seaborne raid on Sparta via the Eurotas valley, and prompted some repairs to the city-wall. By the early 70s, however, peace was sufficiently restored for the young Cicero to emulate Aemilius Paullus and pay a tourist's visit to Sparta, though he came as a student rather than a conqueror.

In 49 civil war broke out at the highest level within the Roman Empire, between the rival forces of Pompey and Julius Caesar. The Greeks as a whole were within Pompey's sphere, and the Spartans like the others had little choice but to comply with his request for troops when Greece briefly became the main theatre of the Civil War. Spartan coinage of the period confirms that kingship of any form was then defunct; Polybius's interesting if flawed comparison of the Spartan constitution and the Roman Republican constitution, which involved likening the Spartan dual kingship to the Roman dual consulship, would have had no purchase whatsoever. But, as we shall see, monarchy at Sparta had by no means had its day.

Pompey was killed in Egypt in 48, and Caesar assumed sole governance of the Roman world under the title of Dictator. Though he was assassinated in 44, the Roman world was tending inexorably towards a form of monarchy, and that was eventually achieved effectively and lastingly by Julius Caesar's adopted son and heir, Octavian, better known to history under his assumed name of Augustus. In 42, when Octavian was but 19, and when Greece was under the authority of the conservative republican Marcus Brutus, the Spartans boldly, if not rashly, declared their support for Octavian and his then political associate, Mark Antony (Marcus Antonius). That move, together with the shelter they provided in 40 to Octavian's future wife Livia, was to prove hugely provident and providential, as Augustus first defeated Antony at Actium in 31 and then settled himself as the first Roman emperor (in all but name) in 27. As the only mainland Greek city to have supported Octavian at Actium, Sparta 'for a while was the cynosure of the newly created (in 27 BC) province of Achaia'.[3] In 21 Augustus went so far as to dignify the city with his own presence and dine with the local officials.

The last Spartan hero (if that is the right term) to grace our history is Gaius Julius Eurycles, who by his very name tells us that we have entered a new, Rome-dominated world. He owed his *nomen* (family name) Julius to the fact that he was awarded the Roman citizenship as a gift from the most famous Julius of all in his day, Gaius Julius Octavianus Caesar Augustus, otherwise known to us as Octavian or Augustus, but to his contemporaries usually as plain Caesar. It was to honour Eurycles, in part, that Augustus paid the above-mentioned visit to Sparta. Eurycles stood then at the pinnacle of the system of euergetism, politically inspired public generosity, on which Sparta by now relied, like other Greek cities, to meet both its ordinary and its extraordinary expenditure. It was therefore in Augustus's as well as Eurycles' interests that Eurycles should be provided with the necessary wherewithal for his benefactions. And well provided he certainly was.

Strabo, the contemporary Greek geographer from Asia Minor, spoke of Eurycles's position as one of 'presidency' (*epistasia*) over the Spartans, and referred to him as their 'leader' or 'commander' (*hêgemôn*). So, once again, Sparta had a *de facto* monarch, as if Sparta, like Egypt according to Herodotus, really could not do without kings. Augustus, who was himself a de facto monarch over the entire Roman world, would have understood and sympathized. Eurycles naturally, like Areus, issued coins with the message '(minted) under Eurycles'. And with the huge wealth he owned, that – thanks probably to Livia's intervention – included possession of the offshore island of Cythera, he made vastly generous outlays on ceremonial and consumption. Conspicuous among the buildings he funded were the rebuilt theatre, the Peloponnese's second biggest, used, not for Athenian-style tragic and comic plays of course, but rather for political demonstrations; a gymnasium; and an aqueduct. Conspicuous among his other areas of concern was official religion; indeed, he can be said to have presided over something of a religious revival, involving the performance of sacrifices in Sparta's name to Helen and the Dioscuri (Castor and Pollux, brothers of Helen, as we saw towards the beginning of this book) at Sparta, and to Poseidon (formerly Pohoidan in the local dialect) at Taenarum in southern Mani.

The story of Menelaus and his stunningly beautiful but unfaithful wife Helen exercised a perennial attraction for Greek storytellers from Homer onwards. Here, an Athenian vase-painter of the time of the Persian Wars recalls the original East-West conflict by depicting Menelaus at the moment when, after ten long years of fighting, he at last gets a grip on his errant wife once again. Helen of Troy, daughter of Tyndareus (or Zeus) and Leda, was by origin Helen of Sparta. According to the *Odyssey*, she returned there with Menelaus to play her allotted role as his stately queen.

Such religious antiquarianism should have appealed to Augustus, as it was surely calculated to. But other actions of Eurycles did not. Perhaps he overplayed his hand in reasserting Sparta's control over the liberated, formerly Perioecic coastal cities of Laconia. Perhaps he showed himself too friendly to Livia's son and Augustus's stepson, Tiberius, when the latter had fallen very publicly out of favour with his stepfather in 6 BC. Whatever the cause, Eurycles was twice put on trial before Augustus, deprived of his 'presidency', and exiled. He died, a disgraced exile, before 2 BC, the year in which Augustus completed his own rise to autocratic power by receiving from the Senate the title of 'Father of the Fatherland' (Pater Patriae): in other words, founder of a hereditary dynasty.

When Augustus ended his long life and reign fifteen years later, however, in AD 14, Eurycles's successors were well placed to curry imperial favour with the new emperor, Tiberius, and have themselves reinstated as imperial Rome's favourites and Sparta's rulers. A son of Eurycles was called 'Laco' ('Spartan') and a son of his 'Spartiaticus' (the Latin form of Greek 'Spartiates'). Tradition thus continued to be reinvented, in a thoroughly Spartan sort of way.

10

THE LEGACY:
LEONIDAS LIVES!

This final chapter will offer a brief discussion of the development of the Spartan myth or legend, from antiquity to today, using Leonidas as the linking thread. He did not quite become a legend in his own lifetime, but the Thermopylae legend that sprang up at once after his death centred around his leadership and heroic feats. His own legend has certainly not suffered from neglect since antiquity, and is indeed as I write set to receive the full Hollywood treatment – again. Before we scale those dizzy heights, we must first briefly review what little is known of his life leading up to his climactic self-sacrificial death.

We know of a number of Spartans called Leon (meaning 'lion'). It was a fairly obvious name to employ in a warlike society, close to wild nature, the aristocratic families of which, including the two royal houses, claimed descent from lion-slaying Heracles. Not surprisingly, therefore, Leon was used as a royal name, but we know of only two Spartans called Leonidas (which means 'descendant of Leon'), both of them kings from the royal house of the Agiads. By far the more famous of the two was our present subject, Leonidas I.

He was probably born in about 540, and his very birth is not the least interesting or important thing about him. For he was born to his father's first wife, but only after his father had had a legitimate son, Cleomenes, with a second – and apparently bigamous – wife. Herodotus wrote that Anaxandridas' bigamy was 'totally un-Spartan': maybe so, but it did not prevent Cleomenes from assuming the throne on his father's death in about 520 and becoming indeed one of the most powerful and colourful Spartan rulers of this or any age. After Cleomenes' birth Anaxandridas achieved, finally, successful conception with his original wife – hence, first, Dorieus, and then two further sons, Leonidas and Cleombrotus.

Thus Leonidas was one of four sons of his father Anaxandridas, the second to be born to his first wife, the third son overall. If he was indeed born about 540, then he would have been of marriageable age by normal Spartan standards by about 510 at the latest, yet Leonidas either married a woman unknown and then was widowed or divorced, or he chose not to marry at all until his one known marriage – in the later 490s to Gorgo (*see* Chapter 3 for her biography). Since Gorgo was a royal princess, a *patrouchos* (heiress) and his step-niece into the bargain, there is every reason for thinking that Leonidas might have deliberately delayed his marriage for dynastic as well as economic purposes until Gorgo was at the normal marriage age for Spartan young women, in her late teens.

In about 490 or 489, his elder half-brother Cleomenes I committed an idiosyncratic form of *hara-kiri* and ended thereby both his life and his tenure of the Agiad throne. Did he jump – or was he pushed, and if so, was he pushed by Leonidas? The finger of suspicion has been pointed at Leonidas for putative regicide, but nothing can be proven, and perhaps, if there had been serious evidence or even suspicion of his complicity, he might not have been chosen for his lead role at Thermopylae a decade later.

With Gorgo, he had one son, Pleistarchus, which put him on a level footing with the special bodyguard of 300 Spartans who were chosen to accompany him to Thermopylae in part because they all had living sons. However, that was not, presumably, the only or even the main reason why he rather than his Eurypontid co-king Leotychidas was selected to lead what was officially the advance Spartan party to the pass. At any rate, his subsequent behaviour as commander fully justified the state's decision. The quality of Leonidas' deeds is not in question. He matched them, remarkably, with his words. Two of his especially *bons mots* show that in laconic gallows humour he could compete with the best of them. When asked by Xerxes to surrender his arms and submit to the might of Persia, he is said to have replied, in just two Greek words (*molôn labe*), 'come and get them yourself'. To his men, at break of the third and final day of the resistance in the pass, he reportedly said something like 'Eat a hearty breakfast, as tonight we shall dine in Hades.' This was an oblique reference to the fact that Spartans when in Sparta took just the one compulsory meal a day, the communal evening mess meal.

During the battle for Thermopylae there was an Homeric moment on the third and final day when some of the few remaining Spartiates fought to the death to try to prevent the Persians getting hold of Leonidas' corpse, for all the world as if they were Homer's Greeks at Troy fighting to preserve the dead Patroclus for proper burial by Achilles. In the end, of course, they were in no position to prevent the Persians from doing whatever they liked to Leonidas' body, and one persistent Greek story was that the Persians mutilated it. An anecdote told by Herodotus reinforces this story in reverse: after the Greeks' victory at Plataea in 479, one Greek hothead suggested to the Spartan commander-in-chief, Pausanias, that he should have the corpse of the Persian commander Mardonius mutilated in revenge. Pausanias' cold, blunt and entirely admirable response was to tell him that that was not the Greek way.

Whether or not Leonidas' corpse really was mutilated, his remains – or what were considered to be them – were brought back to Sparta for reburial forty years later. The site of his death had, however, been marked since soon after 480 by a stone lion, a *leôn* that will have permanently recalled Leonidas. Whereas ordinary Spartans who died abroad on campaign were buried on the spot, and commemorated at home by gravemarkers bearing the laconic information that such and such 'died in war', it was apparently normal Spartan practice to bring back the bodies of their kings for burial in Sparta, embalming them in wax or honey as necessary. That was not possible in the case of Leonidas, and in the place of his corpse a simulated image was prepared for burial. To compensate, he was given a splendid version of the extraordinary funeral rites ('more than befitted a human being', in Xenophon's phrase) that were reserved for all kings, rites that to Herodotus' well-informed eyes seemed more barbarian, specifically Scythian, than typically Greek.

As far as these can be reconstructed, they involved horsemen first riding around the vast territory of the Spartan state, summoning mourners from every Perioecic and every Helot family in the land, men as well as women. In Sparta itself, all public business was suspended, and a ten-day period of national mourning was decreed. Public debts were rescinded, some prisoners were released. The actual ceremony went off with a great deal of din, caused both by the (exceptionally permitted) wailing of the female mourners and by the crashing and bashing of metal vessels. For a moment the social and political structure of the Spartan *polis* was held in a state of suspended animation until *'Le roi est mort!'* could be followed by a triumphant *'Vive le roi!'* – provided of course there was no succession dispute, as there quite often was. Leonidas' (re)burial in Sparta in about 440 came at a delicate moment of international relations, with Spartan opinions veering between peacemaking and bellicosity towards Athens during the currency of the Peace of 445. Perhaps the belated funeral rites were intended to reconcile all Spartan domestic factions by compelling their attention on an agreed object that recalled Sparta's glory days of leading the triumphant resistance to Persia – a role since usurped by, or handed over to, Athens.

All Spartan kings were, in my considered view, treated as heroes in the technical sense after their death: that is, they were venerated with religious cult as heroes, superhuman demi-gods. However, in the case of Leonidas, the veneration was understandably given an exceptionally high definition, and in the Hellenistic era the Spartans built a permanent shrine, the Leonidaeum, and inaugurated an annual Leonidaea festival in his honour. This festival was refounded late in the reign of the Roman Emperor Trajan (AD 98–117), probably just when – and because – Trajan was warring against the ancient Persians' descendants, the Parthians, and the refoundation was financed by a benefactor with the splendidly Graeco-Roman name of C. Iulius Agesilaus. In its Roman-period guise the festival was accompanied by a fair, to which the Spartans, in direct contravention of their ancestors' habitual xenophobia, deliberately sought to attract travelling merchants by exempting them from the usual local sales and import taxes. There is even mention of a publicly regulated bank of commercial exchange in operation, something the Spartans of Leonidas' own day could not have begun to contemplate let alone tolerate or encourage.

In the mid-second century of our era when Pausanias the Periegete from Asia Minor passed through Sparta, he found the Spartans actively cultivating the claims of their city as a shrine to the memory of the Graeco–Persian Wars of six or more centuries earlier. The memorial for Leonidas found its place on his itinerary along with the tomb of admiral Eurybiadas, the memorials for Regent Pausanias and the Thermopylae dead, and the so-called Persian Stoa in the agora. Pausanias can be quite easily placed within the context of the general movement of cultural recuperation known for short as the Second Sophistic: Leonidas was an obvious hero of the Greek past for contemporary rhetoricians and sophists to praise, even if their praise was often overdone and rightly earned a satirical putdown from the brilliantly witty Lucian.

Plutarch, on the other hand, another ornament of the Second Sophistic, would not have dreamt of satirizing Leonidas. On the contrary, he wrote a biography of him, though this unfortunately has not come down to us. Instead, we have the apophthegms attributed to Leonidas in the allegedly Plutarchan *Sayings of Kings and Commanders* and the more authentically Plutarchan sayings that Plutarch incorporated in extant *Lives* such as those of Lycurgus and Cleomenes III (reigned 236–221). To quote from the latter:

> *It is said that, when the Leonidas of olden times was*
> *asked to give his view of the quality of Tyrtaeus as*
> *a poet, he replied: 'A fine one for arousing the spirits*
> *of the young.' This was on the grounds that the poems*
> *filled the young with such enthusiasm that they stopped*
> *worrying about their own lives in battle.* [1]

Thus, in the work of an author of the second century AD, via a remark attributed to a king of the fifth century BC, the reader is taken back to the Spartans' 'national' poet of the seventh century BC, altogether a span of some 800 years of tradition.

In the following, third century AD, the Christian apologist Origen (*c.* 185–253) appealed to pagan precedent in his war of words with the pagan Celsus. He did not scruple to suggest that the central Christian mystery of Christ's passion and death might be illuminated by a comparison with the self-chosen and avoidable death of Leonidas. A century later, as the struggle between pagan and Christian (and indeed Christian and Christian) intensified, Synesius of Cyrene was proud to proclaim his supposed Spartan lineage, and more particularly his descent – like Leonidas' – from Eurysthenes, one of the supposed founders of the two Spartan royal houses. Synesius' bookishness was hardly an ancient Spartan trait, but his passionate devotion to hunting in his pre-Christian days would not have struck his supposed Spartan ancestors as at all odd.

Such kinship claims, made by whole communities as well as individuals, are attested from as early as the fifth century BC, but they became common currency throughout the Greek world from the Hellenistic era (last three centuries BC) onwards. For example, in the early third century BC, the High Priest of Jerusalem even laid claim to the common descent of the Jews and the Spartans from Abraham and Moses. Such a boast of course had more to do with contemporary political necessity than with genealogical accuracy and authenticity. As for the factuality of Synesius' claim, Cyrene was actually founded from Thera in the seventh century BC, and the further belief – also attested in Herodotus – that Thera (modern Santorini) was itself founded from Sparta was more than a little dubitable. Synesius' particular immediate aim, perhaps optimistic and certainly self-serving, was to liken his struggle against the nomads ravaging Cyrenaica to Leonidas' struggle to defend Greece against the Persian invaders. Though far from qualifying as the last of the pagans (he subsequently became a bishop and converted to Christianity...), Synesius marks a suitable point of exit from the ancient world.

The Renaissance was more of a Western than an Eastern, more of a Roman than a Hellenic, intellectual and cultural movement. One exception to that rule was a man who bridged the divide between East and West, Ciriaco dei Pizzicolli, a merchant more familiarly known after his place of Italian origin as Cyriac of Ancona. To him, we owe a travelogue of 1447 that outdid even Pausanias the Periegete in its jeremiad-like *recherche du temps perdu*. Among a long list of Spartan warriors of yore whose absence he lamented as he approached Sparta via Mistra (then still, just, capital of the Despotate of the Morea, but shortly to succumb to the Ottoman Turks) was, inevitably, Leonidas.

Moving from one end of Europe to the other, we find, in the later sixteenth century, the Scottish humanist and historian George Buchanan (in 1579) praising Leonidas, along with Agesilaus II and others, as true kings, by contrast with modern monarchs too much sunk in luxury. He was opposed, however, by Algernon Blackwood (in 1581), who took the constitutionalist view that, in Sparta, kings enjoyed merely the name and empty title of king rather than the substance of kingly power. At almost exactly the same moment Michel de Montaigne was writing as follows in his essay 'On the Cannibals' (1580) – not perhaps the most obvious place to look for such a remark:

> ... *there are triumphant defeats that rival victories.*
> *Salamis, Plataea, Mycale and Sicily* [he means the Battle
> of Himera, legendarily fought on the same day as Salamis]
> *are the fairest sister-victories under the sun, yet they would*

never dare compare their combined glory with the glorious
defeat of King Leonidas and his men in the pass
of Thermopylae.[2]

This is a typically acute observation. Though a defeat in fact, Thermopylae had come to look uncommonly like a victory, really.

Montaigne's fellow-countryman Fénelon almost a century later used Leonidas, his only Spartan, as a character in one of his *Dialogues des Morts*. The idea and title of the work were borrowed ultimately from Lucian (who staged imaginary dialogues, both intrinsically plausible and historically possible, and neither). However, the notion of a dialogue between a Spartan king and Great King Xerxes of Persia was taken rather from Herodotus (even though strictly Herodotus' Demaratus was by then an ex-king). Like Buchanan, Fénelon depicted Leonidas as a true king, in contrast to Xerxes, and painted him in thoroughly local Spartan colours:

I exercized my kingship on condition that I led a hard, sober
and industrious life, just like that of my people. I was king
solely to defend my fatherland and to ensure the rule of law.
My kingship gave me the power to do good without permitting
me the license to do evil.[3]

Xerxes, alas, was for Fénelon simply 'too powerful and too fortunate' a king; had he not been so, he 'would have been a quite honourable man'.

Not long after, at the very end of the seventeenth century, Leonidas' exploits in defence of freedom were briefly glorified across the Channel on the English stage. The author drew a contrast between these and the deplorable factionalism of Regent Pausanias in an otherwise unmemorable English play named after the latter, for which Purcell wrote the incidental music (1696). Far more effective and deserving of commemoration was the glorification of Leonidas by Richard 'Leonidas' Glover in his famous poem of that title originally published in 1737, a high point in the Leonidas legend. Glover's Leonidas is a patriot to the core, a public-spirited lover of freedom and observer of austere self-denial opposed in principle to the luxurious Persians who languished under 'The absolute controulment of their King' Xerxes.

This extensive work started the process of constructing a modern myth that was to evolve from a literary paradigm in Glover's hands into a rallying cry both for and against revolution. In the shape of the Victorian public school tradition inaugurated by Thomas Arnold of Rugby and continued into the twentieth century by Kurt Hahn's Gordonstoun, it has centrally informed one of the most powerful vectors of British or English political and cultural identity. The legendary classical paradigm of eighteenth-century ideals thus became of central importance to the Classical tradition as a whole. Here is a perfect local illustration of the continually changing reception of Classical antiquity that has dominated so many aspects of European culture since the Renaissance.

The cult of Thermopylae was hardly peculiar to England, however. The national wars of the end of the eighteenth century and above all the growth of philhellenism prepared the way for what might be called without exaggeration 'the Age of Leonidas' in Europe in the early nineteenth century. The most splendid single manifestation by far of this cultural phenomenon is Jacques-Louis David's painting *Léonidas at Thermopylae*, first exhibited in 1814 but many years in the preparation. Napoleon, apparently ignorant of or unmoved by the Montaigne line on Thermopylae, asked, when he went to view it, why David had bothered to paint the defeated. Subsequent viewers have mostly not shared the limited Napoleonic vision and have almost unanimously agreed that it was worth the trip to the Louvre.

The foreground is occupied by helmeted warriors and naked youths, in a variety of poses and attitudes, the whole very formally and symmetrically composed and disposed. Behind them on the right, battle is joined between Greeks and Persians, to the accompaniment of trumpeters; on the left, warriors in helmets and Spartan-style red cloaks brandish

Overleaf: Léonidas at Thermopylae (1814), by J.-L. David (Louvre)

wreaths in the direction of a similarly attired warrior who appears to be carving a rupestral inscription (actually a slightly foxed French translation of part of the Simonidean 'Go, tell the Spartans...' epigram) with the hilt of his sword. The still centre of the painting, and the painting's central figure, is of course Leonidas. He too is depicted heroically nude but for his cloak, which flows over his left shoulder and under his body, a pair of sandals, and a notably fancy plumed helmet. His shield is slung by its strap over his left shoulder, forming a kind of backrest. In his left hand he holds a spear, in his right he grasps a sword, the scabbard of which provocatively covers, while simultaneously drawing attention to, what popular newspapers would now call his manhood. David was himself homosexual, and it is no accident that the viewer's eye is drawn first to Leonidas' sexuality and then to the highlighted buttocks of the prancing youth at the right of the frame. David considered the work his masterpiece, asking rhetorically at the very end of his life 'I suppose you know that no one but David could have painted Leonidas?'

Yet splendid though this is, it should not be allowed to eclipse the beginnings of the Greeks' own recuperation of their past and cultural heritage. An early illustration is the 'Patriotic Hymn' of Constantinos Rhigas (1798), inspired obviously by the Marseillaise, which contains a stirring address to the spirit of Leonidas. Byron too, the best-known of the philhellenes, echoed and sought to encourage that native strain in his *Childe Harold's Pilgrimage* of 1812:

> *Sons of the Greeks, arise!*
> ...
> *Brave shades of chiefs and sages,*
> *Behold the coming strife!*
> *Hellenes of past ages,*
> *Oh, start again to life!*
> ...
> *Sparta, Sparta, why in slumbers*
> *Lethargic dost thou lie?*

Awake, and join in numbers
With Athens, old ally!
Leonidas recalling,
That chief of ancient song,
Who saved ye once from falling,
The terrible! the strong!

Some four years later, J. M. Gandy, a follower of the classicizing architect Sir John Soane, composed 'The Persian Porch and the Place of Consultation of the Lacedaemonians', a remarkable two-dimensional 'reconstruction' of Sparta's only sizeable architectural monument of the fifth century BC, the Persian Stoa or Portico constructed presumably during the 470s. Needless to add, Gandy's imagination outstripped the ancient Spartans' practical and creative capacities by some considerable distance, but the point of interest is that a leading figure on the English architectural scene at a particularly potent and fertile neoclassicizing moment should have chosen to let his fancy loose on the architecturally jejune site of ancient Sparta.

Such visual and verbal rhetoric both Greek and foreign presaged ultimately the Greek War of Independence of 1821, which loosed a flood of patriotic literature in which Leonidas was never far from the centre. The heroic and consciously meditated death of Markos Botzaris prompted Byron to evoke the Leonidas analogy. This was further developed in Michel Pichat's romantic-classical tragedy *Léonidas* of 1825, which climaxed in a powerful prophecy by the Leonidas character concerning the influence of the memory of Sparta.

Far more famous, and memorable, are the lines of Byron's *Don Juan*, taken from the song often referred to as *The Isles of Greece*, in which the English lord assumes the mask of a peripatetic poet entertaining his Greek listeners with the dream 'that Greece might still be free'. Here is the passage that refers specifically to Sparta's and Leonidas' contribution to that dream:

Must we but weep o'er days more blest?
Must we but blush? – Our fathers bled.
Earth! Render back from out thy breast
A remnant of our Spartan dead!
Of the three hundred grant but three.
To make a new Thermopylae![4]

A disabused century later, however, one of the twentieth century's most potent voices, Constantine Cavafy, offered this cautionary corrective:

Honour to those who in the life they lead
define and guard a Thermopylae...
And even more honour is due to them
when they foresee (as many do foresee)
that in the end Ephialtes will make his appearance,
that the Medes will break through after all.[5]

Those who do not relish the thought of the Medes breaking through, or of the perverted uses to which Sparta and images of Sparta were put in Nazi Germany before and during the Second World War, will turn their minds rather to the fine Parian marble torso of a naked male warrior excavated in the theatre area underneath the Spartan acropolis by members of the British School at Athens in the 1920s. This was instantly, understandably, but alas erroneously, labelled 'Leonidas'. Erroneously, because the original was part of a group, not a self-standing statue, and the group was probably affixed to the pediment of a temple and therefore represented a hero or a god, not a mortal man. (Not even a descendant of 'the demigod son of Zeus' Heracles such as Leonidas would have qualified for such representation.) Besides, the date of the surviving sculpture, though admittedly a matter of subjective opinion, is more likely to have been before than after 480. In either case, finally, this was too early for anything like a portrait sculpture properly so called to have been created anywhere in Greece, even in far more individu-alistic Athens, let alone community-minded, corporatist Sparta.

In 1955 the Greek government set up this memorial beside the National Road not far from the site of the Spartans' last stand at Thermopylae in 480 BC (presumed to have taken place on and around a hilltop on the other side of the National Road, where a copy of Simonides's famous 'Go, tell the Spartans...' epigram has been inscribed). The statue is based, of course, on the 'Leonidas' (Ill. p. 119) excavated in Sparta.

Nevertheless, it is this statue of 'Leonidas' that forms the basis for the modern memorial statues erected both in Sparta and at the site of Thermopylae itself. Perhaps no less touching, and revealing, in its way is the copy set up in a New World Sparta – Sparta, Wisconsin, one of hundreds of towns in the States so named. This public statue has been Americanized in all sorts of ways, right down to the incorrect letter 'S' emblazoned on his shield. Actually, the ancient Spartans in battle array called themselves 'Lacedaemonians', not 'Spartans', and it was therefore with the Greek letter Lambda (an inverted V) not Sigma that their shields were distinctively marked.

Leonidas remains the stuff of legend in the mass-est of mass media.

This modern Leonidas, too, is based on the original 'Leonidas' excavated not far away. It is located at the focal point of the main street of modern Sparta, which is named after Constantine Palaeologus (the last emperor of Byzantium). Behind Leonidas rises what passed for an acropolis in ancient Sparta.

In the 1960s a powerful Hollywood movie entitled *The 300 Spartans* gave him star billing, and still today he is thought worthy of the Hollywood treatment, with stars of the stature or at any rate the cost of George Clooney and Bruce Willis said to be in the running to play him in a version of Thermopylae based on Steven Pressfield's bestselling novel, *Gates of Fire* (1998). The pages of the suitably named Amazon Web site devoted to readers' reactions to Pressfield's novel are an illuminating snapshot of the Spartan myth in its latest, Western incarnation.

Leonidas Lives! With him, Sparta does too.

APPENDIX
HUNTING: SPARTAN-STYLE[1]

More people than ever today study Classics, or more or less non-linguistic Classical Civilization or Classical Studies courses, at University. More people than ever seem to want to learn the ancient languages. Yet Classics is not included as of right in the minimum National Curriculum that is prescribed by our British government for all public, state schools; and as a direct result, fewer and fewer study either of those ancient languages at high school before getting to university. There is therefore a constant need for university teachers such as myself to proselytize for the subject, to do a kind of ambassadorial job, providing links between universities and schools, and between universities and a wider general public. This is what the French rather elegantly and etymologically call 'haute vulgarisation', and we more prosaic British 'popularization'. This is not, as I see it, a process of dumbing-down, emphatically not, but rather one of wising up: making the roots – or one of the taproots – of our western civilization more accessible, more user-friendly, reminding people in today's three-minute attention-span culture just how important it is to know where, ultimately, they are coming from, in a cultural sense.

Put another way, it's an example of what the great German classical scholar Wilamowitz called 'giving blood to the ghosts' of antiquity. It is, however, to continue the pun, a very specific sort of bloodletting that I want to consider here. There are I believe, broadly, two chief reasons for wanting to continue to study the ancient Greeks today. First, they are so like us – genuinely ancestral in many fundamental cultural ways. Second – the exact opposite reason – they are so unlike us, also in fundamental ways. For example, their direct participatory democracy was not our relatively bloodless representative democracy; their theatre and athletics were invented and continued to be performed within a crucially religious context. Typically, I prefer to stress the differences between them and us, for critical, scholarly, historiographical reasons. And I do so especially when the Greeks are invoked as our 'ancestors' in order to legitimate, or give a favourable gloss to, some current rather controversial practice or pastime. This is where the politically hot topic of hunting comes in. Somehow, Wilamowitz's analogy seems especially appropriate to a study of ancient Greek and Spartan hunting.

In David Brooks's amusing *Bobos in Paradise: The New Upper Class and How they Got There* (2000) the author comments of the 1950s: 'This was the last great age of socially acceptable boozing. It was still an era when fox hunting and polo didn't seem antiquarian'. Unfortunately, as I see it, in my country it doesn't yet seem quite antiquarian enough. Though legally banned in Scotland, foxhunting with hounds is alive and well in any number of our English shires, though here too it is under legal threat, either of severe restriction or total prohibition, largely on ethical grounds. Were Siegfried Sassoon, an alumnus of my own Cambridge College, Clare, to have lived on for another thirty years, he would surely have been pleased to note the sales of the latest reprint of his lightly fictionalized *Memoirs of a Fox-Hunting Man* (originally published in 1928). On the other hand, I am sure too that a remarkable recent evocation of the mythical Calydonian Boar Hunt, *In the Shape of a Boar* (2000) by the classically educated novelist Lawrence Norfolk, had at least one eye to the current political profile of the more genteel modern form of hunting evoked by Sassoon's *Memoirs*.

It was in this climate of fierce public political debate that there appeared in 1998 Roger Scruton's *On Hunting*, a slim volume of 161 small pages. The echo of the extant treatises of that title by Xenophon (fourth century BC) and Arrian (second century AD), recently edited in one useful volume by the scholar Malcolm Willcock, was deliberate. The opening sentence of Scruton's preface goes like this:

Hunting with hounds is a craft requiring both stamina and skill. It was already well established in antiquity, and Xenophon's treatise on the subject shows how similar were the techniques used by huntsmen in ancient Greece to those used today. Similar too were the attitudes – towards hounds, towards followers of the hunt, and towards the countryside. Dissimilar, however, was the quarry...

One can see why Scruton should want to go back to the Greeks, to invoke their cultural authority at a time when his favourite sport and pastime is under legal governmental threat. And I share his nostalgia, in a certain sense, for a return to the world of ancient Greece. One of my own favourite passages in all Greek literature comes in *Odyssey* Book 17, where Odysseus, in his ragged beggarly disguise, returns to his palace on Ithaca after an absence of twenty years to find the aged dog Argos lying, mangy, tick-ridden, neglected, among the kitchen midden. Master and hound recognize each other, despite their changed appearances, but the effort of recognition proves too much for the old dog, and, in the apt words of Walter Shewring's prose translation, 'the fate of dark death fell on him suddenly when in this twentieth year he had once again set eyes on Odysseus'. How different Argos's condition (in more than one sense) had been twenty years before! For then, as the slave swineherd Eumaeus puts it, 'there was no beast in any nook of bushy woodland that could escape him when he pursued. How sure he was in tracking the prey!' – prey that consisted of wild goats, deer and hares.

However, is it really only the quarry, as Scruton would have it, that distinguishes modern British from ancient Greek hunting? And even if some at least of the techniques used were similar, is it really the case that ancient Greek and modern British attitudes to hunting are 'similar'? Is it indeed possible or useful to speak so broadly and blandly about 'ancient Greek' attitudes to hunting? In the rest of this Appendix I shall be looking at those three aspects in turn: quarry, attitudes, and identity of the hunting group, with special reference to the practices of the ancient Spartans.

It does not require a very lively imagination to grasp the huge differences between the kind of 'hunting' that is carried out today with guns – in North America of deer (as in the movie *The Deerhunter*), or in the Mediterranean countries of small migratory birds – and the kind of hunting that Scruton is exclusively talking about, the hunting of foxes on horseback with hounds. Likewise, despite Scruton's claim about similarity of technique, horseback foxhunting is also very different indeed from all forms of ancient Greek hunting, which took place at the point of contact on foot. For although Greek hunters might initially ride to the place of the hunt, they would then dismount and do the actual hunting on foot.

As a matter of fact, the closest direct parallel in respect of technique as well as quarry between ancient and modern hunting is between ancient hare-hunting and what modern hunters call 'beagling' (after the name of the beagle-hound employed). But beagling is not a terribly glamorous contemporary 'sport', or pastime, and it is hard to imagine that Scruton would have waxed as lyrical in defence of it as he does in defending, or rather positively advocating, foxhunting. Besides, at least one of the objectives in hunting hares in most of ancient Greece is not exactly congruent with our modern conceptions and practice, though it was essential to the ancient Greek patterns of thought and behaviour. For hares were a characteristic form of lover's gift, more precisely one of the hallmarks of the pederastic relationship of homoeroticism that most modern legal systems now outlaw on moral grounds as child-abuse. We shall return to the erotic dimension of ancient Greek hunting when we come to look in more detail at attitudes. But, to complete our discussion of the quarry, let us end by considering two further simply huge differences between ancient Greek and modern British or American practices of hunting: boar-hunting and man-hunting.

Scruton himself mentions the hunting of wild boar, to which Xenophon devotes a chapter of his treatise. What he does not mention, despite some amateur attempts at a sociology and social anthropology of modern hunting, is that the ancient Greek boar-hunt – unlike the modern British foxhunt – was a manhood test in the most literal sense, a very suitable test of the sort of *andreia* (manliness, virility) that would be required paradigmatically of a Greek hoplite on the battlefield. Boarhunting was also in a symbolic sense both a rite of passage, technically speaking, and – in all cities but Sparta – a mark of elite social distinction. Scruton is keen – too keen – to stress what he sees as the demotic, cross-class quality of his foxhunting. But few Greeks had the horses and equipment to ride off to the boarhunt, and those who did would use slaves – another fact that Scruton disingenuously or innocently obscures – to act as beaters, netkeepers, grooms and other indispensable support personnel. Only in Sparta, with its ample resources of Helots, and its insistence on the value of hunting as a form of military training for all, would ordinary citizens also take part in this highly dangerous 'pastime'. But it is doubtful that Scruton would wish to single out Sparta as his ancestral model hunting society.

The mention of slaves raises the issue of manhunting. In a slave society such as Classical Athens, a characteristic form of servile resistance to enslavement was flight. The most conspicuous single example of this on record occurred at the end of the Athenian War, when, if we are to believe Thucydides, 'more than two times 10,000 slaves' ran away under cover of Sparta's occupation of part of Athens's home territory. Normally, slaves could run away only in ones and twos, in dribs and drabs. But so regular and persistent was such slave flight that it gave rise to the phenomenon of the professional slave-catcher (*drapetagôgos*). He

– and his dogs – practised what could doubtless be a highly lucrative trade. Another, very different sort of ancient Greek slave society was Sparta, and we shall revisit this issue of difference between Athens and Sparta in another connection later on. For now, what is salient is that manhunting was a systematic part of the everyday relations between Spartans and their servile underclass of (Greek) Helots. Helot-hunting – Helot-culling – in Sparta was not, in other words, a sign of systemic dysfunction, like servile flight at Athens. Rather it was a 'normal' occurrence, a key part of the battery of repressive techniques deployed by the Spartans against the Helots under the legalized veneer of their annual declaration of war against them. In Sparta, then, hunting and war were indeed solidary activities, with a peculiarly Spartan twist.

From differences of quarry, with their rather disturbing implications for differences of social structure, both between ancient and modern societies and within ancient Greece itself, I turn now to essential differences in the metaphorical aspects of hunting. It is a commonplace that hunting terminology is built into our own everyday English vocabulary in a routine, unthreatening way. We academics 'hunt', for instance, for a reference in the library, as a matter of course. Hunting, that is, has infiltrated our everyday English vocabulary at a number of social levels and semantic registers. So too in ancient Greece. In Alain Schnapp's brilliant monograph on the texts and images of ancient Greek hunting, the third chapter – the first substantive one – is entitled precisely '*La métaphore du chasseur*'.

However, it is there that any useful or usable similarity or analogy between ancient and modern hunting metaphors ends. Schnapp's work as a whole is entitled *Le chasseur et la cité*, indicating that hunting in ancient Greece did not exist as a purely social or economic phenomenon but had its place within and only within the all-embracing compass of the polis. It was political in a way that modern hunting cannot possibly be. The book's subtitle, moreover, is *Chasse et érotique dans la Grèce ancienne*. No doubt, erotics and eroticism have had and will have their place in modern hunting scenarios, though Adrian Phillips in his Xenophon commentary remarks intriguingly that 'for some [hunting] will even banish "thoughts of love"'. But the point is that erotics and eroticism are not straightforwardly or directly to be seen as the objective, or even one of the main objectives, of the whole modern hunting phenomenon.

This key differential sets us on the right interpretative track, I think, the track of emphasising difference between us and them, between ancient and modern. Foxhunting today, that is to say, is by no means as 'natural' or elemental as Scruton would like to persuade us; it is very far from being second nature, so to speak. That was, arguably, very much nearer to being the case in Greek antiquity – when, it is salutary to recall, not even the concept of human (let alone animal) rights had been developed.

That brings me to my next and final topic: who, really, were the Greeks to whom Scruton purports to appeal as being relevantly ancestral and authoritative? The ancient Greeks themselves were very aware that they were by no means all identical culturally, but they almost all agreed that they had more in common with each other than not – with one exception: the Spartans. The ancient tradition, fostered by the Spartans themselves and promoted especially by the Athenians, was that Sparta was 'other', crucially different in basic ways from all other Greek cities and societies. Awareness of the propaganda dimension of this Spartan 'mirage' or 'myth' has provoked some modern scholars into claiming that really Sparta was not that different. I beg to disagree, for all sorts of reasons, political, social, economic, religious and so on, and not least for a reason that has to do directly with our present topic. Spartan hunting, I wish to argue, differed *toto caelo* from hunting as practised in any other contemporary Greek city. This is not a novel point of view by any means, but it is, I think, worth briefly stating the rudiments of the case again, if only to show how problematic any appeal to the authority of the ancient Greeks in fact must be.

At the heart of the Spartans' overall political system (*politeia*) was their practice of communal dining or messing, and it was on continued participation in this that the exercise of full Spartan 'citizenship' (*politeia* in another sense) depended. There were only two legitimate excuses for missing the compulsory evening mess-meal: first, the performance of a necessary sacrifice; and, second, hunting. Spartan hunting was directed to the same quarry as that of other Greeks such as the Athenians – deer, boar, hares, etc. But unlike at Athens, hunting in Sparta could not conceivably be described as a leisure-time activity, let alone a sport. Nor were the fruits of the chase used, as far as we know, in the repertoire of a Spartan lover's or would-be lover's advances to his junior male beloved. Rather, Spartan hunting of animals was a deadly serious business, and the products of the chase were contributed routinely to the common meal.

Even more remarkably different from, at any rate, certain kinds of Athenian hunting, was the fact that the Spartan community officially encouraged all Spartans, whatever their economic, political or social status, to engage regularly in hunting, ostensibly for military training motives. Thus horses and hunting dogs – which were privately owned – and Helots – who were not privately owned but were certainly attached compulsorily to the service of individual Spartan masters and mistresses – were all required to be made available on demand to any Spartan who wished to hunt. Ordinary poorer Spartans would indeed wish to take advantage of this requirement, partly for military reasons but also to enable them to provide extra delicacies for their messes and so keep up with the richer Spartans who gave produce off their bigger estates.

The Spartans, being Spartans, moreover, took great pride in and paid great attention to, the breeding of horses, dogs, and – presumably – Helots of the very highest hunting quality. A tract of land in the Taygetus foothills not far from Sparta was labelled prosaically Therai, 'the Hunting Grounds'. Some of the most memorable images in all sixth-century Lakonian black-figure vase-painting are those attributed to the Hunt Painter.[2] Our illustration on p. 71, for example, the name vase of the Hunt Painter, shows a characteristic 'porthole' depiction of a hunting scene. Emphasis is placed on the necessity for close almost instinctive co-operation between the hunters, one of whom is shown as fully adult with a beard as well as long hair, the other as longhaired but still beardless, probably still learning the ropes from his senior mentor. In the illustration, p. 87, a characteristic hoplite figure is depicted together with his Argos, as it were, his faithful hunting-dog. In the illustration, p. 112, there is represented a rather earlier terracotta amphora bearing relief decoration, that served as a grave-marker. On one side of the vase is a scene of a successful hunt, just the sort of image that a good Spartan would wish to take with him to the next world. Finally, mock-hunting was certainly incorporated centrally in at any rate the revived Agoge, the Spartans' comprehensive educational system, of Hellenistic and Roman times. But it was probably included already in the Classical period Agoge, since key ritual manifestations of that cycle were staged within the sanctuary of Artemis Orthia, who was a goddess of fertility, growth and the wild margins, closely associated with the hunting of wild beasts.

However, this official political dedication to the hunting of animals is not the most remarkable feature of Spartan hunting by any manner of means. That, of course, was the manhunting of Helots both individually and collectively that I have already mentioned. This officially sanctioned practice served simultaneously as a way of policing the Helots through a form of state terror, and also as a manhood test for the individual Spartan pre-adults selected honorifically to serve within the Crypteia. It is in the context of state-sponsored Helot-hunting that Aristotle's bitter criticism of the Spartans' unique state educational system is, I think, most telling. The Spartan sort of education, he observed, was systematically defective, in that it aimed to inculcate only one kind of virtue, martial courage, and tended therefore to turn out 'beast-like', specifically wolf-like, Spartans.

Wolves, notoriously, are accomplished hunters and killers. 'Wolfish' Apollo (Apollo Lyceius), whose title is perhaps echoed in the name of the supposed founder of that Spartan educational system, Lycurgus ('Wolf-Worker'), was thus the divine patron of a practice that presumably not even Roger Scruton would wish to invoke as ancestral legitimation of his own pastime of choice.

YOU MAY ALSO LIKE...

On Sparta
by Plutarch

A War Like No Other: How the Athenians...
by Victor Hanson

Thermopylae: The Battle for the West
by Ernle Bradford

Wars of the Ancient Greeks (Smithsonian...
by Victor Davis Hanson

A History of Sparta: 950-192 B.C.
by William George Grieve Forrest

receipt or (ii) for product not carried by Barnes & Noble or Barnes & Noble.com.

Policy on receipt may appear in two sections.

Return Policy

<u>With a sales receipt or Barnes & Noble.com packing slip,</u> a full refund in the original form of payment will be issued from any Barnes & Noble Booksellers store for returns of undamaged NOOKs, new and unread books, and unopened and undamaged music CDs, DVDs, and audio books made within 14 days of purchase from a Barnes & Noble Booksellers store or Barnes & Noble.com with the below exceptions:

A store credit for the purchase price will be issued (i) for purchases made by check less than 7 days prior to the date of return, (ii) when a gift receipt is presented within 60 days of purchase, (iii) for textbooks, or (iv) for products purchased at Barnes & Noble College

NOTES

These notes are confined to referencing the ancient sources translated in the text. All translations are my own.

General Introduction

1. Thucydides Book IV, chapter 40. See also Strassler ed. 1996.
2. Plutarch, *Life of Agesilaus*, ch. 6. See Shipley 1997 in the Further Reading.

Chapter 1

1. Herodotus Book I, ch. 4 (see also ch. 3). See also Marincola ed. 1996.
2. Herodotus II.120 (see chs 113-120).
3. Herodotus VI.61.
4. Sappho fragment 23. See also West 1993.
5. Sappho fragment 16.
6. Aristophanes, *Lysistrata*, lines 78-84.
7. Aristophanes, *Lysistrata*, lines 1296-1315.
8. Herodotus I.65.
9. Plutarch, *Life of Lycurgus*, ch. 6. See also Talbert ed. 1988.
10. Pindar, lyric fragment, quoted in Plutarch, *Lycurgus*, ch. 21.
11. Terpander, lyric fragment, quoted in Plutarch, *Lycurgus*, ch. 21.

Chapter 2

1. Herodotus VII.152.
2. Herodotus I, Preface.
3. Herodotus VIII.65.

Chapter 3
1. Herodotus VI.65.
2. Plutarch, *Sayings of Spartan Women*, Gorgo no. 1 (*Moralia* 240d).
3. Plutarch, *Sayings of Spartan Women*, Gorgo no. 4 (*Moralia* 240e).
4. Plutarch, *Sayings of Spartan Women*, Gorgo no. 5 (*Moralia* 240e).
5. Herodotus VII.226.
6. Simonides, epigram, quoted in Herodotus VII.228.
7. Simonides, quoted in Athenaeus XII.536ab. See Campbell ed. 1991.
8. Simonides, elegy fragment 11. See also West ed. 1993; Boedeker & Sider eds. 2001.
9. Simonides, epigram, quoted in Thucydides I.132.

Chapter 4
1. Thucydides I.19.
2. Herodotus IX.37.

Chapter 5
1. Aristotle, *Politics*, Book II, p. 1270.
2. Alcman, *Partheneion* fr. 1. See also West ed. 1993.
3. Xenophon, *Hellenica* [*History of Greece*] Book VI, chapter 4, section 16.
4. Plutarch, *Sayings of Spartan Women*, Argileonis (*Moralia* 240c).

Chapter 6
1. Thucydides IV.121.
2. Thucydides V.70.
3. Thucydides V.75.

Chapter 7
1. The biography of Cynisca that follows is a modified version of the relecvant chapter in Cartledge 2000.
2. *Palatine Anthology* XIII.16.
3. Plutarch, *Sayings of Spartans*, Agesilaus no. 71 (*Moralia* 213f); also *Moralia* 189f, Lycurgus, no. 5; 227c, Lycurgus, no. 11; *Life of Lycurgus*, ch. 13.
4. Xenophon, *Hellenica* V.3.16.

Chapter 8
1. Plutarch, *Sayings of Kings and Commanders*, Archidamus (*Moralia* 191e); see also *Moralia* 219a, Archidamos, no. 8.
2. Arrian, *Anabasis* [*The Campaigns of Alexander the Great*] Book I, chapter 16.
3. Pausanias, *Guide to Greece*, Book IX, chapter 15. See Levi 1971.
4. Plutarch, *Agesilaus*, 30. See also Shipley 1997.

Chapter 9
1. Aristotle, *Politics*, Book II, p. 1270.
2. Erskine 1990.
3. A. Spawforth in Cartledge & Spawforth 2001: 99.

Chapter 10
1. Plutarch, *Life of Cleomenes*, chapter 2. See also Talbert ed. 1988.
2. M. de Montaigne, 'On the Cannibals', in Essays, ed. M.A. Screech, *The Complete Essays*, Harmonsdworth 1993, p.238.
3. Fénelon, *Dialogue XL*, quoted from Rawson 1969/1991: 220 (my translation).
4. Lord Byron, *Don Juan*, Canto.
5. Those verses are from Constantine Cavafy's 'Thermopylae', in the translation of Edmund Keeley and Philip Sherrard (= Keeley & Sherrard no. 15).

Appendix
1. This new Appendix is based on the James Loeb lecture, entitled 'Blood for the Ancient Greek Ghosts: Hunting for a New Past', that I delivered at Harvard University on 15 December 2000. For their kind invitation, I thank most warmly the Junior Faculty of the Department of the Classics, especially my friend and collaborator Nino Luraghi, and my other genial and congenial host, Professor Gloria Ferrari Pinney.

2. Though formally it is not possible to state categorically that the Hunt Painter was representing genre-scenes of everyday Spartan life rather than Calydonian or other mythical boar-hunts, I think Alain Schnapp has argued pretty convincingly and conclusively for the former interpretation.

FURTHER READING

(see Select Bibliography for full titles)

GENERAL

i. Books and Articles on Sparta
Cartledge 1987, 2001a, 2001b; Cartledge & Spawforth 2001; Chrimnes 1949/1999; Den Boer 1954; Finley 1968/1981; Fitzhardinge 1980; Forrest 1968; Hodkinson 1983, 1986, 1989, 1996, 1997b, 1999b, 2000; Hodkinson & Powell eds. 1989; Hooker 1980; Huxley 1962; Jones 1967; Malkin 1994; Oliva 1971; Poralla & Bradford 1985/1913; Powell ed. 1989; Powell & Hodkinson eds 1994.

ii. Literary Sources [see also ch. 9]
Boedeker & Sider eds. 2001; David 1982/3; Campbell ed. 1991; Marincola ed. 1996; Moore 1983; Shipley 1997; Starr 1965/1979; Strassler ed. 1996; Talbert ed. 1988; West ed. 1993.

iii. Spartan Archaeology
Boardman 1963; Cartledge 1976a; Cavanagh et al. 1996, forthcoming; Cavanagh & Walker eds 1998; Congdon 1981; Dawkins ed. 1929; Dickins 1908; Fitzhardinge 1980; Hodkinson 1998; Pipili 1987; Powell 1989; Steinhauer 1978.

iv. Spartan Politics
Adcock & Mosley 1975; Andrewes 1956; Bonner & Smith 1942; Cartledge 1976b, 1978, 1980; David 1985; Herman 1987; Jeffery 1961/1990, 1976; MacDowell 1986; de Ste. Croix 1972; Staveley 1972.

v. Spartan Society (incl. Helots)
Bryant 1996; Cartledge 1981a, 1985, 1992; David 1989a, 1989b, 1992, 1993; Dickins 1929; Ducat 1999; Figueira 1984; Garlan 1988; Garland 1995; van Gennep 1960/1909; Golden 1998; Hodkinson 1996, 1997a, 1997b, 1999a; Hunt 1998; Kennell 1995; Oliva 1971; Pettersson 1992; de Ste. Croix 1981; Scanlon

1988; Vernant 1991; Vidal-Naquet 1968, 1986a, 1986b.

vi. Spartan Warfare
Adcock 1957; Cartledge 1977, 1996; Ferguson 1918; Hanson 1989, ed. 1991; Lazenby 1985.

vii. Historical Novels
Pressfield 1998; Manfredi 2002/1988.

Chapter 1
Andrewes 1956; de Polignac 1995; Svenbro 1993.

Chapter 2
Cawkwell 1993.

Chapter 3
Lazenby 1985.

Chapter 4
de Ste. Croix 1972: esp. ch. 4.

Chapter 5
Bradford 1986; Bruit & Schmitt 1992; Calame 1997; Cartledge 1981b; Congdon 1981; Kunstler 1983, 1987; Lacey 1968/1980; Parker 1989; Pettersson 1992; Pomeroy 1976, 1997, 2002, ed. 1991; Stewart 1997; Zweig 1993.

Chapter 6
de Ste. Croix 1972.

Chapter 7
Cartledge 1987/2000; Hodkinson 1996.

Chapter 8
Hodkinson 1996.

Chapter 9
Cartledge & Spawforth 1989/2001.

Chapter 10
Cartledge 1999; Finley 1962a; Jenkyns 1980; Ollier 1933-43/1973; Rawson 1969/1991; Tigerstedt 1965-78; Turner 1981.

Appendix
Anderson 1985; Barringer 2000; Cartledge & Waterfield 1997 [the Xenophontic treatise *On Hunting*]; David 1993; Lane Fox 1996; Norfolk 2000; Parisinou 2002; Phillips & Willcock 1999; Scanlon 1988, 2002; Schnapp 1997.

SELECT BIBLIOGRAPHY

ADCOCK, F.E. (1957) *The Greek and Macedonian Art of War*, California & London

ADCOCK, F.E. & D.J. MOSLEY (1975) *Diplomacy in Ancient Greece*, London

ANDERSON, J.K. 1985 Hunting in the Ancient World, Berkeley

ANDREWES, A. (1956) *The Greek Tyrants*, London

BARRINGER, J.M. (2001) *The Hunt in Ancient Greece*, Baltimore & London

BOARDMAN, J. (1963) 'Artemis Orthia and chronology', *ABSA* 58: 1-7

BOEDEKER, D. & SIDER, D. (2001) eds. *The New Simonides: Contexts of Praise and Desire*, Oxford

BONNER, R.J. & G. SMITH (1942) 'Administration of Justice in Sparta', *Classical Philology* 37: 113-29

BRADFORD, A.S. (1977) *A Prosopography of Lacedaemonians from the death of Alexander the Great, 323 B.C., to the sack of Sparta by Alaric*, Munich

BRADFORD, A.S. (1986) 'Gynaikokratoumenoi: did Spartan women rule Spartan men?', *The Ancient World* 14: 13-18

BRUIT-ZAIDMAN, L. & P. SCHMITT-PANTEL (1992) *Religion in the Ancient Greek City*, ed. and trans. P.A. Cartledge, Cambridge

BRYANT, J.M. (1996) *Moral Codes and Social Structure in Ancient Greece. A sociology of Greek Ethics from Homer to the Epicureans and Stoics*, Albany, N.Y.

CAMPBELL, D.A. (1991) ed. *Greek Lyric* vol. III (Loeb Classical Library), Cambridge, MA

CALAME, C. (1997) *Choruses of Young Women in Ancient Greece. Their Morphology, Religious Role, and Social Functions* (Lanham, MD & London 1997)]

CARTLEDGE, P.A. (1976a) 'Did Spartan citizens ever practise a manual *tekhne*?', *Liverpool Classical Monthly* 1: 115-19

CARTLEDGE, P.A. (1976b) 'The new Spartan treaty', *LCM* 1: 87-92

CARTLEDGE, P.A. (1977) 'Hoplites and Heroes: Sparta's contribution to the technique of ancient warfare', *JHS* 97: 11-27 [repr. in German trans., with add., in Christ ed. 1986: 387-425, 470]

CARTLEDGE, P.A. (1978), 'Literacy in the Spartan oligarchy', *Journal of Hellenic Studies* 98: 25-37 repr in Cartledge 2001b

CARTLEDGE, P.A. (1980) 'The peculiar position of Sparta in the development of the Greek city-state', *Proceedings of the Royal Irish Academy* 80C: 91-108 repr in Cartledge 2001b

CARTLEDGE, P.A. (1981a) 'The politics of Spartan pederasty', *Proceedings of the Cambridge Philological Society* n.s. 27: 17-36 [repr. with add. in Siems ed. 1988: 385-415] repr. in Cartledge 2001b

CARTLEDGE, P.A. (1981b) 'Spartan wives: liberation or licence?', *Classical Quarterly* n.s. 31: 84-105 repr in Cartledge 2001b

CARTLEDGE, P.A. (1985) 'Rebels and *Sambos* in Classical Greece: a comparative view' in Cartledge & Harvey eds 1985: 16-46 repr in Cartledge 2001b

CARTLEDGE, P.A. (1987) *Agesilaos and the Crisis of Sparta*, London & Baltimore [repr. in paperback 2000]

CARTLEDGE, P.A. (1992) 'A Spartan education' in *Apodosis. Essays prsented to Dr W.W. Cruickshank to mark his eightieth birthday*, London: 10-19 [St Paul's School, privately printed] repr in Cartledge 2001b

CARTLEDGE, P.A. (1996) 'La nascita degli opliti e l'organizzazione militare" in S. Settis ed. *I Greci II. Una Storia Greca 1. Formazione*, Turin, 681-714 repr in English in Cartledge 2001b

CARTLEDGE, P.A. (1999) 'The Socratics' Sparta and Rousseau's' in Hodkinson & Powell eds 1999: 311-37

CARTLEDGE, P.A. (2000) *The Greeks: Crucible of Civilization*, New York [repr. London 2001]

CARTLEDGE, P.A. (2001a) *Sparta and Lakonia. A regional history 1300-362 BC*, 2nd edn London, Henley & Boston

CARTLEDGE, P.A. (2001b) *Spartan Reflections*, London & California

CARTLEDGE, P.A. (2002) *The Greeks. A portrait of Self and Others*, 2nd edn, Oxford [German trans., with Nachwort, Stuttgart 1998]

CARTLEDGE, P.A. & A.J.S. SPAWFORTH (2001) *Hellenistic and Roman Sparta: a tale of two cities*, rev. edn London & New York

CARTLEDGE, P.A. & R. WATERFIELD (1997) eds. Xenophon 'On Hunting' in *Xenophon: Hiero the Tyrant & other Treatises*, London, 123-62

CAVANAGH, W.G., J.H. CROUWEL, R.W.V. CATLING & D.J.G. SHIPLEY (1996) *Continuity and Change in a Greek Rural Landscape: the Lakonia Survey II: Archaeological Data*, British School at Athens, Supplementary Volume 27, London

CAVANAGH, W.G., J.H. CROUWEL, R.W.V. CATLING & D.J.G. SHIPLEY (forthcoming) *Continuity and Change in a Greek Rural Landscape: the Lakonia Survey I: Methodology and Interpretation*, British School at Athens, Supplementary Volume 26, London

CAVANAGH, W.G. & WALKER, S.E.C. (1998) eds *Sparta in Laconia* (Proceedings of the 19th British Museum Classical Colloquium: B.S.A. Studies 4), London

CAWKWELL, G.L. (1993) 'Cleomenes', *Mnemosyne* 4th ser. 46: 506-27

CHRIMES, K.M.T. (1949) *Ancient Sparta. A Re-examination of the evidence*, Manchester [repr. Oxford 1999]

CONGDON, L.O.K. (1981) *Caryatid Mirrors of Ancient Greece*, Mainz

DAVID, E. (1982/3) 'Aristotle on Sparta', *Ancient Society* 13/14: 67-103

DAVID, E. (1985) 'The trial of Spartan kings', *Revue internationale des Droits de l'Antiquité* 32: 131-40

DAVID, E. (1989a) 'Dress in Spartan society', *The Ancient World* 19: 3-13

DAVID, E. (1989b) 'Laughter in Spartan society' in Powell ed. 1989: 1-25

DAVID, E. (1992) 'Sparta's social hair', *Eranos* 90: 11-21

DAVID, E. (1993) 'Hunting in Spartan society and consciousness', *Echos du Monde Classique/Classical Views* 37: 393-417

DAWKINS, R.M. (1929) ed. *The Sanctuary of Artemis Orthia At Sparta. Excavated and described by members of the British School at Athens, 1906-1910 (Journal of Hellenic Studies* Supp. V), London

DEN BOER, W. (1954) *Laconian Studies*, Amsterdam

DICKINS, G. (1908) 'The art of Sparta', *Burlington Magazine* 14: 66-84

DICKINS, G. (1929) 'The terracotta masks' in Dawkins ed. 1929: 163-86

DUCAT, J. (1999) 'Perspectives on Spartan education in the classical period' in Hodkinson & Powell eds 1999: 43-66

ERSKINE, A.W. (1990) *The Hellenistic Stoa. Political Thought and Action*, London

FERGUSON, W.S. (1918) 'The Zulus and the Spartans: a comparison of their military systems', *Harvard African Studies* 2: 197-234

FIGUEIRA, T.J. (1984) 'Mess contributions and subsistence at Sparta', *Transactions of the American Philological Association* 114: 87-109

FINLEY, M.I. (1962a) 'The myth of Sparta', *The Listener*, August 2: 171-3

FINLEY, M.I. (1968) 'Sparta' in J.-P. Vernant ed. *Problèmes de la guerre en Grèce ancienne*, Paris: 141-60 [repr. in Finley 1981: 24-40, 1986a: 161-77

FINLEY, M.I. (1981) *Economy and Society in Ancient Greece*, ed. B.D. Shaw & R.P. Saller, London [repr. Harmondsworth 1983]

FITZHARDINGE, L.F. (1980) *The Spartans*, London & N.Y.

FORREST, W.G. (1968) *A History of Sparta 950-192 B.C.*, London [repr. 1980]

GARLAN, Y. (1988) *Slavery in Ancient Greece*, Ithaca & London [French original 1982]

GARLAND, R. (1995) *In the Eye of the Beholder. Deformity and disability in the Graeco-Roman world*, London.

GENNEP, A. VAN (1960) *The Rites of Passage*, London [French original 1909]

GOLDEN, M. (1998) *Sport and Society in Ancient Greece*, Cambridge

GRIFFITHS, A. H. (1989) 'Was Kleomenes mad?' in Powell ed. 1989: 51-78

HANSON, V.D. (1989) *The Western Way of War: infantry battle in classical Greece*, New York [rev. edn, California 2000]

HANSON, V.D. (1991) ed. *Hoplites. The Classical Greek Battle Experience*, London & New York

HERMAN, G. (1987) *Ritualised Friendship and the Greek City*, Cambridge

HODKINSON, S. (1983) 'Social order and the conflict of values in Classical Sparta', *Chiron* 13: 239-81

HODKINSON, S. (1986) 'Land tenure and inheritance in Classical Sparta', *Classical Quarterly* n.s. 36: 378-406

HODKINSON, S. (1989) 'Inheritance, marriage and demography. Perspectives upon the decline and success of Classical Sparta' in Powell ed. 1989: 79-121

HODKINSON, S. (1996) 'Spartan society in the fourth century: crisis and continuity' in P. Carlier ed. *Le IVe siècle av. J.-C. Approches historiographiques*, Paris, 85-101

HODKINSON, S. (1997a) 'Servile and free dependants of the classical Spartan "oikos"' in M.Moggi & G. Cordiano eds *Schiavi e Dipendenti nell' ambito dell' 'oikos' e della 'familia'*, Pisa: 45-71

HODKINSON, S. (1997b) 'The development of Spartan society and institutions in the archaic period' in Mitchell & Rhodes eds 1997: 83-102

HODKINSON, S. (1998) 'Patterns of bronze dedications at Spartan sanctuaries, c. 650-350 BC: towards a quantified database of material and religious investment' in Cavanagh & Walker eds 1998: 55-63

HODKINSON, S. (1999a) 'An agonistic culture? Athletic competition in archaic and classical Spartan society' in Hodkinson & Powell eds 1999: 147-87

HODKINSON, S. (1999b) 'Introduction' in Hodkinson & Powell eds 1999: ix-xxvi

HODKINSON, S. (2000) *Property and Wealth in Classical Sparta*, London

HODKINSON, S. & C.A. POWELL (1999) eds *Sparta: New Perspectives*, London

HOOKER, J.T. (1980) *The Ancient Spartans*, London

HUNT, P. (1998) *Slaves, Warfare, and Ideology in the Greek Historians*, Cambridge

HUXLEY, G.L. (1962) *Early Sparta*, London

JEFFERY, L.H. (1961) *The Local Scripts of Archaic Greece*, Oxford [rev. edn by A.W. Johnston 1990]

JEFFERY, L.H. (1976) *Archaic Greece. The City-States c.700-500 B.C.*, London

JENKYNS, R. (1980) *The Victorians and Ancient Greece*, Oxford

JONES, A.H.M. (1967) *Sparta*, Oxford

KENNELL, N.M. (1995) *The Gymnasium of Virtue. Education and Culture in Ancient Sparta*, Chapel Hill & London

KUNSTLER, B.L. (1983) 'Women and the Development of the Spartan Polis. A Study of Sex Roles in Classical Antiquity', diss. Boston University

KUNSTLER, B.L. (1987) 'Family dynamics and female power in ancient Sparta' in M. Skinner ed. *Rescuing Creusa. New Methodological Approaches to Women in Antiquity (Helios* Supp. 13.2), Austin, TX: 32-48

LACEY, W.K. (1968) *The Family in Classical Greece*, London [repr. Auckland 1980]

LANE FOX, R. (1996) 'Ancient hunting: from Homer to Polybios' in G. Shipley & J. Salmon eds. *Human Landscapes in Classical Antiquity*, London & New York, 119-53

LEVI, P. (1971) ed. & trans. *Pausanias. Guide to Greece*, 2 vols, Harmondsworth

LAZENBY, J.F. (1985) *The Spartan Army*, Warminster

MACDOWELL, D.M. (1986) *Spartan Law*, Edinburgh

MALKIN, I. (1994) *Myth and Territory in the Spartan Mediterranean*, Cambridge

MANFREDI, V.M. (2002) *Spartan*, London [Italian original, 1988]

MITCHELL, L.G. & P.J. RHODES (1997) eds *The Development of the Polis in Archaic Greece* , London & New York

MOORE, J.M. (1983) *Aristotle and Xenophon on Democracy and Oligarchy*, 2nd edn, Cambridge

MOSSÉ, C. (1991) 'Women in the Spartan Revolutions of the Third Century B.C.' in S. Pomeroy ed. *Women's History & Ancient History*, Chapel Hill & London, 138-53

NORFOLD, L. (2000) *In the Shape of a Boar*, London

OLIVA, P. (1971) *Sparta and its Social Problems*, Amsterdam & Prague

OLLIER, F. (1933-43) *Le mirage spartiate*, Paris [repr. in 1 vol., New York, 1973]

PARSININOU, E. (2002) 'The "language" of female hunting outfit in ancient Greece' in L. Llewellyn-Jones ed. *Women's Dress in the Ancient Greek World*, London, 55-72

PARKER, R. (1989) 'Spartan Religion' in Powell ed. 1989: 142-72

PETTERSSON, M. (1992) *Cults of Apollo at Sparta. The Hyakinthia, the Gymnopaidiai and the Karneia*, Stockholm

PHILLIPS, A.A. & M.M. WILLCOCK (1999) eds. *Xenophon & Arrian On Hunting with Hounds*, Warminster

PIPILI, M. (1987) *Laconian Iconography of the Sixth Century B.C.*, Oxford

POLIGNAC, F. DE (1995) *Cults, Territory, and the Origins of the Greek City-State*, 2nd edn, Chicago [French original 1984]

POMEROY, S.B. (1976) *Goddesses, Whores, Wives and Slaves: women in classical antiquity*, London

POMEROY, S.B. (1997) *Families in Classical and Hellenistic Greece. Representations and realities*, Oxford

POMEROY, S.B. (2002) *The Women of Sparta*, New York

POMEROY, S.B. (1991) ed. *Women's History and Ancient History*, Chapel Hill, NC, & London

PORALLA, P. & A.S. BRADFORD (1985) *A Prosopography of Lacedaemonians from the earliest times to the death of Alexander the Great (X - 323 B.C.)/ Prosopographie der Lakedaimonier bis auf die Zeit Alexanders des Grossen*, 2nd edn, Chicago [original German edition, 1913]

POWELL, A. (1989) 'Mendacity and Sparta's use of the visual' in Powell ed. 1989: 173-192

POWELL, A. (2001) *Athens and Sparta. Constructing Greek Political and Social History to 323 BC*, 2nd edn, London

POWELL, A. (1989) ed. *Classical Sparta: techniques behind her success*, London & New York

POWELL, A. (1995) ed. *The Greek World*, London & New York

POWELL, A. & S. HODKINSON (1994) eds *The Shadow of Sparta*, London & New York

PRESSFIELD, S. (1998) *Gates of Fire*, New York

RAWSON, E. (1969) *The Spartan Tradition in European Thought*, Oxford [repr. 1991]

STE. CROIX, G.E.M. DE (1972), *The Origins of the Peloponnesian War*, London & Ithaca

STE. CROIX, G.E.M. DE (1983) *The Class Struggle in the Ancient Greek World. From the Archaic Age to the Arab Conquests*, corrected impr., London & Ithaca [original 1981]

SCANLON, T.F. (1988) '*Virgineum gymnasium*: Spartan females and early Greek athletics' in W.J. Raschke ed. 1988: 185-216

SCANLON, T.F. (2002) *Eros & Greek Athletics*, New York

SCHAPS, D.M. (1979) *Economic Rights of Women in Ancient Greece*, Edinburgh

SCHNAPP, A. (1997) *Le chasseur et la cité. Chasse et érotique dans la Grèce ancienne*, Paris

SHIPLEY, G. (2000)*The Greek World After Alexander 323-30 BC*, London & New York

SHIPLEY, D.R. (1997) *Plutarch's Life of Agesilaos*, Oxford

STARR, C.G. (1965) 'The credibility of early Spartan history', *Historia* 14: 257-72 [repr. in Starr 1979: 144-59]

STARR, C.G. (1979) *Essays on Ancient History. A Selection of Articles and Reviews*, ed. A. Ferrill & T. Kelly, Leiden

STAVELEY, E.S. (1972) *Greek and Roman Voting and Elections*, London & New Yor

STRASSLER, R.B. (1996) ed. *The Landmark Thucydides*, New York

STEINHAUER, G. (1978) *The Museum of Sparta*, Athens

STEWART, A. (1997) *Art, Desire and the Body in Ancient Greece*, Cambridge

SVENVRO, J. (1993) *Phrasikleia. An Anthropology of Reading in Ancient Greece*, Ithaca [French original 1988]

TALBERT, R. (1988) ed. *Plutarch on Sparta*, Harmondsworth

TIGERSTEDT, E.N. (1965-78) *The Legend of Sparta in Classical Antiquity*, 3 vols, Stockholm, Uppsala & Göteborg

TOD, M.N. (1933) 'A Spartan grave on Attic soil', *Greece & Rome* 2: 108-11

TURNER, F.M. (1981) *The Greek Heritage in Victorian Britain*, New Haven & London

VERNANT, J.-P. (1991) 'Between shame and glory: the identity of the young Spartan warrior' in *Mortals and Immortals. Collected Essays*, ed. F. Zeitlin, Princeton: 220-43

VIDAL-NAQUET, P. (1968) 'The Black Hunter and the origin of the Athenian *ephebia*', *Proceedings of the Cambridge Philological Society* n.s. 14: 49-64 [repr. in Vidal-Naquet 1986a: 106-28]

VIDAL-NAQUET, P. (1986a) *The Black Hunter. Forms of Thought and Forms of Society in the Greek World*, trans. A. Szegedy-Maszak, Baltimore & London

VIDAL-NAQUET, P. (1986b) 'The Black Hunter revisited', *Proceedings of the Cambridge Philological Society* n.s. 32: 126-44

WEST, M.L. (1993) ed. *Greek Lyric Poetry*, Oxford

ZWEIG, B. (1993) 'The only women to give birth to men: a gynocentric, cross-cultural view of women in ancient Sparta' in M. de Forest ed. *Women's Power, Men's Game: Essays in Classical Antiquity in honor of Joy King*, Wasconda, IL: 32-53

PICTURE CREDITS

Maps

p. 18–19. The Classical Greek World. Courtesy of Routledge (*Atlas of Classical History*, 1985).

p. 20. The Peloponneses. With permission of the Cambridge University Press (*Cambridge Ancient History*, vol. III, 1954).

p. 26. Laconia and Messenia. Courtesy of Nick Sekunda and reproduced with permission.

p. 44. Sparta's western territory: Mesenia. Courtesy of Nino Luraghi (Journal of Hellenic Studies, no. 122).

Illustrations

p. 30–31. View of Sparta town. The Society for the Promotion of Hellenic Studies.

p. 49. Relief on four-sided block of bluish-grey marble. Sparta Museum. Photo Hannibal.

p. 49. Reverse of four-sided block. Sparta Museum. Photo Hannibal.

p. 59. Sanctuary of Artemis Orthia Temple. Paul Cartledge.

p. 63. Lycurgus statue, Sparta. Michelle Jones/Ancient Art and Architecture Collection Ltd.

p. 68. Bronze statuette of warrior, *c.* 490 BC Wadsworth Athenaeum, Hartford, CT.

p. 68. Bronze hoplite warrior figurine, mid-sixth century BC. The British Museum #1929.10-16.6.

p. 71. Boar hunt *kylix, c.* 540 BC (Louvre E 670). Antikensammiung, Staatliche Museen zu Berlin, Preussischer Kulturbsitz.

p. 74–75. The Second Messenian War (*c.* 670–50). Osprey Publishing.

p. 89. Bronze hoplite figurine, sanctuary of Apollo Korynthos, later sixth century BC (14789). Deutsches Archäologisches Institut, Athens.

p. 94. Bronze Heracles. Staatl. Museen Kassel. Photographs A570 and A572.

p. 99. Bronze Krater from Vix, France, later sixth-century (Mus. of Chatillon-sur-Seine). The Bridgeman Art Library.

p. 110. Perioecic hoplite hero-relief from Areopolis (NM 2368). E. Kunze/ Deutsches Archäologisches Institut, Athens.

p. 114. Terracotta amphora, *c.* 600 BC. Sparta Museum # 5395.

p. 115. Ivory warship plaque, later seventh century (NM 3462). H. Wagner/ Deutsches Archäologisches Institut, Athens.

p. 121. Marble statue, *c.* 490-480 BC. G. T. Garvey/Ancient Art and Architecture Collection Ltd.

p. 138. Apulian red-figure vase, *c.* 420 BC. Davis Museum and Cultural Center, Wellesley College.

p. 168. Bronze figurine, later sixth century. The Fotomas Index.

p. 173. Bronze mirror from Lousoi, Arcadia, sixth century. Sparta Museum.

p. 175. Marble statue, sixth century. Sparta Museum #364.

p. 184. Bronze shield. American School of Classical Studies at Athens: Agora Excavations.

p. 199. Lysander. Hulton Archive.

p. 231. Bronze arrowheads from Tsakona, Laconia. British School at Athens.

p. 255. Menelaus & Helen: Athenian red-figure vase attributed to the Foundry Painter, *c.* 480 BC. Wadsworth Museum.

p. 266–67. J.-L. David's *Léonidas at Thermopylae*, Louvre, Paris. The Bridgeman Art Library.

p. 271. Thermopylae memorial, Thermopylae. G. T. Garvey/Ancient Art and Architecture Collection Ltd.

p. 272. Leonidas statue, Sparta. R. Sheridan/Ancient Art and Architecture Collection Ltd.

While every effort has been made to trace the copyright holders for illustrations featured in this book, the publishers will be glad to make proper acknowledgements in future editions in the event that any regrettable omissions have occurred at the time of going to press.

INDEX

ALSO AVAILABLE FROM VINTAGE/ANCHOR

CARNAGE AND CULTURE
Landmark Battles in the Rise to Western Power
by Victor Davis Hanson

Examining nine landmark battles from ancient to modern times—
from Salamis, where outnumbered Greeks devastated the slave army
of Xerxes, to Cortes's conquest of Mexico to the Tet offensive—
Victor Davis Hanson explains why the armies of the West have been
the most lethal and effective of any fighting forces of the world.
History/Military/0-385-72038-6

ON THE ORIGINS OF WAR
And the Preservation of Peace
by Donald Kagan

War has been a fact of life for centuries on end. By relating the ancient
confrontations between Athens and Sparta and between Rome and
Carthage with the two calamitous world wars and the Cuban Missile
Crisis, renowned historian Donald Kagan reveals new and surprising
insights into the nature of war—and peace.
History/Military/0-385-42375-6

MEMORY AND THE MEDITERRANEAN
by Fernand Braudel

A grand sweep of history by Fernand Braudel, *Memory and the
Mediterranean* chronicles the Mediterranean's immeasurably rich
past during its foundational period from prehistory to classical antiquity, illuminating nothing less than the bedrock of our civilization
and the very origins of Western culture.
History/Ancient/0-375-70399-3

IMAGINING ATLANTIS
by Richard Ellis

Ever since Plato created the legend of the lost island of Atlantis, it has
endured as a part of the mythologies of many different cultures, yet
there is no proof that Atlantis ever existed. Intrigued by the inex-
haustible appeal of the myth, Richard Ellis plunges into this rich
topic, investigating the roots of the legend and following its various
manifestations into the present.
History/Mythology/0-375-70582-1

WAR AND OUR WORLD
by John Keegan

Is war a natural condition of humankind? What are the origins of war? Is the modern state dependent on warfare? How does war affect the individual? Can there be an end to war? In a series of concise essays, John Keegan, widely considered the greatest military historian of our time, addresses these questions with a breathtaking knowledge of history and attempts to understand why war remains the single greatest affliction of humanity.

History/Military/0-375-70520-1

I, CLAUDIUS
From the Autobiography of Tiberius Claudius
by Robert Graves

Despised as a weakling and dismissed as an idiot because of his physical infirmities, Tiberius Claudius survived the intrigues and poisonings that marked the reigns of Augustus, Tiberius, and the mad Caligula to become emperor of Rome in 41 A.D. *I, Claudius* is written as Claudius's autobiography and stands as one of the modern classics of historical fiction.

Fiction/Literature/0-679-72477-X

SAILING THE WINE-DARK SEA
Why the Greeks Matter
by Thomas Cahill

In *Sailing the Wine-Dark Sea*, Thomas Cahill explores the vast legacy of the ancient Greeks. From the origins of Greek culture in the migrations of armed Indo-European tribes into Attica and onto the Peloponnesian peninsula, to the formation of city-states, to the birth of Western literature, poetry, drama, philosophy, art, and architecture, Cahill makes the distant past vitally relevant to the present.

History/Greece/0-385-49554-4

VINTAGE/ANCHOR BOOKS
Available at your local bookstore, or call toll-free to order:
1-800-793-2665 (credit cards only)